PRAISE FOR PHILIP HESKETH
AND HIS BOOKS:

'It does exactly what it says on the cover. It's a great book that will show you how to be more persuasive and influential. So if you want to be more persuasive and influential... read it.'

Ged Shields, Vice President of Marketing, Ronseal

'The Government would do well to appoint someone to teach us all how persuasion and influence work. I believe it's one of the key skills for everyone who wants to get on in life or business to learn. I'd give the job without hesitation, or even an interview, to Phil Hesketh. This book is the definitive guide to being more persuasive and influential.'

Steve McDermott, author of the bestselling
How to Be a Complete and Utter Failure in Life,
Work and Everything **and winner of the European**
Business Speaker of the Year award

'Superb content coupled with excellent delivery means there is something for everyone. An incredibly valuable book'

Chris Norman, Managing Director, Johnson
& Johnson (DePuy UK/Ireland)

'If you only read one book on how to be more persuasive and influential – this is it. A modern classic.'

Paul McGee, The Sumo Guy, author of the bestselling
S.U.M.O. (Shut Up, Move On)

How to Persuade And Influence People

Powerful techniques to get your own way more often

Philip Hesketh

CAPSTONE
be inspired!
™

Library of Congress Cataloguing-in-Publication Data

9780857080424

A catalogue record for this book is available from the British Library.

Set in 11.5 on 14pt Adobe Caslon Pro-Regular by aptara

Printed in Great Britain by TJ International Ltd, Padstow, Cornwall

CONTENTS

PREFACE

It's often said that nothing under the sun is really new. There are just new twists on existing themes. So when I set out to write a book on persuasion—a subject that's been around ever since early caveman first encouraged his fellow cave dwellers to see things his way with the aid of a big club—I admit to being a little apprehensive. At one point I even considered the idea of setting up a 'Plagiarism Advice Bureau' to counter any criticism. But then I guess somebody has already done that too. The bottom line is that you just don't know if someone has had the same idea as you.

The first version of this book was called *Life's a Game So Fix the Odds*. I was happy with it in 2005 and it has sold well throughout the world. But five years on and with so many rich and various experiences as a professional speaker on the psychology of persuasion and influence—plus all the research I had both done and come across over that period—it seemed right to revisit, rewrite and retitle the book.

Like everyone else I learn from other people. I read books, commission research, read other people's research, and present workshops and seminars from Ashton to Adelaide, from Dewsbury to Dubai. And from Pwllheli to Philadelphia.

I possibly observe what is going on around me more keenly than most: I study other people's reactions to situations with great assiduity. And after five years I felt that my book could be improved.

I think it is the better for it.

I hope you agree.

Philip Hesketh, 2010

PART 1

THE STARTING POINT— PEOPLE, BELIEFS AND RELATIONSHIPS

Daring to Begin

The Role of the Subconscious in Influence

How to be More Liked by More People

How to Remember People's Names

How to Develop Good Relationships

1

DARING TO BEGIN

In successful relationships, people never stand still. They're always moving forward and evolving to make their relationship even more successful. Happy and successful people continually work on their skills and their ability to be more persuasive and influential. So when you are going through a change in your life, you always need to counteract the uncertainty that generates with hope that things will get better. And the greater the degree of hope, the more positive vibes you give off to those around you and the greater the chance of a positive outcome and long-term success.

Research among businesses going through change reveals that employees who are hopeful of providing worthwhile solutions are much more likely to produce positive results. Why? Because people with hope enjoy themselves more and are a great deal more productive.

You no doubt want others to say 'yes' to you more often. You would like to get your own way most of the time. You want to be more persuasive and influential, so people will do what you want them to do. That's what this book is about.

It teaches you specific techniques that allow you to become more influential and persuasive. Techniques that enable you to get your own way more often, whether you are in business—hoping to find ways of convincing colleagues and potential clients—or looking for ways to improve your relationships.

I also explore the difference between persuasion and influence. Persuasion is often something we 'do' to people—and most people don't want to be persuaded. Have you ever gone home after a day's shopping and said to whoever you live with, 'Guess what someone sold me today?'

I didn't think so. If you said to a friend 'I've been persuaded to do this', you almost certainly didn't feel good about it. Because persuasion is something we *do* to people. And influence is something that we *have*.

HOPE

So it is with hope that I start to write this book. It is a Tuesday evening in England. It's cold, dark and miserable. In fact, it's snowing.

But not for me.

For me it's a Wednesday morning and I'm sitting overlooking the bay in Russell, Bay of Islands, New Zealand. It's a lovely summer's day with just a little cloud. An early morning walker ambles by; the ducks float happily and the world is at one.

For me it is an epiphanic moment.

My story is of a lifetime of studying persuasion, influence, communication and relationships. I have been fascinated by how and why we do what we do. Though one is never sure, I think that the process of study began when a neighbour of my parents in Ashton-under-Lyne gave me a copy of Dale Carnegie's *How to Win Friends and Influence People*. It was then, at the age of about 16, that I decided to live my life with the principles of that book in mind. Many years later, in my first year as a professional speaker on the psychology of persuasion, I vowed not to write a book until I could write one that was better than the book I had read all those years before. Carnegie's book rightly remains a classic. You are the better for reading it.

But I had also set myself a number of goals in deciding to become a professional speaker. First, I wanted to become the best and most sought-after speaker on the planet, bar none. Secondly, I wanted to become a Professor at Harvard and speak at the likes of Oxford, Cambridge and Yale universities. Thirdly, I wanted to write a bestselling book, and fourthly, I wanted to change the weather in February. If you've ever visited the north of England you'll understand why. And finally, I set a goal for my son Daniel and I: one day to play live, together, on stage with the great Ralph McTell. That's my dream. Naturally, it doesn't figure highly on Ralph's list of goals, but remember what this book is all about: learning how to persuade and influence other people to do what you want them to do. Look out, Ralph.

And so I sit in the Bay of Islands in the North Island of New Zealand, having achieved one of my goals. I have changed the weather in February. For me, at least.

This book is not just about understanding how the process of influence works and making yourself happier, it's also about challenging yourself to establish what your goals are. It is about you deciding on your own equivalent of hope, of changing the weather in February, and how to achieve it.

For you.

Life is a game and this book helps you to improve the odds.

DARE TO BEGIN

But I said that I wouldn't write a book until I could write a better one than Dale Carnegie's classic. So why now? Will it be better? I don't know. But I do know that there may never be a better time than this one to start.

So I'm taking my own advice and daring to begin. I don't want to work in a biscuit factory again, but I'm glad I did. Two night shifts at Hills was more than enough for me.

Instead, I want to go to Kansas City and see if everything is up to date there. I want to go to Alexandria and have an ice-cold beer. I want to go to Nashville and play the guitar. They're not so keen, obviously, but it's what I want. I want to drive down Route 66 to see if I can get my kicks there. I want to stand on the corner in Winslow, Arizona and see if it is such a fine sight to see. I want to meet a Wichita lineman. At some point in my life, I want to actually be 24 hours from Tulsa. I want to sail on *Kon-Tiki*. I want to fly with eagles and swim with dolphins. I want to go for it all or die trying.

The first step in achieving your goals is to believe that you can. But you also need the courage to recognize that sometimes you are simply not physically or mentally able to fulfil a dream; so you do what you can and move on. Remember, life and happiness are about the journey and not the destination. In my previous life as an ad man for 25 years, I was often asked the question, 'How do I become a director?' My answer was always, 'Start behaving like one now.'

So I begin this book because I can. Because I can't think of a better time to start than when it's dark and snowing in England in February and I'm overlooking the bay in Russell, having just finished breakfast.

However, before I start on persuasion and influence, an apology.

I am of the view that there is no need to use swear words. The English language is rich and deep and there are many words you can use when you feel that something is nonsense, whether it's an idea, a belief or a point of view. You disagree, you think it's wrong, very wrong. In fact, you think it's rubbish. You get my drift?

Well, despite my best efforts, I can't find a word that effectively conveys what my dad would call 'absolute balderdash'. So I invented a word: 'horrocks'. It means that I think a theory or view is horribly wrong. I'm afraid, dear reader, I use it 12 times in this book, including this one here.

Bear with me.

Just as studies have shown that people who score high on hope cope better with disease, illness and pain, so I find that because I expect people to say yes to me—to do what I want them to do—it happens more often than if I assume I am going to fail.

And so I ask you to read this book with hope.

I will not only share with you techniques to improve your ability to persuade and influence, improve your reputation and get your own way more often, I will also give you the secrets to happiness and the purpose of life.

Time to begin.

2

THE ROLE OF THE SUBCONSCIOUS IN INFLUENCE

In the decades-long battle of the colas, Coke continues to outsell Pepsi. Not because it costs less or tastes nicer, but because we, the consumer, just think that it's better. Let me explain.

Back in the early 1980s, a series of taste tests found that most people actually preferred the taste of Pepsi over Coke. Provided, that is, they were blindfolded during the challenge and couldn't see which one they were drinking. However, run the challenge without the blindfolds and the results were almost always reversed. Coca Cola—or Coke as it is universally known—proved itself time again to be the real thing. But why?

Well, years later, Reed Montague and his team at the Neuro-imaging Laboratory in Houston came up with an answer. His researchers discovered that the ventral putamen—one of the brain's reward centres—behaved differently when people used only taste information than when they also had brand identification.

So brainwashed are you by years of advertising telling you that Coke is better, that when you see a can and take a swig your ventral putamen thinks 'bingo'. My words, not Montague's.

Technically speaking, this area of the brain is hijacked and the neuron connections go straight to your dorsolateral prefrontal cortex, which is the area concerned with opinions. So your brain is telling you that you love the taste even though your taste buds may be screaming for you to gag.

Therefore, the first thing you should know about your preference for Coke or Pepsi is that you don't really know what you are doing, so deep in your brain is the belief about certain brands. That explains why it's such a hard job not only to get people to change their mind about brands regardless of how good the product might be, but also to get people to change their mind on anything. The stronger someone feels about something, the more difficult it is for them to change their view. You might well have that frustration yourself.

But the second thing you should know about Coke is who really won the cola war. Not the customer, for a start. If you go to any bar and ask for Coca-Cola you will often get the reply, 'Will Pepsi be OK?' That's because bars that sell Pepsi don't sell Coke, and vice versa. Maybe these establishments would gain a marketing advantage if they were able to offer both.

Incidentally, if you were Coca-Cola and you knew that people liked your brand but preferred the taste of Pepsi, what would you do to strengthen your market position? Of course, you would bring out New Coke, which tasted more like Pepsi. This is exactly what the company did, with disastrous consequences. It just goes to show that you can't fool all the people all the time.

BELIEFS

Along with five partners, I set up an advertising agency in 1986 called Advertising Principles. In the ensuing years we handled some major brands. The focus of the agency was to convince people to buy those clients' brands. My personal focus was on getting new business for the agency. And what always fascinated me more than anything was how brands worked. That is to say, how consumers have beliefs about brands; and indeed, in some cases, blind faith in a brand. We used to do the '625 Test'—which I'll explain later—for a beer brand, which illustrated what Dr Montague also found: that people believe in brands (i.e. an idea) and continue to believe in them, despite being faced with subsequent, over-whelming evidence that contradicts their belief. It's a bit like believing in Father Christmas when you are little.

I loved Father Christmas. I truly believed he existed and loved me. I'd seen him. My parents, friends, aunts and uncles all told me he was real and I trusted them to tell me the truth. And what better evidence was there than on the morning of December 25th? 'He's been!' The thing is—I don't want to ruin it for you here—but it wasn't true, was it? It was just a belief. Many people have beliefs that aren't true. People believe not only in their chosen brands but also in their chosen opinions. Or sometimes the opinion that was given to them by their mother, father, favourite uncle, or even old boss who promised, 'If I want your opinion, I'll give it to you.' They—and you—have all sorts of beliefs and if you're going to become more persuasive as a result of reading this book, we need to start here.

With beliefs. In particular, the beliefs of the people you want to persuade. Because it doesn't matter whether the beliefs are true or not. People have beliefs, and they are held in the subconscious.

15 years after setting up Advertising Principles, I enrolled on a course at Harvard Business School. That had been one of my goals since I visited the place on holiday some years

before. After all, if I was to be a professor at Harvard, I needed to study there as a starting point. You'll remember that I also set myself the goals of playing live with Ralph McTell, being the best professional speaker on the planet, going to New Zealand and, of course, changing the weather in February. One of my partners at Advertising Principles, Bernie May, came with me. The lecture I most remember was when Professor Gerald Zaltman was speaking on the subject of the subconscious.

'95% of our thoughts are subconscious,' he said.

'*Wow!*' I thought. That means 95% of our thoughts are not within our control! Frankly, I doubted him. I thought he'd made it up. So I put my hand up and asked the question, 'How do we know it's 95%, Professor Zaltman? Why *that* figure?'

He paused. 'Do you mean beyond the fact that I, a professor at Harvard, who have written 14 books on the subject, am a past President of the Association for Consumer Research, have an AB from Bates College, an MBA from the University of Chicago, a PhD from the John Hopkins University and am widely regarded as the world's leading authority on the subconscious, say so?'

Oh dear. You know those times when you've put one foot in and there's no getting it out again? You have foolishly said something that if you'd thought about it a little more you would never, ever say? He basically changed the lecture and told us about the subconscious. The point was that what people *say* they do isn't necessarily what they *actually* do.

UNDERSTANDING WHAT PEOPLE THINK

I sat in, or listened to, dozens and dozens of focus groups when I worked in advertising and I drew three conclusions. First, most people, most of the time, don't know why they do what they do. Secondly, they don't really know why they buy what they buy. And thirdly, people lie; not always consciously, either. People interpret events in different ways. How they see things is not how you see things.

For instance, people may say what they think the researcher wants them to say, or what will impress others. People often struggle to understand themselves and why they've done what they have. Even 'accompanied shops'—when a shopper is escorted by a researcher, who prompts them and asks them why they're choosing one brand over another—have enormous flaws from a research point of view. And, on top of all that, most people don't know why they're doing what they're doing anyway!

Take personal care and beauty products such as perfumes and cosmetics. They invoke deep thoughts and feelings about what Professor Zaltman calls 'social bonding'. How someone grips a product in their hand tells you more about how they really feel about it than what they say. What is communicated through body language is far more believable than words and tone of voice. My wife often doesn't need to say anything to communicate. Words don't even reach 1%: she can do whole paragraphs with a single glance.

Nevertheless, I believe that Professor Albert Mehrabian's 1960s studies, which concluded that 55% of communication is through body language, 38% is tone of voice and 7% is the actual words spoken, are horrocks. Or rather, the way they've been interpreted make them so.

His research is out of date—The Beatles were releasing *Sgt Pepper's* and Sandie Shaw had just won the Eurovision Song Contest with '*Puppet on a String*' when he published his results in May 1967—and was based on his own students simply saying nine different words. However, we remember it because we understand that body language—what we give away by how we act and react—can be revealing.

Yet in reality, body language and tone count for little when we are in rapt attention and learning something very new, very relevant and of high interest. When you are trying to persuade someone, particularly of something quite radical, they will always see and perceive it in terms of their personal frame of reference. And if you don't understand—or at least begin to appreciate—their frame of reference, you will struggle to get your message across.

Remember that famous Institute of Directors' dinner in 1991, when jeweller Gerald Ratner said, 'People ask me how can we afford to sell this stuff so cheap and I say because it's absolute crap'? He couldn't have known what kind of frame of reference he was setting up for his audience. Hidden deep within the subconscious mind of anyone who heard or read about that statement is a frame of reference that Ratner equals crap. It's probably in the same 'box' as Roy Keane equals prawn sandwiches and Brentfords equals nylons, and some people's deep-seated beliefs from their childhood that God is a Catholic and therefore anyone who is not a Catholic will not be able to enter Heaven; or at the very least, they won't get a good seat.

Nevertheless, the fact is that we all have subconscious beliefs and it doesn't matter whether or not they are true. If we believe something, we look for evidence to support our belief—and we usually find it.

So persuasion is not just about turning features into benefits, but about understanding as much as we can about how the person we are trying to persuade thinks.

I was in town recently in a menswear store. The owner of the shop asked me if I wanted any help. 'No thanks,' I said, 'I'm just browsing.' As I was doing just that, another guy came in with his 'significant other'. They were smartly dressed and as they walked into the shop the owner again said, 'Can I help you?' The man smiled and said, in a very polite way, 'I'm looking for a BOSS suit. I like the brand BOSS. Do you sell BOSS?'

The shop didn't sell BOSS. So what would you do if you were the guy who owns it? Let me give you three options:

1　Tell the customer that you don't sell BOSS but you know where he could find it.
2　Say that you agree that BOSS is a fine brand, that you can understand why he likes it and although you don't sell it yourself, you have something similar.
3　Say that you agree that BOSS is a fine brand and ask him what in particular he likes about it so that you have the best chance of matching his need to something you do have in the shop.

Clearly option 1 is helpful, but you have little or no chance of making a sale. And you are reading this book, I hope, because you want to influence people to buy what you sell. Option 2 is a much better answer but you're still guessing. Option 3 is clearly the best. People like people who respect their opinions.

Incidentally, shall I tell you what the shop owner actually did? He said, 'We all like BOSS sir, but can you afford their prices?' The guy looked him straight in the eye and replied, 'Yes I can.' And promptly walked out of the shop!

You can't insult people and hope to persuade them. One can only guess how many people the customer told that story to over the following weeks—people who were potential customers for a friendly menswear store that relies on personal recommendation! Will he ever go back to a shop that questions his ability to buy a particular brand?

The point is that the potential buyer had a belief. His belief was—and almost certainly *still is*—that BOSS is an excellent brand and it's the brand for him. The belief is a deep-rooted one and it's also an emotional one. He likes people who also like BOSS because people like people who a) are like them, b) like what they like and c) have similar beliefs.

The lesson of this whole book—if you want to skip the rest of the chapters and find the 'key', the 'nugget', the 'kernel'—is this: listen with rapt attention and understand that people have different opinions to you before you speak. The starting point for persuasion is to accept that the other person's belief system may be quite different to yours. And if you are going to persuade them to do what *you* want them to do, you need to find out more about *their* beliefs and views. You need to know what they believe in. You need to know what *motivates* them.

HORSE AND RIDER

I want you to imagine that the person you're trying to persuade is riding a horse. The horse is 95% of the whole and the person is the other 5%. The horse is the subconscious mind and the rider is the conscious mind. If you are to persuade the person to change their opinion and buy into your idea, it's like asking them to change the direction and speed of the horse. And, get this, the person you are trying to persuade is not in control of their horse!

Makes it a bit tricky now, doesn't it? But that is what persuasion is all about.

It's about understanding how your horse—your subconscious—gives away what you are thinking to the other person. It's about seeing how the other person's horse reacts. It is also about understanding that you have to persuade the other person's horse.

It is the subconscious, or the 'cognitive unconscious', that explains why decisions are emotional.

People buy emotionally and justify logically. Indeed, all decisions are made emotionally. The justification can be terribly logical, but the decision to buy is emotional. The post-purchase justification process is what psychology terms 'cognitive dissonance'. Logic is the language of and for the conscious mind. Emotion is the language of and for the subconscious mind.

The banking and credit industry would be structured very, very differently if we only bought logically. If no one needed 'retail therapy'. If we only bought what we could afford. If we only bought what we needed and not what we wanted.

I love the whole concept of placebos. Who's kidding whom here? You are *told* a particular prescription will be good for you (and your horse believes it) and, hey presto, so often the 'miracle drug', which is just a sugar pill, actually improves your physical condition. You just trained your horse by tricking it into believing that you will get better.

When I was a Boy Scout we used to go on camping holidays. The Scout Leader was Alan Fish. Alan hadn't done a degree in psychology, but he knew a thing or two about small boys. He bought dozens of aspirins and put them into 10 different small boxes. He carefully labelled the boxes according to different parts of the body. There were 'knee pills', 'headache pills', 'back pills' and so on.

If a boy had an injury, cut or bruise, Alan would painstakingly go through all the boxes to make sure he selected the right pill: the 'specialist' pill for the ailment. And it appeased every one of us. There was a bit of a to-do when a lad fell on his coccyx, but apart from that the scheme worked quite well.

It was my introduction to psychology.

People say, 'I've tried to give up smoking but I can't.' When you keep saying that, who's the person who hears you the most?

You! And your horse holds the belief that you can't give up smoking. Ever.

People often say to me, 'I wish I could lose weight.' I tell them I have a five-second talk that, if they follow the instructions in it, will guarantee they will not only lose weight and live a healthier lifestyle but be happier too. So if you want to lose weight, live a healthier lifestyle, be happier with your own body and be happier too, here's the secret:

+ Eat less
+ Eat better
+ Exercise more
+ Take personal responsibility to do those three things

I'm fascinated by how my own subconscious works. If I need to wake up early to catch a plane or a train, I always wake up early. I have trained my horse to do so without any effort!

I'm also fascinated by persuasion and influence and how they work—which is what this book is all about.

3

HOW TO BE MORE LIKED BY MORE PEOPLE

(AND AS A RESULT BECOME MORE PERSUASIVE AND INFLUENTIAL)

When I was at school in Ashton, I used to work in a bakery on Saturdays. Not only did I earn a day's pay and still finish in time to play football in the afternoon, I also got to drive a big van. I would drive around from market to market delivering bread, buns, cakes and what my mother endearingly referred to as 'fancies'. We started promptly at 6 a.m. and I would leave home to walk to the bakery at half-past five. It fascinated me that everyone I saw said 'hello' to each other. At that early hour there were only a few souls about and there was always an acknowledgement. By seven o'clock or so the effect ended, simply because there were more people about.

It's similar now whenever I'm running (my sons call it jogging, but I like to refer to it as running)—there's always a nod of the head from other runners. An acknowledgement, because we're doing the same thing. And when I took my sons to university, the other dads and I acknowledged each other as we carried the music systems and books and other accoutrements of student life into their halls of residence. Not only were we doing the same thing, we tended to be dressed alike too, what I call the Tony Blair School of Casual Wear for the Over-40s: chinos, deck shoes and an open-necked, button-down denim shirt.

People like people who are like them. People like people who dress and behave like they do. In meetings it's good to have a coffee together—not because you need the coffee, but because you are sharing an experience. You are 'alike'.

When golfers meet, the conversation naturally turns to handicaps. Now, I'm not what you would call a 'natural' at golf. I think it's God's way of making me humble. But when a golfer I've just met asks me my handicap, I seem to get one of two reactions. If they're a good golfer—my definition is they're expected to score par on at least one hole—they react with an 'oh dear' expression. They're not eager to play with me because I'm not like them. Conversely, if their handicap is in the 20s they tend to slap me on the back, shake my hand and say something like, 'That's great, we're both rubbish—we must have a game!'

The whole purpose of the handicap system is to allow golfers of different abilities to play against each other and enjoy the competition. Why is that?

Because people like people who are like them. It's why you need first to agree that BOSS is a good brand. People like people who dress and behave like they do. You can only do so much about how you look, but you can do a lot about how you dress. And, just as importantly, you can influence what you share with others about what you believe in. People like people who agree with them. People like people who mirror their actions and body language. People like people who respect their beliefs and values. Those might include the importance of timekeeping, having clean shoes or just not saying 'I hate dogs' when it's manifestly obvious the other person is a dog lover.

It's the things we have in common that help create relationships and the differences that make other people interesting or irritating.

Have you ever been to a football match and been part of a Mexican Wave? You get a nice feeling of doing something together—we are alike. The men in suits and ladies in hats in the directors' box don't participate; they are saying they are not like us. And we don't like people who don't want to be like us and do what we are doing, so we boo them!

Watch the same people in that crowd enter a church, a library, a hospital waiting room or an expensive hotel. We behave as we do there not only because we think we should, but because everyone else is acting in a hushed, reverent manner.

People like people who truly listen to them. People like people who flatter them and talk about their interests. People like people who remember their name. People like people who show a real and genuine interest in them. People like people who are like them.

Birds of a feather flock together.

Regrettably, there's a flipside to that coin. People often don't like other people for no good reason than that they're not like them. For evidence, take religious intolerance and bigotry down the ages. Wars have been caused and continue to be fought, and the root of them is often simply that people don't like people who are not like them. They don't believe in the same things.

I live in Yorkshire and I was born and raised in Lanca-shire. It's over 500 years since Henry VII married Princess Elizabeth of York, uniting the warring Houses of Lancaster and York, but the rivalry remains. People like to 'belong' and the natural corollary to belonging is disliking those who don't belong. Ask the people in Dubai what they think of the folk in live in Abu Dhabi, Liverpool fans what they think of people who support Manchester United, see what the Kiwis say about the Aussies. Go to a cricket match between India and Pakistan. I could go on. It's natural.

So should you be a chameleon? Because people are far easier to persuade if they like you, the essence of selling is to make it easier for people to buy. The process starts with the relationship. And that, in turn, starts with how much other people like you and respect you.

Let's look at the key issues here.

FIRST IMPRESSIONS

A whole host of research projects have been undertaken to discover exactly how long it takes to form a lasting first impression. My summary is that 90% of the time, 90% of people form 90% of their first impression of you within 90 seconds. And typically, before you've spoken, what you wear and the way you walk and hold yourself are the key elements in that first impression. If you're going to persuade someone you have never met before, you need to think about all those issues.

I believe that people effectively 'plot' you on a First Impressions scale that has 'Like you/Don't like you' on the vertical axis and what might best be described as 'Respect you/ Don't respect you' on the horizontal axis (see Figure 3.1).

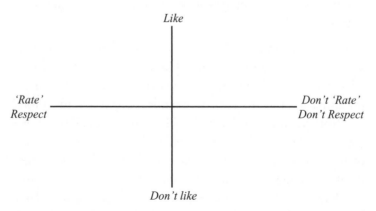

Like

'Rate'
Respect

Don't 'Rate'
Don't Respect

Don't like

Figure 3.1 on First Impressions

There is, of course, another axis. It's referred to sometimes as 'Love at first sight'. The French call it *un coup de foudre*, a bolt of lightning. It's about love and lust and passion. It's the degree of instant physical and sexual attraction between two people, their 'chemistry'.

Despite the fact that you can, of course, change your opinion of someone (and he or she of you), the initial opinion that is formed is immovable. Have you ever heard someone say, 'I never liked him from the beginning'?

Persuasion and influence begin with the relationship. And that, in turn, begins with the first impression. When I worked in advertising, no company ever appointed our agency. *People* at the company appointed the *people* at the agency.

Because people buy people first. The press release would always say something like, 'We very much liked the agency's strategic input and the creative solutions were radical, innovative and on brief blah blah blah.' We almost always, like every other agency and PR company, wrote the quote ourselves and although there was some truth in it, the real truth was that the people at the client end liked the people at the agency.

They *liked* them. They could relate to them. They had confidence in them. And yes, they thought they would deliver the creative product.

When I worked in Newcastle I represented an ad agency called Riley Advertising. I went to see someone called Josie Pottinger at a large local company. We had three or four meetings and at that tender age and stage of my career, I couldn't work out why she didn't want to use our agency. We were nearer geographically, could offer a better service at a reduced price and presented a number of benefits over her London-based agency. But she didn't appoint us. When

I left to work for the office in Manchester, I introduced her to my replacement in Newcastle, Norma Barclay. Within a month, Norma had won the account and the 1% commission that went with it.

I was obviously a little frustrated and curious and I asked Norma to chat to Josie and find out what the decider had been. Josie said, 'I always thought Phil made a lot of sense. I could see we would get a better service at a better price. I was sure it would be a sound decision. I just didn't particularly like him.'

Oh no! Not that she didn't like me, but that I didn't *spot* she didn't like me. Because people buy people first. The first impression really counts in the persuasion process. And it's the non-verbal signals that matter in making the first impression.

NON-VERBAL SIGNALS

I read recently that Prince Charles holds and plays with his cufflinks in the way he does because he's 'chained to the monarchy'. Horrocks. It's just displacement activity. It's something to do because he's a little nervous. But that 'something to do' gives him away.

How do we tell if our body is sending the right signals? And how do we read those of others?

Basically, if you're bored, you're likely to be boring. If you don't really want to be somewhere, your body gives it away. In contrast, enthusiasm is contagious and it's communicated by body language. If you don't have any enthusiasm, get another job.

It would be easy to dismiss this as obvious, but approaching a new meeting with someone expecting a positive outcome actually does make a difference, according to research by

Dr Danu Anthony Stinson at the University of Waterloo in Canada. He's been able to back up the idea of the self-fulfilling prophecy in first impressions. Namely, whatever you expect to happen, probably will. That's because your behaviour influences that of the other person. So if you go in there all meek and mild like a lamb to the slaughter, the chances are you'll be chewed up and spat out, if you'll pardon my French.

Stinson proved that what psychologists call the 'acceptance prophecy' holds true by arranging a series of blind dates between men and women. Half the men were told that the women they were going to meet were a little anxious about the date and half were told that their blind date was an experienced man-eating vixen with a sixth sense for bullshit. He may not have used those exact words, but that was the nub of it. The result of the blind date experiment showed that the men who met the 'nervous' women behaved in a warm, friendly and relaxed manner. Their prior knowledge of their date's anxiety had the opposite effect on them and made them feel more confident in comparison and – here's the clincher – much more likeable. However, it was a different story for the men who met the cross between Bette Davis and Myra Hindley. Their nervousness and fear of rejection were naturally heightened and let's just say they didn't even steal a kiss.

In summary, the guys who were confident got on better with the women, whereas the ones who approached the meeting fearing rejection came across as colder and didn't get on with the women at all. Just as importantly, an independent panel of researchers who observed each date liked the personality of the confident guys much more than the others.

So be a social and business optimist. Approach every meeting expecting to be liked and more often than not you will be.

EYE MOVEMENTS

If you want to know what someone thinks of you, look at their eye movements. When we first meet someone we tend to look from eye to eye, across the bridge of the nose. If you've ever wondered where to look when you're meeting someone in a business situation, simply look at the gap between their eyes at the bridge of their nose. You don't want to stare because it embarrasses them, but you don't want to be continually averting your gaze because they begin to distrust you. (This is all going on in their subconscious, by the way.)

Interestingly, with friends, the gaze tends to drop below eye level and moves into a triangle shape around the two eyes and the mouth. And if a couple start getting into what my mother calls 'a bit of something going on', the triangle gets bigger. It widens at the bottom and they start to look at each other's mouths. So if you want to know if someone likes you in *that* way, look to see if they're staring at your mouth. If they are, they subconsciously want to kiss you…

It's a well-researched fact that if someone finds you attractive, their pupil size increases and so does their blink rate. So if you find someone attractive and want to test them out, increase your blink rate. If they feel the same way about you, they'll unconsciously begin to match your blink rate. This is called 'mirroring' and get this—they won't know they're doing it!

MIRRORING

So people like people who are like them. And people are easier to persuade if they like you. So how do you 'cheat'? How do you get them to like you? Particularly if physically and perhaps in terms of age you're not that alike?

Well, the first step is to believe they are going to like you and the second step is to look really, really interested. Raise your eyebrows in a positive way, lean forward and smile. And the third step?

Mirroring.

Basically, you do whatever they do. If they fold their arms and lean against a door, do that. If they lean forward in an 'I'll confide in you' sort of way, then lean forward too. When they reach for their cup of coffee, so do you. If they stroke their chin and look pensive, you do the same. If their feet point towards you they are being open—so follow them.

But not too close, or else it looks like you've read a book or been on a course.

The secret is to let them feel that they're on the same 'wavelength' as you. Give them the impression that you understand their mood and circumstances and truly empathize with it. Do it. It works.

Now you know but they don't. Unless they've read this book too.

And sometimes it's just natural, isn't it? Sometimes it feels as though you are numbers on the radio dial. You meet someone and you know you are on the same frequency.

But this book and the benefit I hope you get from it apply when things are not so natural. Not everyone likes everyone else easily. For all of us, some people are simpler to like than others. The thing is, if you want to be more persuasive, you need people to like you more—even when it's not so natural.

There's a flipside to 'love at first sight' too, isn't there? When love is over and the embers are all that's left of the fire that once burned, and all the signals are clear, we tend to avoid them. Sometimes lovers merely drift apart and it's as natural as the tide going out. When you are lying beside the one you once loved is when you feel the most alone. And we avoid the feelings and the little voice that talks to us, just as we try to avoid an unpleasant time. We know it's coming but we don't want to face it. Complicated stuff, love. Let's get back to persuasion.

But before we go into more detail about how you improve the impression people have of you, remember that *you* are always forming an opinion of the person you are meeting too. Let me give you this thought.

Each year, over £20 billion is inherited by British individuals. We are the first generation to benefit in such enormous numbers from our parents having property, and it was the buying of property in the 1950s and 1960s that is now triggering the largest transfer of wealth in the history of money. First impressions have always been deceptive, but even more so now if you're wondering whether somebody's got enough money to buy your product or service. In other words, don't *you* judge a book by its cover.

IMPROVING THE IMPRESSION YOU MAKE

When we come to the section in the book on negotiation, you'll find out that one of the key things is to be fully aware of what your body is saying to the other person. The important lesson us: do not let your body do what it naturally wants to do.

So what are the key issues for managing the impression you make?

+ **Be on time and reduce the chance of someone finding something offensive or off-putting about you.** Have clean fingernails, clean shoes and be appropriately dressed. One of my clients always wears cufflinks. All his senior people do. It's his thing. It's his standard. So I wear cufflinks when I go to see him.

I clearly remember working with Mike Moran when he was at what was then Pharmacia. We met in a Little Chef in Cumbria. I had, quite frankly, not thought through the implications of visiting vets and farmers in the Lake District. It was in the third vet's surgery with all around me dressed in browns and tweeds and me in my blue suit, white shirt and Armani tie that it really got to me. 'Who's the city slicker then?' said the receptionist just in earshot as Mike and I went in to see the vet. So it's not always about looking like a tailor's dummy, is it?

+ **Expect to be liked.** Feel positive and alive and tell your body. If you're happy, tell your face. If you're not feeling positive, fake it for a day or go home.

+ **Prepare well and think about how you can make a good impression.** Don't sit down in someone's office or boardroom until they point to where they want you to sit.

I once blew a presentation to a major company in the north of England because I sat in the chairman's favourite seat. Throughout the presentation his whole body language was negative. He wasn't ever really interested. And it was only as we were packing away our flip charts and slides that the marketing manager said. 'I perhaps should have told you the chairman only ever likes to sit in that chair.'

+ **Listen with rapt attention.** Look very, very interested. Right at that very moment they are the only person who matters to you. People tend to listen with the intention of saying something. Some people even listen with the sole intent of 'topping' your story. Anything you say, they have been at a better or bigger one. Anything you have seen, they have seen a longer and wider one. They know someone more senior. They know someone who took longer, ran faster, went further and so on.

If you want people to like you, don't top their stories. Listen with rapt attention. Listen simply so that you can truly understand how they *feel* about what they're saying. Listen so that you see things from their point of view. They will like you more and you might learn something too.

✦ **Flatter them and talk about their interests.** Most people are interested in three main things: themselves, their pleasures and their problems. So talk about them.

If you are meeting someone you need to persuade, flatter them by reading up on their subject. When I go to see a potential client I look at their website and print off a page or two. I let them casually see that I have the copy and they always, always comment on the fact that I've taken the trouble to look at their website. They like that. And so do I.

Say things like: 'That must be really enjoyable', 'How did you feel when that happened?', 'That's quite a story', 'You must be very proud', 'That's fascinating'.

But be sincere. Be honest. Be genuinely interested in the other person. Don't be a charlatan.

CHOOSE WHO YOU INTRODUCE YOURSELF TO

Finally, when you go to a conference at which you know no one, do you just wander up to the first person you see or do you do your homework, have a good look at the delegate list and plan who you speak to and, indeed, sit next to? Well, some more research tells us whether or not that matters.

I saw a movie recently in which a bunch of ageing friends went on one last road trip together across the wastelands of the Mid West on Harley-Davidsons. It was rather like a reunion of old university pals that I attend. We don't own motor bikes, we tend to meet up in the wastelands of Berkshire and stay put in a comfy hotel called Caddy Palace.

The point is that all six of us met on the very first day of university as freshers and have remained firm friends ever since. That's despite sharing a flat in Newcastle for three years with all the inherent squabbling and subsequent deep resentment over things like cooking rotas and washing your smalls in the sink. A habit I've now managed to kick.

Our children think it's amazing that our friendships formed on the very first day of university should have lasted for more than 30 years. But is it so unusual? Dr Mitja Back of the University of Leipzig subjected brand new psychology students to a nerve-wracking first day. At their introductory session students were told to sit randomly. Then each fretting fresher had to introduce themselves from the podium. Immediately after their presentation everyone else was asked to rate that person on two scales: how much they liked them and whether they would like to get to know them more.

The results showed that people liked—and wanted to be friends with—the people they had initially sat next to. That's fairly understandable.

However, the most interesting results were revealed one year later when the students were well settled into the course, had mixed extensively with other students and knew each other much better. Surely that first day when the lecturer tortured them with random seat allocations, public introductions and instant judgements couldn't still influence their friendships?

It did. Even after a year, students who had sat on the same row as each other on that very first day liked each other better. And for those who had sat right next to each other, the level of liking was even higher.

Why should this be? Well, perhaps when we're in a brand new social environment we're anxious to make a connection with someone. Anyone. And when we find someone to talk to—an island of acceptance in a sea of strangers—we're so relieved that we're more likely to form a lasting bond.

So in the future, if you go to a conference where you know no one, be selective about the person you first introduce yourself to. Choose who you want to be with. You may be with them for a very long time...

4

HOW TO REMEMBER PEOPLE'S NAMES

People are flattered if you have taken the trouble to remember their name because it shows you care. You make them feel important. On my courses I often ask, 'Who's bad at remembering people's names?' I can guarantee at least 30% will put their hand up, often with a glow of pride at just how bad they are.

It's horrocks!

It's just a belief. One delegate said to me, 'My brother's memory is as bad as mine—we both think we're an only child.' A nice line (and probably an old joke), but the five-step plan to remembering people's names starts with the belief that you can. I'm a big fan of acronyms and this is the first of quite a number of them. But if the acronym is relevant, repeated and distinctly different, it's going to help, isn't it?

The five-step plan to remembering people's names is incorporated in the acronym BLUFF.

B is for Believe you can. Shed all thought of your inability to remember people's names. It's only a belief and, like most beliefs, it's just that. It's not true. So stop saying, 'I've always been bad at remembering people's names.' Stop saying, 'I can't remember people's names.' *Now.*

L is for Listen. Remember we talked about listening with rapt attention? According to my research, most people don't actually hear the other person's name in the first place but carry on chatting anyway. After only 30 seconds it seems too late to say, 'I can't remember your name.' That's because you never got it in the first place. So if you don't catch what someone says, *ask them again for their name.* Do you know, in all the time I've been doing this, if I don't quite catch someone's name and I say, 'I'm sorry, I didn't quite catch your name', no one has ever said, 'I gave you my name once and I won't tell you again.' They never feel upset or offended. Indeed, they are usually flattered that I want to know their name. So listen, and if you don't hear it, ask them to repeat it. Not rocket science, is it? So ask if you don't hear their name the first time.

U is for Use it. Use their name straight away. Immediately. Bounce it straight back to them, more than once. Not so many times that it sounds like you've read a book on how to remember people's names, but these first 60 seconds are critical if you want to remember their name. And you do. Because they'll like it. And they'll like you if you can remember their name. And the more they like you, the better your chance of being persuasive.

F is for Face. Their face. You need to link their name with their face, even if it's a simple case of looking at them directly and picturing them as you say their name.

And the final **F** is for File it or write it down. As soon as you can. Certainly if you are in a meeting and there are several people to work with, write their names down in the positions they are sitting, so at least in the meeting you can glance at your notes. John is sitting next to Joanne, and so on.

After the meeting or encounter, file your list. How often, if you do write down people's names, do you go back to your notes as soon after the meeting as you can to make notes on those you have met? The clothes they wore? Their habits, interests, football team, even their birthday? If this person, or these people, you have met are important to you and you need to persuade them over a period of time, collect all the information you can. Gather not only information on their name but also their interests. If they give you a business card, write on the back (amazing how few people use both sides of a business card, isn't it?) anything you can remember about them. As a minimum, write down where and when you met them. Finally, write in your diary alongside the appointment the people you met and a line about them.

I was in Marks & Spencer in Harrogate recently. I popped in to buy some shirts and socks. I bumped into an acquaintance. 'Hi Sally,' I said. 'How are you?' She paused and then stopped and said hello and how was I and how were the children and it was manifestly obvious she couldn't remember my name. That's okay—she doesn't do this for a living. She hasn't been on my course.

But I could tell she was trying to remember my name, so I helped her out. 'Chris said to me this morning, "Phil, you need to go to M&S and buy some white shirts. Why don't you pop in now and get me the gift tokens while you're there?"'

Sally visibly lightened up. *Now* she had my name and my wife's. And she continued to use my name for the rest of the conversation. So use your own name to help people out and help them remember you. Use your partner's or friend's name in a group or social situation. You want to be remembered by the people you're trying to persuade, don't you?

5

HOW TO DEVELOP GOOD RELATIONSHIPS

I want you to imagine your Christmas card list. If you are typical, you will find on that list a handful of people whom you might describe as 'very close friends'. The kind of friends who, when you call them on the telephone, you don't need to say who you are; you just start talking. No introductions necessary. Close friends whom you confide in, turn to, rely on and trust.

Then there's the next 'tranche' of friends. You don't have quite the same close relationship but you get on very well, you see each other socially and are happy to be in their company. And there's more than a handful of them.

Then there are the people you know and like but don't see a lot of. You might know them but not know their children's names. Friends, yes, but not in the inner circle. There are more of them. They're all the other people on your list.

This is the circle of friendships (see Figure 5.1).

This is how it is. Then there are the people you know but don't really know at all. When you meet you struggle to get past ritual and cliché. 'How are you?' 'Nice weather for ducks.' 'Did you take long to get here?' etc. They might not even be on your Christmas card list.

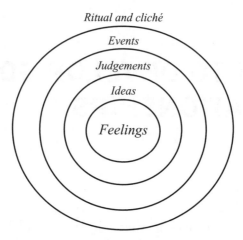

Figure 5.1　The Circle of Relationships

Do you have the same dilemma of most established couples, that once you've started sending and receiving Christmas cards you just keep going ad infinitum? No 'annual review' but rather, 'They always send us one so we'll send them one.' And throughout the year you have developed good relationships with other people but don't bother to send a card. Funny world, isn't it?

But the Christmas card list illustrates how relationships work. The friends on the inside of your circle have progressed there because you have common ground, common interests. They're usually (but not exclusively) people like you. And you love them.

I remember Prince Charles being pilloried by the press when he was asked if he loved the then Lady Diana Spencer. 'Yes,' he said, 'whatever that is.' I think he was referring to *love* and not Diana. To be fair to him, love is such an inadequate and insufficient word, isn't it? It's like saying that what is between black and white is all grey. One shade. It's like saying that green is the colour that comprehensively describes all the colours you can see from the top of Pen-y-Ghent.

Did you know that the Inuit have over a dozen words for 'snow' because it matters to them to be able to describe the difference? When an Inuit comes back home after catching the breakfast and his wife says, 'What's it like out?' there's not much point in him replying, 'It looks like snow.' She wants to know what kind of snow so that she can wear the right kind of footwear. 'It's not a stiletto day, darling' would be much more useful.

I love many people, but none of them in the same way. Not even women since I threw away the manual in my late teens. I don't even love the immediate members of my family in the same way. But there aren't easily accessible words to help me communicate all those things. It's nice stuff, love, but it's complicated.

You can discuss feelings (and you don't need to have known each other very long for all this to happen) with people you know well and with people you like. Not just ideas, views and opinions, but how you feel about things. It's a deeper relationship when you can talk about how you feel about something. And the word 'feel' is like the word 'love'. If you want to be truly persuasive, I want you to consider that the word 'feel' is as inadequate as the word 'love'. As inadequate as the Inuit would feel if they could only use one word for snow.

THE THREE PARTS TO EVERY CONVERSATION

My wife said to me recently, 'Don't buy me flowers from the petrol station.' And she said it in a staccato, abrupt manner with a very strong emphasis on each word. The facts are clear: I bought my wife some flowers. But it's not the facts that matter—it's the feelings. She went on to say,

'I wouldn't mind if you had gone to the petrol station to buy me flowers and when you arrived, decided that you may as well also buy some petrol. But it wasn't that way round, was it? It was an afterthought.'

Every conversation you ever have with anyone has three parts:

+ Facts
+ Feelings
+ After effects

It wasn't the flowers that were the issue; it was that there was no real thought to their purchase. Why do people wrap presents? Because it shows they care. It wasn't the flowers, it was the effort I didn't go to that matters. And that influences what people think of you. When someone says to you, 'Well, with all due respect...', you immediately feel slighted and feel that they have no respect for you and your opinions.

I was speaking at an academic conference recently when one speaker, making a reference to a fellow academic's work, said, 'In Peter's otherwise excellent book...' The after effects of that may well last a lifetime. It's not simply the facts of what you say; what really matters is how people feel about what you say. If you say the wrong thing it may scar the relationship for a lifetime.

In Chapter 2 I made reference to Gerald Ratner saying that his own product was crap. The day before he made that statement people were happy to buy his products. He was one of the most successful jewellery retailers the UK has ever seen. But the day after he said that people stopped buying his products. Within a very short period his business was bust, he was out of a job and the Ratner name was never again seen on the high street. It wasn't the facts of the jewellery, was it? It was identical. The products didn't change. What changed was people's feelings about the brand and about the relationship between themselves and the retailer. And the after effects have lasted for Gerald's life time. I've met Gerald. He's a nice man and a good man. He just made a mistake. He hurt people's feelings and it cost him his business.

Throughout this book I'm going to talk a lot about establishing the other person's need. Their deep need, how they *feel* about what it is you're trying to persuade them to do.

I want to take you on to a higher plane of understanding of how persuasion works so that you become more persuasive. And to do that you need to understand how other people *feel*.

Because until you discuss how your persuadee feels about a situation, you're stuck in facts and logic, in discussing events and what you've watched on television. You're simply turning features into benefits. At its worst, you're only talking ritual and cliché. And people buy emotionally.

The logical part of persuading is the tip of the iceberg we all see, but what really matters is the bit we don't. And I'm sure you know enough about icebergs to know that's the big bit.

So it's not just what you say but how people perceive you. It's people's feelings that really matter. And sometimes you can say the wrong thing, it hurts people's feelings and the after effects can last a lifetime.

When we come to discuss how buying and selling actually work, we will see how good planning reduces ritual and cliché and helps speed up the process as well as interesting the buyer. People are far more interested in knowing how much you care before wanting to know what you know. You have to find out how your persuadee *feels* about the situation. You need to move into the circle of relationships and communication so that you get past ritual and cliché and move into the circle.

MOVE INTO THE INNER CIRCLE BUT DON'T GET TOO NEAR THE VIOLINS

Allow me to explain.

In an orchestra the musicians sit in a semi-circle. The conductor is in the centre. Right at the edge of the circle are the drums. Big guys with that strange leopard skin tied around the midriff and on that, a drum. All manner of people making a noise, but on their own not very tuneful, as anyone who has a child with a drum kit will testify.

As you move towards the conductor the next instruments are the trumpets, trombones, French horns and tubas. A bit more interesting to listen to but again, on their own not easy on the ear.

Then it gets more interesting. As you get still nearer to the conductor you get bassoons and then the flutes, oboes, piano and harps. And finally the violas, cellos and violins. Ah, yes, the violins.

And so it is with the circle of relationships. If you want to be persuasive, imagine the person you want to persuade as the conductor. You need to move into their circle—the 'inner circle'. If you don't form any emotional bond and don't truly empathize, you are just a loud drum. You make a noise but no one wants to listen. As you move closer by establishing the emotional bond, you start making music you both enjoy.

But be careful not to get too close. Beware of getting in there with the violins where they can pull on your heartstrings. Work colleagues who socialize and get to know each other's families often have a problem discussing a difficult issue. Sales people who get too close to their buyers frequently find it difficult to move back into harsh commercial reality and deliver bad news. They tend to be too soft on negotiation to the extent that they forget whom they work for.

So establish the other person's emotional needs and have genuine interest and empathy. However, you can get too near to the flame. We all need people we can play the violin with and they with us. But be aware that that's a different type of relationship.

Networking has always been a popular way to build up business contacts and establish relationships with potential clients. In the twenty-first century we have speed dating and social networking, which is something of an oxymoron as you can do it sat at home with a laptop. Instead of discovering whether someone shares our love of the theatre or fine wine, we want to know their business plan for the next 12 months. But just how much should you reveal about yourself to your new-found friends? And exactly how far can you take a business relationship before it starts to become counterproductive?

A study by Michael Norton of Harvard Business School endorses the view that you shouldn't get to know another person too well and risk getting too close to the violins. According to the research, familiarity really does breed contempt. Not surprisingly, when asked, 80% of businesspeople said they preferred to do business with people they know. Better the devil and all that. But when they were shown a series of general traits broadly representative of businesspeople just like them, an interesting thing happened. The more traits they were shown about a supposed individual, the less they liked them.

Why should this be so? I mean, we were getting along so well. The answer, according to the researchers, is that the more we discover about a person, the more chance there is of uncovering a trait we don't like. And once we do that, it colours our view of that person regardless of all the other positive traits that we admire. So, for example, you might not want to reveal that you're a Manchester United fan when trying to get a sale on Merseyside. Or that you like to go seal clubbing in the winter with a bunch of old university chums. The moment you reveal something about yourself that others don't like, it's downhill all the way.

Fat cat company directors of failing financial institutions in the early part of the twenty-first century went from hero to zero before you could say £1 million pension payoff. MPs were able to undo a lifetime of achievement when it was suddenly revealed that they'd been claiming for a Peruvian foot slave to clip their toenails twice a week. (I think I made that one up, but you never know.)

As I say in my Desiderata: Never outstay your welcome; guests and fish both begin to smell after three days. So next time you are at a conference with various business associates, give them a bit of space and make yourself scarce for at least part of it. Once they see a dissimilar (and therefore unlikeable) trait during their conversation with you, it will negatively affect the way they perceive the rest of your traits; even things about you they might have liked. And on no account tell that hilarious anecdote about the mystery couple you discovered in a laundry closet at last year's event. You never know who might not find it very funny.

THE TISSUE PAPER THEORY

Number 2 son and I were chatting about his childhood. I asked him if he could remember me changing his nappies. 'No.' Helping him to ride a bike? 'No.' Teaching him how to swim with his little arm bands on at Coppice Baths? 'No.'

The conversation went on. I began to think that all the love and care and attention and time I'd spent with him were wasted. But they weren't, were they? I saw him as an egg in its fragile shell in a tin box. And every act of kindness, all the things I had done for him and his brothers, were like individual layers of tissue paper. And as he grew and eventually went to university, it was the layers of tissue paper in the tin box that would protect him, give him confidence and allow him to feel—and continue to be—strong.

Indeed, when a chicken bursts out of the egg, it isn't an overnight or instant sensation, is it? It has been slowly but surely incubating in the egg until the time was right. And just as the chicken has been nurtured, so too had number 2 son.

It's the same with your potential client, customer and persuadee. If you are in the business of building relationships with your clients, customers, colleagues and friends, remember that every act of kindness is another layer of tissue paper. Every time you listen with rapt attention, remember their name and listen to how they feel with genuine empathy, you are adding more tissue paper. And every time you don't do what you say you are going to do, you add an irritant within the layers. Every time you say you think they are wrong, you're adding a little broken glass.

And if you lie to the person you are trying to persuade you may never, ever recover. Because when trust is broken it sometimes can't be repaired.

After appointing us to create the advertising for his brand, Roger Cooper, the MD of Ideal Standard, asked me if we would like to do some PR on the appointment. Of course we would. He insisted in no uncertain terms that he needed to approve the press release and, while I happily agreed, he seemed a little over-zealous in his request. I asked him why and he told me this story.

He had appointed a well-known London agency some years earlier and had insisted on seeing any press release before it went out, to which they agreed. Unfortunately for the new agency, the marketing manager at Ideal Standard, Jenny Rustomji, had a son who worked in the press office at *Campaign* magazine. It was Jenny's son who received a press release from the agency with regard to their appointment by Ideal Standard.

Roger, of course, got to find out about this and was understandably upset because he hadn't seen the release. He allowed the agency to come up to Hull for the briefing meeting before asking them if they had sent a release without him seeing it. They told him they had absolutely not issued a press release. After a number of opportunities for the agency to come clean, he produced the faxed release. He then released the agency.

Trust had been broken irrevocably and that was the end of the relationship.

CONSTRUCTIVE CRITICISM

I speak at seminars and conferences all around the world. I ask delegates if they have ever been offered any 'constructive criticism' and most tell me they have. I ask them which of the two words they pick up on most and how they feel. Everyone tells me the same tale: they feel they are going to be criticized.

Full stop. Nothing constructive about it.

Why is that? Offering 'constructive criticism' can be a powerful way to effect a positive change in a person's behaviour. The problem is that like most things to do with construction, you have to take great care when laying the foundations. Otherwise you just dig a hole that you can't get out of.

For instance, telling somebody that they're a lazy good-for-nothing whose total lack of knowledge, skill and endeavour means they will never amount to anything in life is not likely to encourage them to try harder. I still have no idea why my headmaster wrote that on my report.

The bottom line is that while constructive criticism should encourage, just about any other form of criticism is destructive, since it usually merely highlights a problem and rarely gives tips on a solution. In my experience of offering 'constructive criticism' I found that three things happened:

1 People took it personally and didn't like me.
2 They disagreed and their knee-jerk reaction was along the lines of 'But…' and 'The thing is…' or simply, 'You don't understand.'
3 They reacted. Not straightaway usually, but afterwards. They spoke to their friends and asked their friends for their view. And guess what? Most times their friend gave them the view they were looking for. They wanted evidence to support their view and went in search of it. And they could find it with their friends.

As a result there was little or no gain—but a lot lost.

So after years of providing constructive criticism to employees and, in the main, managing to dodge flying fists and avoid temper tantrums, here's my thoughts on how to do it effectively.

First of all, you have to build trust and show that you care, because nobody willingly takes advice from someone they think doesn't have their best interests at heart. That's why double glazing salespeople have such a tough time. So make sure you praise people whenever they do something good. People like to have their efforts recognized and, over time, this will help them to consider your comments as valid, relevant and welcome. Put down tissue paper first. Regularly tell people what you think they are good at—with no 'but' and no 'however'.

Then, when you do come to offer something a little more critical, they are much more likely to take it. You have developed the relationship well enough to give them confidence that you care about them. That you trust them and they trust you.

Let's suppose someone does something that is not very clever. Something that causes you to lose either money or face with a client. Often it will be the result of a genuine mistake rather than a malicious error, and the chances are they know exactly what they did wrong. I found that most people knew what they were doing wrong and what they needed to work on. So say to yourself, 'How can I get the other person to say, "I have a weakness here?" and how can I get them to identify what areas we need to look at?' Often it is as simple as that: ask them where they think they can improve and develop.

A good technique is to give of yourself first. You say that you think you can improve and point out something you are endeavouring to be better at. Then get the other person to acknowledge the mistake by asking them which areas of their work they can improve or develop. If they introduce the subject rather than you, it's a lot easier to talk about. So rather than admonish and criticize, you need to sympathize, encourage and ask questions. Don't concentrate on what went wrong, but rather on what they need to do to put it right. That's constructive criticism. Of course, if it turns out that their error was malicious you should string them up by the thumbs and take a long lunch. That can work too.

The real issue is that you need to have built up trust. And how do you develop trust apart from always being 100% honest and doing what you say you are going to do?

Rapt attention is the highest form of flattery. It helps develop trust. If you want to be persuasive, you need to listen with rapt attention. You have to see things from the other person's point of view. What most people do is simply give information without thinking about how the recipient can receive it.

I listen to radio traffic announcements. Invariably they tell us what they know, such as an accident at a particular road junction, using their frame of reference and knowledge. Anyone driving through Leeds will hear stuff like 'Chained Bar is very busy, so avoid it.' Where's Chained Bar? Anyone who knows it will probably already know to avoid it in the rush hour. 'A lorry has shed its load of strawberry preserve completely blocking the Woodhead Pass. Drivers are advised to seek an alternative route to avoid the jam.' That's not much good for motorists who don't know that the Wood-head Pass is five miles ahead of them on the A628. And how about suggesting an alternative route?

Still, the 'jam' joke was good. I just had to throw that in.

SAYING THE RIGHT THINGS AND ASKING THE RIGHT QUESTIONS

Each of those traffic announcements is a classic case of telling people what the announcer wants to tell them and not what they need to know. How often do you receive a message on your voicemail where the person leaves you their telephone number so quickly you have to repeat the message at least once because you couldn't catch it the first time? In hotels, the room service menu is often beautifully designed with some out-of-focus picture of a tomato on the front and wonderful descriptions of the 'bed of lettuce', but what I really want to know is what number to dial to get it.

And that's in the small print, because the designer doesn't like the look of it. On business cards, why is the contact telephone number often so small that you need to put your glasses on to see it?

Movies on television take far too long to tell us the names of the technicians such as the sound recordist or wardrobe person. When those names do appear, they whizz past so fast you can't read them. That's because the producers don't expect us to want to know, but they feel obliged to tell us anyway.

I hate to see channel brand names on television. I want to watch the programme without a constant reminder that I'm watching the Geographic Channel or the Paramount Channel or the Adult Channel. (*Note to editor: delete that last one.*) (*No—ed.*) I mean, why do Channel 5 bosses insist on having their logo on screen all the time? It's not for our enjoyment, is it? They're telling us what they want to tell us and not what we want to know.

How often do you tell people what you want to tell them and not what they want to know? With the exception of filing in your tax return, it's bad form.

For most men, deciding what to wear for an evening is a reasonably straightforward procedure. First, we decide whether it's casual, formal or black tie; and secondly, we need to make sure that we wear the right colour shoes. For some men that's about it.

If like me, you're a man and you're married to a woman, you may have wondered what to do when she says, 'Should I wear the red dress or the black dress?' Naturally, for Chris de Burgh it would be the red dress that has made him millions, but most men don't think in such terms.

There are five key steps in the process of finishing with a happy outcome. Follow these steps assiduously.

1   Be very, very interested in whether it's the black
    dress or the red dress. If you are not actually
    interested, do your best to fake it. Glance away from
    the newspaper momentarily at the very least.
2   Be as indecisive as her, as this creates empathy.
3   Importantly, ask her which dress she prefers.
4   This is the most important step: ask her why she
    prefers one dress over the other.
5   Agree with her.

This needs to take a little time. If you rush it you appear to
be insincere and uninterested and you need to go back to
step one again.

So on other occasions when you're trying to influence
someone, what can you say that is persuasive and will help
you build a relationship so that you can achieve what you
want?

Well, here are the top three things to start saying and the
top ten questions to ask to ensure you will be more liked by
more people and, as a result, become more persuasive and
influential.

THE TOP THREE THINGS TO START SAYING

Robert Emmons from the University of California and
Michael McCullough from the University of Miami have
done a number of studies on gratitude. Psychologists and
scientists are latecomers to the concept of gratitude; reli-
gions and philosophers have pretty much always embraced
gratitude as an integral component of health and general
well-being. What their experiments have involved are
comparing the subsequent well-being of people who kept
'gratitude journals' on a weekly basis versus those who either

didn't keep a journal or took note of all the bad and unfortunate things that happened to them each week.

The people who simply jotted down the things they were grateful for and itemized the good things that happened to them each week were subsequently found to exercise more regularly, reported fewer negative physical symptoms, felt better about their lives as a whole, and were more optimistic about the upcoming weeks compared to those who recorded hassles or neutral life events. Children who practise 'grateful thinking' have more positive attitudes towards school and their families.

Telling people what you like about them and telling them what they are good at—and generally being grateful—also actually affects your health and general well-being. So for two different but very good reasons, you need to tell people what you like about them and also what you think they're really good at. Be sincere, honest and genuine. And, better still, tell them when there are other people around.

1 'I'll tell you what I like about you'

This is, I believe, the most persuasive thing you can ever say to anyone—provided you know what you are going to say next. If you say it and the person you are talking to says, 'What's that?' and you reply, 'I don't know, I read it in a book', it doesn't work.

You also need to make sure you don't say something like, 'How do you ignore all those horrible things that people say about you behind your back?' Not good.

As well as being flattering, you need to be absolutely sincere, honest and genuine. Everyone wants to know what you like about them. They will like you more and if they like you more it will be easier to persuade them. It helps build a real relationship. But you have to be honest in your compliment.

2 'I'll tell you what I think you're really good at'

This is at the very heart of how dolphins are trained to jump through hoops. It's what is known as 'operant conditioning', whereby the dolphin is conditioned to an activity (jumping through a hoop) by positive behaviour being rewarded. If, when the dolphin exhibits certain behaviour, it is followed by something that the dolphin likes, then it's highly probable that the behaviour will occur again. And if the trainer's response is not agreeable, the dolphin will eventually tend to avoid that particular behaviour.

Positive reinforcement is the most effective means of influencing behaviour. In effect, it's an extension of the first point and is great to use with work colleagues. Again, you have to be sincere. If you have a colleague you don't get on with as well as you might, talk to their best friend about what you admire about them and what you think they're really good at. Be honest, sincere and genuine.

What does their buddy do? Goes and tells their friend, of course. And they, in turn, will like you more and that helps you build that relationship.

Football managers hopeful of signing a new player do it all the time. They talk in the press about his 'great qualities' and how he would be 'an asset to any team'. They have already started to influence the player. And when the player does become a member of the squad he wants to play for the manager; he is motivated. So be sure to find out what a person is really good at and tell them so—particularly if you're talking to a loved one.

I believe these first two things to start saying are at the heart of being a great company. The view that 'people are your greatest asset' really needs a caveat. Your *best* people are definitely your greatest asset; but what about the ones you have question marks about? The fact is, all the successful companies I see have got, in the main, the right people— and in the right jobs. If you have that *and* you develop them and you keep telling them what they're good at, you usually have a growing company with a happy team of people on board too. And isn't that what we all want?

When my wife and I bought three sofas from a large furniture store—the negotiation is in a later chapter—the sofas were delivered by a couple of burly guys. They were both what might be described as 'big units'. They were extremely polite and not only wore white gloves to reduce the chance of marking the sofas as they carried them in, but also wore small, plastic covers over their shoes, which they carefully put on as they came into the house and took off as they went back to the van for another sofa. When the sofas were in the lounge they then puffed up the cushions and, when they were happy, one of them turned to me and said, 'Is everything to your complete satisfaction?' He'd been trained to say that. And he was sincere. And the whole experience was past my expectation and certainly I was more than satisfied.

So I called the sales person at the department store, Sue Taylor. I explained who I was and she remembered we were due to take delivery that day. This is how the conversation went:

> 'Hi Sue. It's Phil Hesketh. I've just taken delivery of the sofas.'
> 'What's wrong?'
> 'Nothing's wrong. I just wondered if you could do me a favour.'
> 'Yes, by all means.'

'Can you tell the boss of the guys who've just delivered the sofas that they were excellent? Exemplary. They are a credit to you.'
'Well, yes. Sure.'
'How often does this happen?'
'What? People call to say well done and thank you?'
'Yep.'
'You are the first.'

Now why is that? Why don't we say 'well done' more often? Let's think it through. It takes me all of two minutes and I enjoy the conversation. Giving people good news is enjoyable. Sue gets a glow; she has a satisfied customer. So do the delivery guys. (They hopefully get to know I called.) Their boss feels like his training is worthwhile. And his boss too. And hopefully there will be conversations at their respective homes that night. All positive.

3 'I can see it from your point of view'

A key focus of this book is to see things from the other person's point of view. Arguably, that's the definition of empathy. If you say 'I agree with you', you lose your position. But if you say 'I don't agree', you lose empathy. So to say 'I can see it from your point of view' has the other person thinking that you understand their position. However, it has a flaw.

The flaw is that if 'I can see it from your point of view' is quickly followed by 'but...', you may as well not bother. The secret is always to follow it with '... and ...'. If you do always use 'and', you will find yourself being more conciliatory and persuasive. You can still make the point you want to make and the other person will like you more *and* you will continue to build empathy.

Indeed, avoid the word 'but' whenever you can—it's inherently confrontational.

THE TOP TEN QUESTIONS TO ASK

As a young salesman for Procter & Gamble, I once had a disagreement with a supermarket manager over a packet of washing powder. Well, to be a little more accurate, about 500 packets. The problem was, he wasn't actually there when I wrote the order and I filled his warehouse with two years' worth of detergent. It was a Friday afternoon and I had a sales target to meet, so 500 units of new Fairy Snow with built-in fabric conditioner seemed like a reasonable deal.

I am not making this up.

When I returned a week later he was still fuming with rage, although I noted his hands were suspiciously soft as he grabbed me by the neck.

I placated him with the cheery news that this new, improved product was not only guaranteed to remove grease and grime but also knock spots off Ariel and Persil. He wasn't convinced. I tried to reason that if we put it all on display like a huge pyramid it would sell. He didn't go for that either, pointing out that if the place flooded it would resemble Foam Night in an Ibiza club disco.

What should I have done in that situation? Let me fast forward to the conclusion of an interesting piece of research by Rick van Baaren of Radboud University Nijmegen in the Netherlands. He found that waiters who identically match a customer's verbalizations after receiving an order increase the amount of tips they get by 50%. In other words, they repeat back the order, word for word. No paraphrasing, no tacit agreement, and definitely no use of the ubiquitous 'OK'. But why?

Well, people want to be sure that you both hear and understand them. They want to feel that you know what is really important to them. Ditto, angry customers with a problem.

It's not enough to say 'I understand you are frustrated' since this just makes them more angry. Instead, you need to repeat the problem back to them, using the words they used, before offering a solution. This makes your solution sound more plausible, coming as it does immediately after stating the problem. People like people who show a genuine desire to understand their situation, an unfeigned interest in what is the most important thing to them.

As your persuadee is speaking to you, use their language when you respond. If someone says to you, 'Well, I'm fed up because you can't get anything done round here', don't turn to them and say, 'What makes you so annoyed about it?' They haven't said that they were annoyed, they said that they were 'fed up because they can't get anything done round here'; so use their words back to them. Use the same sort of language rather than imposing your own way of saying what they say. Using the same language is a key indicator to them that you understand them. Or, in other words, go with the flow.

All of these questions have one thing in common: they allow you to 'go with the flow', giving you the information and the opportunity to influence.

1 'What is the most important thing to you about...?'

It could be argued that Socrates set the standard for all subsequent Western philosophy in the fifth century by asking questions like 'What is the most important thing to you about...?' Socrates has gone down in history as one of the greatest educators and he taught by asking questions and thus drawing out answers from his pupils. People's opinions of you are directly related to the quality of the questions you ask. If you wish to build a good relationship, it is absolutely key to find out what is the most important thing to your friend, or potential client, about what you are doing, or the service or product you are offering.

Ask more questions to find the other person's real interests and motivations. The top question to ask is a great one to ask your life partner, if you have one. You just fill in the appropriate words at the end, in that case 'What is the most important thing to you about our relationship?'

Back to the supermarket manager and his detergent mountain. If I'd known then what I know now, I might have persuaded him to give it a go. Instead, I had to remove the stock on the threat of him never buying from me again. And 'new' Fairy Snow, even with added fabric conditioner, never did clean up the market. They should have called it 'Fairly Slow' because that's how it sold. If you're interested, I've still got a garage full.

2 'Why do you ask?'

We had a Bosnian cleaning lady at home at a time when my eldest son was in Canada on a year out after finishing university. My conversations with Senka tended to be based on, 'Hello, Senka. How are you?' 'I'm fine thanks, Phil. How are you?' I would then make myself a coffee and go back to my office.

One day she asked how David was in Canada. 'Fine, thanks, Senka.'

'Is he safe?' she said.

'Yes, he's safe.'

'Everything's OK with him; there are no problems?'

As I replied in the affirmative, it was only after she asked her fifth question about my son's well-being that I said, 'Why do you ask?'

'Because,' she began, clearly holding back the tears, 'my son has just gone to America and it's the first time he's been away from home and I'm really worried about him.'

She wasn't concerned about my son at all, was she? She was concerned about hers. Naturally, I sacked her on the spot. Only kidding.

So if someone is asking you the same question in more than one way, ask them why. Then you get to know their concerns, which in turn leads to greater understanding and greater empathy—and a greater ability to persuade them.

I was running a seminar for the Ministry of Defence and the client, Mike, arrived at the first coffee break to check that everyone had turned up and that all was well. He then looked over his shoulder as we were chatting and nodded his head towards the most senior guy in the room, asking, 'What do you think of the colonel then?'

Earlier in this chapter we talked about the three parts to every conversation—facts, feelings and after effects. The facts of this particular question were that he was asking what I thought but the feelings were very clear. Mike didn't like the colonel.

So what would you do in this circumstance? It happens in offices and bars all over the country every day. He doesn't like the colonel and he wants me to agree with him. But the colonel and I have developed a rapport and I quite like the guy. So instead of either lying—and having Mike spread the story I don't like the colonel—or having a debate with Mike, I simply said, 'That's interesting, Mike, why do you ask?'

And off Mike went on a ten-minute rant. Does he really want to know what I think of the colonel or does he just want to tell me what he thinks?

Most people think you are a great conversationalist when they are doing the talking.

3 'How was yours?'

I worked in an office environment for many years. On Monday mornings people would pop their head round the door. 'Morning, Phil. Had a good weekend?' On returning from holiday at the end of August there would be a clutch of people also returning from holiday. 'Hi, Phil. Had a good holiday?' I would always reply to these questions: 'Great, thanks. How was yours?'

Do you know, in all the time I did this no one ever said, 'Hang on. I asked about your holiday.' Or 'No, tell me about your weekend.' The point is that people are usually not interested in your weekend, your holiday or your well-being. They're interested in theirs. So get them to do the talking. It builds up their perception of the amount you care, and that builds empathy. It means they like you more, which in turn gives you a better opportunity to persuade.

One September I was in my regular hairdressers having my usual cut and the barber asked me if I'd been on holiday. I briefly explained that we were going to go to South America but then our plans had to change. My wife wanted to go to London for ten days to see the shows, go to the Old Bailey, Buckingham Palace and so on. I wasn't keen on the idea as I go to London anyway on a pretty regular basis, but I explained how we compromised and went for ten days. I then said, 'But the second half of the holiday was bizarre. Have you been away?'

And he told me that he and his family had been to Spain.

I tested this with all the people who asked if I'd been away. I explained this whole story, ending with 'But the second half of the holiday was bizarre. Have you been away?'

And on no occasion did anyone say, 'So what was bizarre, Phil?'

As I say, most people think *you* are a great conversationalist when *they* are doing the talking.

4 'If you were me, what would you do?'

Case study

It is just after ten o'clock in the morning on a damp and wintry day in Newcastle upon Tyne. My son Daniel, sporting an overcoat, a fashionably tied scarf and a trilby—yes, a trilby hat—is about to leave his upstairs flat as he has a lecture at eleven. As he descends the stairs the doorbell sounds, so he answers the door with hat on and a rucksack over his left shoulder. The man at the door, a slight man in his sixties, is dressed for the cold of the north-east of England in February and has a letter in his hand, an identity badge around his neck and, yes, a trilby on his head.

He shows Daniel the letter for a 'Mrs P. Rowson', at which point Daniel professes his admiration for the accomplished way in which his male flatmate has apparently been concealing his true gender. The older man laughs as Daniel tries to remain cool while transfixed by the TV Licensing Authority stamp at the top of the letter, more than a little conscious of the fact that Daniel, Peter (the aforementioned 'Mrs' Rowson) and their three other flatmates have spent the last six months 'getting round' to buying a TV licence. Predictably enough, the man from the Authority asks whether or not they have a television and Daniel replies whimsically, 'As it happens we don't have a television.'

'Well, I'm sure you won't mind if I pop in to verify that fact,' answers the man.

'You know, I'd actually prefer it if you didn't, as it happens. Now is not a terribly good time.' (Dan is doing his best to effect what he later that day described to me as 'a rather charming, urbane air'.)

'Well,' says our trilbied friend with a wry smile, 'it doesn't quite work like that. Basically if you refuse me entry now, then tomorrow the enforcers come round and they check.'

'Well,' replies Daniel, 'not that we have a TV anyway, but if we were to have one I'm sure there wouldn't be any evidence of one tomorrow.'

'No, I don't suppose there would,' was the reply, 'but we already have evidence that you have a TV. Watching television without a valid licence is a criminal offence. This can lead to prosecution, a court appearance and a fine of up to £1,000. And that doesn't include legal costs.'

£1,000+!

'So what would be the options available to me and my flatmates in this hypothetical situation if we were to have a TV?'

'Well, you either let me in now and I see your hypothetical TV and give you a bill for £1,000, or the enforcer comes round tomorrow and, regardless of whether there is a TV or not, he starts the process that will end with a fine and total costs of over £1,000.'

This is not looking good.

'Nice hat,' says Dan.

'Thanks. I've had it for ages. They seem to be coming back in fashion among students.'

'Very much so. Most of my friends have them. They keep you warm and they are considered to be pretty cool.'

(I am not making this up.)

Daniel senses a pause in the conversation, but notices the man is smiling.

'You must know of another way—what can I do? I'm a poor student. I'm sure you don't enjoy giving these fines out. With all your knowledge of how the TV licensing authorities work, I'm sure you know of another option…'

The man on the doorstep smiles and looks at Daniel, who now delivers line number six.

'If you were me, a poor student, who doesn't mean anyone any harm—in my situation, what would you do?'

He paused and said, 'I'd ring the TV licensing authorities right now and buy a TV licence over the phone. The licence costs just £142.50, so you'll be saving yourself quite a bit. I'd put down on my form that I arrived after you had bought the licence…'

Daniel couldn't help but laugh. 'That's a fabulous idea! I've got my cash card in my pocket, just let me run upstairs and get my phone.'

'No need,' he replied, reaching into his bag. 'You can use mine.'

They chat some more about the numerous benefits of hats and Daniel listens with rapt attention as the man extolled the virtues of the trilby.

Daniel finishes his conversation with the TV licence people, hands back the mobile phone and the man shakes him by the hand and tells the young student the experience has been 'a real pleasure'.

I have absolutely not made up a word of that. Frankly, I don't have enough imagination to do so. And neither, bless him, does Dan. He told the man what he liked about him. He could not see a way out of the situation and as a last resort appealed not only to the guy's better nature but also for a resolution he might just have.

'What would you do?' is a great line to use when someone is extremely angry with you, too. One of the most effective things about it is that it almost forces the other person to see things from your perspective—no need to tell them what you're thinking, feeling or going through. Once you hear the words 'what would *you* do...' it sets off a train of thought that would perhaps otherwise be difficult to instigate. You get to know just how much they want from you. It allows you to understand and then manage expectations.

I've used the line when I worked in advertising, when we had made an error and the client was unhappy. It's a great way not only of finding out how bad things are, but often of finding a solution you are struggling to find yourself.

Real life is always funnier than gags, isn't it?

5 'I wonder if you could help me?'

We all want to feel important. We all want other people to see us as knowledgeable. So starting a request for information with 'I wonder if you can help me?' will invariably produce the answer 'Yes'.

This is because you are making the other person feel important. You are also, in a small way, making them feel obliged to help you because they have said they would.

6 'How do you feel about that?'

Earlier in this chapter, we talked about the importance of appreciating how people feel about your idea, product, service or excuse. That it's never just about the facts. That the feelings are more important than the facts. Particularly if someone has an objection, it is not quite enough to understand the facts of their position. It's barely adequate to say that you acknowledge their point of view. You need to know how they feel and you need them to know that you care, that you genuinely want to understand how they feel.

So use this one. Don't say 'What do you think about that?', ask the other person how they feel. But make sure you do care. Don't say you do if you don't.

And don't forget to ask the people you love the most how *they* feel too.

7 'Can you tell me more about that?'

If people ask you what you think of a particular film, conversation, event or person, what they are also saying is 'Can I tell you what I think?' Most people want to say more about their problems and issues than most of their friends want to listen to.

So if you truly care about someone and want to build your relationship, ask them to tell you more. If you have an angry client, make sure you have given them the opportunity to get everything off their chest before you talk about what to do next. Try it—it works.

8 'What makes you say that?'

Often someone will say something that is contrary to your belief and the temptation is to argue. If you ask 'what makes you say that' in the right, friendly tone, it allows them to articulate where that view or opinion comes from. Importantly, it also gives you the opportunity to explore—with them—whether what they are saying is opinion or fact. We tend to confuse the two. And asking this question gives them the opportunity to realize that what they thought was a fact is actually just an opinion. You can then agree to disagree.

9 'What can I do to help you?'

Or 'How can I help you today?' This is easy enough to use in a shop when you are manifestly after someone's money. The key to this is to use it when a friend or client is struggling with an issue. I find most times people don't want you to *do* anything, they just want you to listen with rapt attention and real empathy.

Finally, it's a great thing to *do* rather than merely a question to ask—and it could be one of the best things you ever do.

10 'What is the most irritating thing about me?'

Ask a friend to tell you the most irritating thing about you. It could turn out to be the biggest step you make towards being persuasive and living your life in a more influential manner. We all have things about us that other people find irritating, or even downright rude and off-putting.

I watched a television programme the other night about a football hooligan fresh out of prison. He had a well-meaning mentor who was trying to help him with the transition from prison to civilian life. Trouble was, the lad couldn't look anyone in the eye. I'm sure I wasn't alone in finding this very off-putting. But probably no one had told him. And his chances of getting a job would have been greatly enhanced by looking interviewers in the eye rather than giving the consistent impression of a shady character who wasn't to be trusted.

The truth is that we all have traits that others don't like. So ask the friends you trust the most to tell you what yours are. Ask them to be sincere, honest, genuine and blunt. Ask them what traits you have that they find irritating. Then resist the temptation to punch their lights out. That's not a good trait either.

Try to stop doing all the things that annoy people.

So back to your Christmas card list. The more you ask these ten questions, the closer you will find people are to you. You will have more friends that you confide in, turn to, rely on and trust.

You will find you have more friends in your inner circle.

PART 2

PERSUASION AND INFLUENCE

The Five Keys to Persuasion and Influence

How to Create Genuine Empathy

Asking Questions and Accepting the Answers

Understanding Implications and Influence

Thinking Long Term and Getting Your Own Way

The Importance of Preparation in Influencing

Different Strokes for Different Folks

6

THE FIVE KEYS TO PERSUASION AND INFLUENCE

There's an untrue but nonetheless widely held view that selling and being persuasive is about talking. That the 'gift of the gab' is the key element to being persuasive.

Horrocks.

Over the years I have asked many, many professional buyers what the key elements are in being persuasive. In other words, who do they buy from and what do they *like* about good persuaders? What they all tell me is that, first, they want the person to be honest. Secondly, they want them to understand needs and frustrations. And they also need to show they genuinely care: to want to be a partner and remain interested after the sale.

My wife and I were staying at the Datai Hotel in Langkawi, Malaysia. Rather than prompting me to enter my pin number when I put my credit card in, the hand-held device asked me, 'Are you sure?' The bathrobes and bathing towels are so thick and sumptuous it takes a full 20 minutes to shoehorn them into your suitcase before checking out.

Only joking.

But the really impressive feature of the hotel is that each and every member of staff knows your name. They simply take the trouble to cross-reference it against your room number and commit it to memory. So every time you buy a drink, order a meal or ring down to reception, they always greet you by name. I asked the manager why they went to such trouble and he said, 'Because this is our standard, Mr Cameron'.

I like to travel incognito.

And that, I guess, is why I like it there. They take the trouble to bother. They set themselves a certain high standard and are proud to live up to it. Naturally, they charge a premium for this level of cosseting, but it's also the reason that in their peak periods they have a return rate of over 85%. And it's not as if guests go back to explore the island further. There's so precious little of it that if you want to take a leisurely drive around its perimeter it's advisable to have a late breakfast or you'll be back before lunchtime.

No, the reason they can charge top dollar and guests return time and again is because they have very, very, high standards. And care for their guests' comfort is central to those standards.

So here is the first key to persuasion and influence.

1. PEOPLE DON'T CARE HOW MUCH YOU KNOW UNTIL THEY KNOW HOW MUCH YOU CARE

Every morning the hotel staff get together to discuss who is arriving that day. They are reminded of any idiosyncrasies of returning guests and particular requests that any new arrival has made in advance. They even talk about which flight they are on and will therefore be able to anticipate whether the new guest will want, breakfast, lunch or dinner on arrival. All of this takes a little extra time, but none of it costs any extra money.

So is this approach beyond the reach of other businesses? Is it beyond your reach? Could you set such a high standard in your business, maximize your assets, charge a premium and make more money? Is it really possible to satisfy your customers to such a degree that they will always keep coming back for more? And who needs rhetorical questions anyway?

The answer is clear. Don't settle for mediocrity, aim for excellence. Not only in your business life but in your relationships too. In an earlier chapter we talked about the three parts to every conversation and the fact that it's not only the facts but rather the feelings. And they, in turn, lead to the after effects. When the staff at the Datai take the trouble to remember your name, it gives you a great feeling. And the after effects of a great holiday are down to the feelings.

So often I hear people ask how someone's family is and then launch into relating the progress of their own children, without allowing the person to answer the question. The fact is, they don't really want to know. So show you care and have a genuine interest before you speak.

2 ESTABLISH THE OTHER PERSON'S EMOTIONAL NEEDS

People buy from people who are like them or, at least, act and behave like them and have similar values. People will like you if you behave like them and mirror their body language.

Have you ever heard anyone say, 'He's a regular guy, he's quite nice but he just listens too much'? Effective persuaders listen more than they talk.

So your persuadee must truly believe in you. They must believe that you are more concerned with their situation than you are about simply getting your own way. They must believe that you will do whatever is necessary that's in their interests. Without trust and the belief that you will do what you say you are going to do, all the benefits, added value or discounts don't mean a thing. You have to be sincerely interested in their situation to be a top persuader.

And you have to be honest.

People buy emotionally and justify logically. Everything you have ever bought has been bought emotionally. The clothes you are wearing right now, the watch on your wrist, the car you drive, the house you live in, the restaurant you last had a meal in, the brands you have in your pantry and fridge—everything. Why else would there be as many as 20 brands of bottled water in the average UK supermarket? You can't really tell the difference, can you?

You need to establish not only the other person's logical, stated needs, but also their emotional needs. You typically only do that when you have a relationship. And you only have a relationship when the other person likes you.

Start using the top ten questions from the last chapter to find out what is important to the other person and what matters to them.

It's a bit of an effort, isn't it? But being professional is an effort, isn't it? It's not what you do, it's the way that you do it. And that's what gets results. As Bananarama once put it.

3 THE ESSENCE OF PERSUADING IS TO MAKE IT EASY FOR PEOPLE TO BUY

As a good persuader you need to be continually saying to yourself, 'Can I make this easier?' Most of my clients' products and services solve *problems* the buyer has, so the better you understand and have true empathy with their problem, the better the chance of being persuasive—and the better you ease the buyer's pain, the better for you.

Why are instructions on the back of ready-meals in such small type? If the essence of persuading is to make it easier for people to buy, making it easier for things to be *used* will increase the likelihood of the product being bought again.

All airports have signs as you enter for long-term parking and short-term parking. But how short is short term? Is it less than an hour or less than a day? Why not make it easy to decide, easy to buy?

I love how we're presented with attractive items to buy while standing at the supermarket checkout. Isn't that a superb example of making it easy for people to buy? You have time to kill, a desire to do something and an open basket. But I feel many retailers miss opportunities of this nature. When I'm buying shoes, what do I look at when the assistant has gone to get me my size to try on? Should I not be looking at other items that I might be interested in?

I'm surprised when dentists' waiting rooms only have old copies of *Horse and Hound* or *Cosmopolitan*. My mood and circumstance are such that I'm interested in dental care, and yet so few dentists I see make it easy for me to buy toothbrushes, toothpaste, dental floss and so on. You could also get sunglasses at opticians, or crèches in menswear departments so that dads can look at a leisurely pace and find it easy to buy.

Of course, many companies do this well. But the 'Do you want fries with that?' mentality doesn't necessarily permeate all the way through to shop assistants in dry cleaners (stay crease), video stores (popcorn), lawnmowers (hedge trimmers) and so on.

Case study

I am walking up a street in a local town. I have had a good meeting with a client, I have plenty of money in my parking meter and it is a lovely sunny day. I pass a menswear shop and see a Sand suit in the window.

I approach the salesman, who, it turns out, is the owner of the shop. He asks if he can help me and I say that I notice he has a Sand suit in the window. Does he have the same suit in dark blue or black in my size, I ask. Yes he does, and he picks the suit off the hook and lays it down on the counter.

This is encouraging. But he then goes on to do something amazing. He says, 'I've nothing against Sand but...' and tells me how the cut and design of another brand are better. He tells me what he knows about this other brand, where they are made and the quality of the fabric. He takes a suit off the hook and lays it on top of 'my' suit.

'My' suit!

Why? I want to buy the Sand suit! Why doesn't he ask me questions? Why doesn't he ask me what I like about Sand suits and why I feel that way? Why does he want to educate me? Why doesn't he make it easy to buy?

I leave the shop and am now looking for a retailer who not only sells Sand suits but will let me buy one; a retailer who doesn't simply want to tell me what he knows.

So make it as easy as possible for your buyer to buy. There are no objections, there are 'issues to address'. You don't have a 'cheaper model', you have one that 'might fit your budget' and is 'excellent value for money'. Don't ask people to sign a contract, ask them if they would like to 'autograph the paperwork'.

And so on.

4 SELL VALUE AND NOT PRICE

People don't want cheap brands but they do want brands cheap.

People want value. The word 'cheap' doesn't necessarily mean that, does it? It carries with it baggage that says 'poor quality'. So what is 'value'? Value is quality divided by price. And by quality I mean perceived quality.

In fashion, men and women often don't want to pay less than a certain amount for a suit because they believe they need to pay that much for the quality they desire. It doesn't matter whether that's true or not; it's their belief.

Because our advertising agency was in Leeds, many potential clients held the belief that we couldn't be as creative as agencies in London. On one occasion a client was interested in giving us a design project but told us that we were not expensive enough. He felt he had to pay more.

But how does value manifest itself as you pay more and more? The Price Perception Curve (Figure 6.1) shows how it works. As you pay more you get less in tangible benefits. A car at £20,000 is arguably twice as good as one at £10,000—but a car at £100,000 can't possibly be 10 times better, can it? Well, logically it can't, but we don't buy logically. The benefits just become more intangible. They become more about image, mystique, ego and perceived benefit.

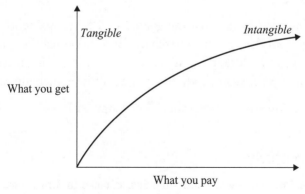

Figure 6.1 The Price Perception Curve

Case study

I am sitting in a hotel in Richmond, Surrey. Well, I say hotel, it's a pub. An old and dirty pub with no hot water and no marmalade. The bar stools that in the evening light were not noticeable are, in the cold light of day, worse than shabby. The owner doesn't care and I won't be coming back. But it's cheap.

Only last week I stayed at the Pennyhill Park Hotel and Country Club, also in Surrey. Hotels don't get much better. The manager, Danny Peccorelli, runs a fine ship with assiduous attention to detail. And it's expensive. Quite rightly.

However, at £150 a night, is it five times better than the one down the road? Well, yes and no. Looking at it logically, each hotel provided me with a clean bed, a cold beer, a hot snack and an early morning call. But I'd rather pay the premium. The benefits are there even though they are intangible. It's about attitude and attention to detail. It's about care. It's about 'value'.

Flowers show you care. If you are responsible for an office, have fresh flowers in reception. It says a lot about the organization.

If you are responsible for a retail outlet or a hotel, make sure every visitor or guest is acknowledged as soon as possible. A wait seems shorter when your customer knows that you are aware of them. And a wait is easier when there's someone to talk to.

In Harrods I notice that the guards and the people who shift boxes from A to B wear aftershave. Body odour can be so off-putting, and a little thing like that shows you are in an establishment where somebody thought about it. Somebody cares.

First impressions, remember? They stay with us.

Case study

It is a Saturday. My youngest son, Seb, is going to Africa tomorrow. He wants to look after monkeys and work with wild animals. He has bought a digital camera on the internet after painstaking research, but it hasn't arrived in the post and isn't going to be here before he flies. So, we go into town. I have agreed to buy him a camera and I will have the one that is somewhere in the postal system.

We find a specialist camera retailer and ask the owner of the shop if he has this particular camera. The good news is that he does, the bad news is that it is £70 more expensive than buying on the web. Seb shows him the printout from the website and he asks the man if he can match the price.

Not only is the answer 'no', we get an education on the costs of running a high-street shop versus selling on the web.

I stand back and watch. Why doesn't the retailer put the camera in Seb's hand and allow him to handle it? Why doesn't he ask him when he needs it? Why doesn't he talk about the intangible benefits such as the fact that the shopkeeper can offer advice and feedback? Such as the fact that the web supplier cannot supply before midnight? My son is willing to pay the premium (he's going away tomorrow) but needs to have the premium justified by intangible benefits.

The shop owner needs to establish my son's emotional needs. He needs to make it easy for him to buy. He needs to talk emotional value and not just price.

We leave the store without buying.

I was responsible for conducting some research for Tetley's beer some years ago. We carried out exit interviews at pubs that were in highly affluent suburban areas and compared them with those in what were known as 'town drinking houses'. One of the key questions was, 'Do you know the price of a pint of beer?' This question was only asked of those people who'd actually bought a pint of beer and the results were interesting.

Less than 50% of the people coming out of the affluent pubs said they knew the price of a pint of beer, but the majority of them were wrong when we asked them for the amount. In contrast, 90% of the customers of the town drinking houses said they knew the price and the vast majority of them were right when they told us the price they paid. You're buying much more than a pint, aren't you? Indeed, for some men in particular, ignoring the price tag is an act of virility.

Another piece of research was the '625 Test' to which I made reference in Chapter 2. We recruited people on the basis that they had a very strong preference for either John Smith's bitter or Tetley's bitter. They were only asked to participate if they would *only* drink one rather than the other. We gave each individual two half glasses of beer and asked them to tell us which one they preferred; that is, which one was their favoured brand. Glass 'A' on the left was Tetley's and glass 'B' on the right was John Smith's. We repeated the same exercise three times. So on four occasions they were given two beers and asked to take a sip from glass 'A' and glass 'B', and report on which they preferred.

Unknown to them, 'A' was *always* Tetley and 'B' was *always* John Smith's. It was called the '625 Test' because they had a one in two chance (i.e. 0.5) each time of telling us which was their favoured brand ($0.5 \times 0.5 \times 0.5 \times 0.5 = 0.0625$).

Over 90% of these men and women who expressed a strong preference for a particular brand did not know one from the other.

Fact.

Did it then change their mind about the brand they didn't like after we told them the results? Not usually.

If you're going to be expensive you need to be consistently expensive. So you need to sell *emotional* value to the buyer, not price. You need to persuade on the emotional footing of value for that individual and not the logical footing of price. In selling, price is often the first objection raised, so later we look at ways of overcoming that by getting away from price and into the emotional value to the other person.

Every client I work with tells me that it's rare for price to be the only and deciding factor in winning and losing business. They all fully appreciate that price is a key factor, a major driver. But they all tell me that what their clients really want is value. Sell value, not price.

5 MANAGE THEIR EXPECTATIONS

Study the works of any great writer and you'll discover a variety of styles and subjects, but one common thread links them all. It's the uncertainty of outcome, a technique used to devastating effect by every popular writer from Shakespeare to Emily Brontë to Dickens. Why? Because it retains the reader's interest and gives their work 'page turner' appeal. Will Othello really kill Desdemona or is he just in a filthy mood that might pass eventually? Should Heathcliff really venture onto that windswept and unforgiving moor without at least buttoning up his coat first? And just when is Oliver Twist going to get that second helping of gruel he craves?

It's not knowing the answers to these burning questions that keeps the reader wanting more. Contemporary writers such as JK Rowling also realize that if you crank up the suspense you're guaranteed to have small children sleeping in the doorways of bookshops around midnight. A bit like a Charles Dickens character, in fact, only with bobble hat and mittens, and a much better reading age.

Of course, Hollywood has always known the value of suspense. Its blockbuster storylines of intrigue and suspense only ever unravel in the final moments of the very last reel. Even now I can vividly recall the shock and horror when I realized that Bambi had been brutally slain. I almost choked on my sherbet dip.

Uncertainty of outcome is what keeps us glued to the screen and on the edge of our seat. A 'cliff-hanger' in a television series has us craving the next episode. A story with an underdog has us watching with bated breath just in case they triumph. Live sporting events where we don't know the outcome are always the most exciting.

Uncertainty of outcome is central to entertainment and to sport. It's at the very kernel of what we enjoy and, perhaps more importantly, it's central to business too—it's what gives us the buzz. If we all knew what would happen when we made business decisions there'd be no thrill.

But what of relationships, and business relationships in particular? They're not about uncertainty of outcome, they're about certainty. The only way to cultivate a good business relationship and to enhance your reputation is to keep on making promises and to keep on keeping them. That way, the only uncertainty for your customer is knowing by how much you are going to surpass their expectations. And that's a certainty.

Good business relationships are not about promises and veneer. They're about certainty of outcome, with a few nice surprises thrown in for good measure. By all means continue to make the promises you need to make that creates demand for your product or service and enables you to charge a premium price. But focus then on surpassing those expectations.

The reputation you have is a very basic equation. It is what people expect of you *minus* what they expected of you.

REPUTATION = EXPERIENCE − EXPECTATION

I recently stayed at the International Hotel in Canary Wharf. Framed on the wall by reception is a sign that rather grandly states: 'The company cannot guarantee the provision of wake-up calls and accepts no liability for any missed telephone calls.' Nice welcome.

This had obviously proved a problem area. Maybe guests had expected to be woken by wood nymphs splashing lightly perfumed cologne on their pillows? No. They just expected the phone to ring. So the hotel has a choice. It can either put in a wake-up call system that actually works or put up a sign that says: 'We might phone you in the morning as you asked us to do; or we might not.' They probably decided that didn't look too good, so got their lawyers to reword it so it looked like a legal disclaimer.

Tell me, when it comes to caring for customers, who do you think needs the wake-up call most?

And what has happened to the hotel's reputation? That's why the fifth key to persuasion and influence—and also the key to you building your own reputation and building good relationships based on trust—is to become known as being reliable and managing the expectations of the other person. As my good friend and former agent in New Zealand, David Glover, likes to say 'I like surprises providing they are nice ones.'

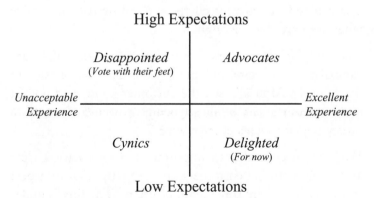

Figure 6.2 Managing Expectations

You have to manage people's expectations. And to do that you have to establish properly what they are. Then don't make over-ambitious promises and work at exceeding the other person's expectations of you.

THE IMPORTANCE OF SAYING 'NO'

This chapter has been about the five keys to persuasion and influence, but it's important to finish on the issue of sometimes being brave enough to say 'no'.

If you want to truly influence an outcome, then you have to be in control of the situation as early as possible. That usually means subtly dictating the topic of conversation. Setting the parameters. Establishing the rules. Defining the ballpark. You need to appear firm without giving the impression of being ruthless. That means learning to say 'no' politely. Prefixing your answer with a compliment is just one way of softening the blow. For example, 'I can see your point and fully understand your request. I get frustrated too that the market sets the price and the painstaking production process dictates the delivery date' is a much better answer than, 'No you can't have it cheaper or sooner'.

Learn to say 'no' to yourself too. We all need to recognize when we have done enough.

'Just say No' may work as a slogan for an anti-drugs campaign, but it's rarely adopted by business people eager to make a sale. After all, isn't the customer king? And doesn't good customer service mean bending over backwards to satisfy the customer's every whim?

Well, not necessarily. It's important that you have a clear 'positioning' so that customers know exactly what to expect from you. There are three main positions. The first is undeniable, out-and-out quality; the second is perceived quality, often created by clever marketing; and the third is value for money, which in turn is a euphemism for low cost.

So you have The Ritz at one end of the scale and budget motels at the other; a Rolls-Royce and a Robin Reliant; a Mont Blanc and a Bic. The trick is to be single-minded in your marketing and develop a name and reputation for one thing in particular. Being a Jack of all trades and a master of none is not only a negative concept, it also confuses the consumer.

Of course, most people in business find it difficult to say 'no' to a chance to make money. It cuts right across a basic ego desire to be popular and busy. However, if you want to be really successful, you need a nailed-down strategy with a specific set of criteria that you stick to. If you try to broaden your customer base with a wider range of products or services, you may enjoy higher initial sales but you'll almost certainly diminish the focus that both existing and potential customers have of you.

The same is true for you as an individual in terms of positioning yourself. If you let people believe you can do anything, they will not expect you to be excellent at anything.

I said you needed a nailed-down strategy—right now it's time for the *nail*.

7

HOW TO CREATE GENUINE EMPATHY

I want you to imagine a dog on a house porch, an American clapboard house porch with granny sitting in her rocking chair taking in the evening air. The dog is whining slowly and softly because he's in a little pain.

The reason that he's experiencing a little pain is because he's lying on a nail. A large nail. But he doesn't move, he just keeps whining.

Doesn't it feel like that for you sometimes when you are trying to persuade someone to your point of view and they don't seem to get it? Why don't they buy into your idea, product, service or excuse?

For the same reason as the dog doesn't move. The nail doesn't hurt enough.

There isn't enough motivation to move. So you have to build the need by either amplifying the pain or explaining the benefits of moving to a different part of the porch.

In certain zoos there are temperature controls underground inside the animal enclosures, near to the public viewing areas. When you go to a zoo you want to see the lions, tigers and jaguars and you want to be as near as possible without being in any danger. So on hot days, the zoo keeper reduces the temperature under the ground nearest to the visitors so the animals lie nearest to the public viewing areas. On cold days they turn the temperature right up so the animals want to be near to where the public are.

That's influence as opposed to persuasion. The animals have been influenced to move, not persuaded.

You need to establish the motivation and mindset of the other person—in this case, the animals. You don't get very far prodding half a ton of lion with a stick and, in today's business environment, you don't get far with only a big stick either. You need to amplify the dog's pain or point out how much better it would be somewhere else, away from the nail.

The NAIL is an acronym in which the N stands for Need.

I once spoke at a Smith & Nephew conference for nurses, people who specialize in deep wound care. During the coffee break I asked a group of nurses what their definition of empathy was. One said to me, 'You can't have empathy with an amputee unless you've lost a limb yourself. You can't have empathy with someone who's got cancer unless you've had cancer and you can't have empathy—real empathy— with someone who's got a bad bed sore unless you've had a bad bed sore. That's how it is.'

While I'm not sure I totally agree with her, there is no doubt that real empathy is a genuine understanding of the other person's situation. True empathy is when you understand the other person's needs.

N IS FOR NEED

Remember the guy looking for a BOSS suit? His need was for a BOSS suit because his belief was that it was an excellent brand and that was the brand for him. If you asked him *why* he liked that brand he would no doubt give you logical reasons: previous experience of the brand, a view on the cut and design being right for him and so on.

But the major issue is that he had an emotional attachment and belief. His need was for a BOSS suit or something very similar, and our retailer lost any chance of selling him a suit when he didn't identify the buyer's need and belief system. Similarly, my retail friend didn't establish my view on the Sand suit.

If you have ever bought a house you will have no doubt considered three key factors:

✦ What is it?
✦ Where is it?
✦ How much?

These *appear* to be the needs, the basic needs.

But buying a house is an emotional decision, isn't it? If you can think about when you bought your house, you became emotional about it. Indeed, if you are honest with yourself, you will acknowledge that you don't really know why you fell in love with it.

When we first viewed the house that would become our family home for over 20 years, my wife glanced over her shoulder at me as we walked in the front door and said with her eyes, 'Say nothing—we're buying this house. This is ours.' We had only seen the view from the front and the hall.

Did you know that women have more facial muscles than men have? Men are just not as able to be as expressive as women.

Remember Gerald Zaltman's 95:5 rule? He declared that most of the time we don't know what we're doing. We justify logically but we buy emotionally. And the needs of the other person you are trying to persuade often need 'teasing' out of them because initially they talk about the logical issues, and they themselves don't really know what they want. That's why we buy the house that costs £20,000 more than we really wanted to pay, or why we have a shiny new two-seater Cabriolet on the drive and a baby on the way.

Here are five things you need to know about customers:

1 People don't always know what they want.
2 They know what they like when they see it.
3 They know whose money it is.
4 Often what they think is important in the buying process is different to what you think should be important.
5 Men and women are very different.

I want you to imagine that you are selling boxes of widgets. You have come to the point in your presentation where you have asked the buyer for a commitment to buy.

You have an ongoing relationship with this buyer and wish to build the relationship further. As you ask for the commitment to buy, the buyer says to you, 'Could I take delivery by the first of the month?'

Now, you *can* ensure delivery by the first of the month. Do you always say 'Yes' and close the sale?

It would be easy to do, but I believe it's best not to. I believe that the best thing to do in those circumstances is to say, 'Is taking delivery by the first of the month important to you?'

This is a variant of the number one of the top ten questions.

There are then basically two options. If it isn't terribly important for him to have delivery by the first of the month, you can establish the range of dates that would be ideal for him, and get back to him as soon as you wish. Nothing lost.

But let's say that having delivery by the first of the month is crucial. Let's suppose that not having delivery by the first of the month would cause headaches for him. Let's suppose he would have a whole bunch of unhappy customers if you couldn't organize delivery by the first of the month.

Now you know his need. And knowing his need, you can build the relationship and/or sell more widgets. You could tell him that you will do everything in your power to ensure delivery but there will be some effort in it. It will involve more than simply putting it down on your order pad. It will involve him being indebted to you for the effort you have expended to establish delivery by the first of the month. Or of course, you could say something like, 'Delivery by the first of the month isn't straightforward. At the moment you are only taking 200 boxes of widgets. If you were to take a full lorry load of 250 boxes then I could ensure delivery by the first of the month.'

When it comes to negotiation, the key element is to establish the other person's need. Don't give anything away that costs you little if it's very important to the other person, but is less important for you.

Now let's role-play the widgets scenario again. You close the sale and your buyer asks, 'Could I take delivery by the first of the month?' but this time you *cannot* ensure delivery by the first of the month. What do you say?

I'm constantly amazed in seminars I run all over the world when I ask this question and people say, 'Tell him you'll do what you can.'

You can't deliver by the first of the month. Fact.

If you say 'I'll do what I can', you are raising the buyer's expectations that you can deliver by the first of the month.

In some cases a buyer will take that as meaning you are *going* to deliver by the first of the month. You have raised his expectation. And you don't want to do that.

What you say is, 'Is taking delivery by the first of the month important to you?'

And again, there are basically two options for the buyer. Option one is that it isn't important. So you needn't have gone into a blind panic and started to think that you have lost the order. You can explain that you can't deliver by the first of the month and discuss what is and isn't possible.

But what about option two, where it is really, really important to him to have delivery by the first of the month? Well, as Tom Hanks uttered the words apparently spoken by Jim Lovell on Apollo 13, 'Houston, we have a problem.' I don't deny that this is a major issue, but when would you prefer to start addressing the issue? Now, or round about the first of the month when the buyer's needs and expectations will have built up?

Just as the value of a service reduces over a period of time, so the degree of disappointment, anger and frustration builds if buyers are expecting one thing and you are expecting something else and at the end of it all the buyers feel they've been duped.

Buyers want honesty first and foremost. Don't you?

Let me give you another example. I was doing some research in a care home for the elderly in preparation for a talk I was due to deliver at a conference on the future of care. I overheard the daughter of a prospective resident in the home say to one of the staff, 'Will mum be given the run of the place'? My immediate thought was, 'Why are you asking that?' It will be for one of two very different reasons. Either she is very keen for mum to have 'the run of the place' and a positive answer will be the right one to satisfy her need; or she will be very concerned that mum is not to be left alone. Mum perhaps may have a history of causing havoc. If so, it might be dangerous if she were to be given the run of the place. So to establish the need it's best to use one of the top ten questions: 'Why do you ask?'

It's better to establish the real need right now for the daughter. It's better to establish the real need right now for the widget buyer and to begin to work out what is and isn't possible for delivery rather than deceiving him. Partly because it's unethical and unacceptable and not very nice; but also because my brief to you was that it was important to build the relationship.

So the answer in all the four possibilities in this scenario is to find out the degree of importance; to find the real, emotional need. Don't guess, don't assume and don't just close the sale and miss the opportunity.

'Is taking delivery by the first of the month important to you?' and 'Why do you ask?' are real killer questions. They help you to find the real need. So find out more about people's needs. And, of course, this isn't only about the commercial world of buying and selling. This is about finding the real needs of the ones you love the most.

Mobile phone operators took an age to realize the real potential of text messaging. Run by adults, they just didn't see young people's needs for quick, cheap and easy communication. If they'd done their research they would have been promoting texting years before they did when they found out the real market.

So the *N* in the NAIL is for Needs. Time for the A in the NAIL and Chapter 8.

8

ASKING QUESTIONS AND ACCEPTING THE ANSWERS

I had an engagement in Corby, Northamptonshire, with a pharmaceutical company. I was due to start at 9.15 a.m. at the client's offices just outside Corby and I was staying at the Hunting Lodge Hotel in Cottingham, just a few miles away. It's a nice hunting lodge, but they don't sell cufflinks.

When I am on a speaking engagement, I wear cufflinks. NLP practitioners call it a 'positive anchor'. I call it getting into the right frame of mind.

And at eight o'clock that morning I realized I had no cufflinks. I went straight down to reception and asked the receptionist if they had any. The answer was 'No'. The best place to buy a pair of cufflinks was Corby. It hasn't got a lot to say for itself, Corby, but surely I would be able to buy a pair of cufflinks easily enough.

I went first to the client's offices and dropped off all my equipment and notes for the day, and was in Corby's at 9 o'clock sharp waiting for the shops to open. The first and most obvious place to buy cufflinks was the local department store, but that only had one pair. Big purple Elvis Presley jobs. Not ideal.

The next menswear shop was for the under-25s and there wasn't a cufflink to be seen. So, at seven minutes past nine and aware that I was due to start the session in eight minutes' time, I arrived in what might best be described as a gentleman's outfitters. Perfect.

You can imagine my body language and my rushed tone of voice when I virtually ran in and saw several pairs of cufflinks that were ideal.

'Can I help you?' the attendant said.

'Yes, I need a pair of cufflinks. These here are fine,' I said, pointing to a simple pair of silver cufflinks with no price marked.

For me, it was obvious what my need was. What would you do? Sell them to me and help me put them on? Surely, that would be the reasonable and sensible thing to do.

He said, 'I have more round the back.' And he turned to get more to show me! He wanted to impress me with his range, and I wanted a pair of cufflinks-to-go and to get out of the shop as quickly as possible.

I said, 'No, no, these are fine. I'll just take these ones.'

And he said, 'Would you like them gift wrapped?'

Gift wrapped? I am not making this up!

I was manifestly in a hurry and he wanted to gift wrap them. In the event, his young assistant helped me on with them and I handed over £10. I'd have gladly paid more, because at the time I had a greater need than most people when buying cufflinks. As I was leaving I heard the older man say to his young assistant, 'Ttttt! Customers…'

The point is that he couldn't accept my need because he didn't recognize it. He didn't even accept the answer to his question.

If you want to be truly persuasive, you have to ask questions and accept the answers. You have to empathize with the other person and see the situation from their point of view. This salesman wanted to sell his cufflinks and present them the way he wanted to, not in a way that was appropriate for me at that time.

We are all guilty of telling people what we want to tell them and not what they want to know. We are all guilty of falling into a formulaic or prescriptive way of selling and persuading regardless of how the other person is feeling.

Stop it.

A IS FOR ASK AND ACCEPT

Everybody has their own particular needs. Yours is to persuade someone to do something. However, you must be patient at the outset and establish the other person's needs first of all. Do this by asking questions and accepting the answers.

Headlines in ads for medical products almost always ask a question, because it immediately gets the reader into a positive and receptive frame of mind. 'Do you suffer from memory loss?' 'Having difficulty sleeping at night?' 'Tense, nervous, headache?' My own personal favourite is the world's greatest one-word headline, 'Piles?' You get the idea.

Start establishing the other person's needs by asking questions and accepting the answers. Stop telling people what you want to tell them and start telling them what they want to know.

'Turn features into benefits.'

Horrocks.

If you see the benefits of your offer as being xyz, it's unlikely your persuadee sees the benefits being xyz. It's more likely to be apxzd. In that order.

In Chapter 6 we talked about the importance of making it easy for people to buy. And developing that important attribute of the good persuader is to ask good questions and to avoid 'showing off' about what you know.

If you want a role model for asking great questions, you could do worse than study Lieutenant Colombo in the old television detective series. Suspects spoke more freely because he lowered their guard. I wouldn't suggest you dress like Colombo or look foolish in front of your buyer, but I do suggest you ask questions in a disarming way to uncover their real needs.

Recently I needed a skip. Not the sort you do with a rope, but one of those big metal bucket things they leave on your drive and all your neighbours help you to fill up with rubbish before the company comes back and takes it away. So I looked up 'Skip Hire' in *Yellow Pages* and made the call to my local skip hire merchant.

'I'd like a skip please.'

'You'll want to know the price then?'

'Er, yes.' (Price was the last thing on my mind, but this is where I was being led.)

'They're £55 + VAT, £75 + VAT, £95 or £135.'

'Plus VAT for the £95 or £135?'

'No, they include VAT. They're builders' skips.'

'How big is each skip?' I asked. Price means nothing; she's telling me what she wants to tell me, not what I want to know.

'They're minis at £55, midis at £75, 6 cubic yards at £95 and the 8 yard builders' skip is the one at £135.'

Now if, like me, you are still wondering at this stage what you need, you are forgiven. I asked if she could explain to me how long and wide the four different skips were.

'What are you putting in the skip?'

At last, she thinks about establishing my need.

'Well, we are having our drive widened and we have rubble and stone to have taken away.'

'Oh, why didn't you say? You need the stone and rubble skips. The midi holds 4 tonnes and the mini about 3 tonnes. They're £75 and £55.'

I am not making this up.

What does four tonnes of bricks look like? I have no idea. Do I need a mini or a midi? Does the £75 and £55 include VAT? I have no idea. (There is no VAT on rubble skips although there is on 'furniture' skips, but VAT is included on these higher-priced skips.)

Are you following this or have you lost the will to live?

I rather imagine this woman is still doing the very same thing now—telling her potential customers what she wants to tell them and not want they want to know in a manner they can understand.

For most people, cubic yards and tonnage, or mini, midi and 'builders' skips', is unknown information. And for us to understand it, we need to connect unknown information with known information.

So the A in the NAIL is for Ask questions and Accept the Answers. Ask for help, too.

One of the interesting things about working with the psychology students at Newcastle University is them over-coming their initial fear of asking people for help. As infants, the word 'no' is one of the first we understand and learn to speak. Yet as we get older it becomes strangely more and more difficult to say. When a friend's car needs a push start, we don't think twice about lending a hand even if we're suffering with a double hernia. Similarly, we're not likely to refuse a motorist's request for directions when he pulls up beside us on a country lane. We feel obliged to have a stab at helping him, even if we've no idea what to do. Because just like the girl in the Rodgers and Hammerstein musical *Oklahoma*, we can't say no.

Given that we know all this about ourselves, why is it that we're so reluctant to ask others for help? Maybe we're too proud or too stubborn, but more likely it's because we're afraid of being embarrassed. Asking others for help in everyday life can show up our weaknesses and even lead to rejection. So we're reluctant to do it.

However, a study by Frank Flynn of Stanford University and Vanessa Lake of Columbia University concluded that we grossly underestimate just how willing other people are to help us out. They got people to ask others to fill in questionnaires, to accompany them to the gym to work out, and even to lend them their mobile phone for the day. But first, they also asked participants to estimate how likely they thought people were to agree to their requests. The results showed that most people underestimated their likely success rate by as much as 100%. In other words, twice as many people were happy to fill in forms, work out with them and hand over their mobiles, than the participants had imagined.

You see, what they hadn't factored into the equation was the social pressure people feel to say yes to certain requests from friends. However much they don't want to do it, it's much more awkward and embarrassing for them to say 'no'. So the conclusion is clear: if you want help, just ask. People are much more likely to help than you think, especially if the request is relatively small.

Remember, most people take pleasure in helping others out from time to time and are unlikely to say no to a reasonable request. However, a word of warning: if a complete stranger asks you to act as a lookout, start up a getaway car or carry something through customs on their behalf, it's probably best to just say no. After all, there's helpful and there's just plain stupid.

On the occasions when you need help yourself, think about whether providing assistance is going to prove burdensome to others. And if so, consider ways of making it easier for them to say no. But then, as they say in Newcastle, 'Shy bairns get nowt.'

THE FLAW IN THE NAIL

As with all acronyms, there are flaws. The flaws in the NAIL lie in 'ask and accept'. The first flaw is that sometimes people lie. So how do you spot them doing it and what do you do about it? The giveaway in lying is in the body language. If the body language is not consistent with what's being said, you need to test the answers that you're given again. And you do that by asking questions, such as, 'Can you tell me more about that?'

The other flaw in 'ask and accept' is that sometimes you know more about a client's requirements than they do. Occasionally a buyer is given a brief by someone, but they don't know the full detail. So again, it's important to test the answers by using such questions as, 'Would it be useful to look at an additional xyz if you're looking at abc?' This way you can tease out the buyer's lack of knowledge.

What I really mean by 'ask and accept' is that you must accept the buyer's attitudes, beliefs, views and thoughts. You don't necessarily accept that they're always telling the truth, nor that they know what they're doing.

Time for Chapter 9.

9

UNDERSTANDING IMPLICATIONS AND INFLUENCE

When I worked in advertising we did some work for the local football club, Leeds United. Bill Fotherby was the managing director well before Peter Ridsdale set to with his 'ego and egg' strategy, which is basically the ego of the chairman egged on by his cohorts, but with little real grasp of economics and no 'Plan B'.

Bill asked me to look at the sales of season tickets and how we might increase the number sold. Buying a Premiership season ticket is for the committed fan. You are paying in advance for 19 games of football. You are paying in July or August for a product you will still be 'consuming' the following May.

And while I don't know of many products that people are willing to queue up for in the rain as football fans do for Cup games (indeed, I don't know of any other product where people will be so blindly loyal for a lifetime regardless of how the product performs), it is clearly a big commitment to make for someone to pay in advance for a variable product. And what of the people who were supporters and wanted to see some of the games, but didn't want to go to all of them?

So we came up with the idea of buying a third of a season ticket. We would split the 19 games into three 'lots' of 6, 6 and 7 games. We would 'grade' the attractiveness of the teams so that each 'lot' was roughly equally attractive and sell a ticket for a third of the season for a third of the price. Less cost and less commitment, but allowing the fan to ensure they would see some games and feel like a real supporter. And once they were committed, hopefully we could go on to sell them two-thirds of a ticket and build them up to being a full season ticket holder.

Brilliant.

Bill liked this idea and suggested we go and see Mavis in the ticket office. Mavis had been working in the ticket office for some years. It was she who saw the queues for the big games. It was she who sold the tickets over the counter to season ticket holders and regular 'match-by-match' buyers alike.

So my colleague Richard and I went to see Mavis and I proudly explained the idea. She listened intently and then looked at us with some contempt.

'You don't understand, do you?'

I looked at her with a look that said, 'What?'

'The people who queue up here,' she said, glancing at the ticket office window, 'don't think further than next week. You come here with your fancy electronic diary systems and your time management ideas and your schedules and you think everybody lives that way. Well, they don't. They live hand to mouth. They don't plan. They don't schedule stuff in their diaries weeks ahead. They queue up at the window.'

So off went Richard and I, with our tails between our legs.

I'd asked Bill questions and accepted the answers. Now I'd asked Mavis questions and had to accept her answers.

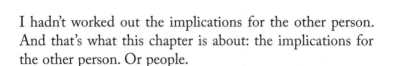

I hadn't worked out the implications for the other person. And that's what this chapter is about: the implications for the other person. Or people.

I IS FOR IMPLICATIONS AND INFLUENCE

My wife and my third son, Sebastian, share a car. When Seb had just started to drive, what was then my wife's car was due to be replaced. So off she and I went one bright and cheerful Saturday morning in January to look at various cars.

Now, neither of us is passionate about cars. In fact, we are not really interested at all. Different strokes for different folks. I could spend all day looking at guitars (and have done—lovely days), and my wife could happily spend all day looking for a dress, but cars? Frankly, we would both be happy if we bought a car and were back home in time for morning coffee.

I do like the smell of a new car, though, don't you? What a great emotional trigger. To the best of my knowledge no one has been able to bottle it and produce aerosols of the stuff. It's as emotive as baking bread when buying a house, garlic and tomato as the ferry pulls into Napoli, and cigarettes and cheap burgers when you go to a big football match.

Back to the story.

Having been to a couple of other dealerships, we arrived at the local VW dealership just after lunch. We were greeted by a young saleswoman about 23 years old. She asked what we were looking for and we explained that we were looking for a hatchback. She, in turn, explained there was effectively a choice of two: the Golf and the Polo. The car will probably do less than 5,000 miles a year and was not a major investment, so we said we would like to look at the Polo.

The conversation went on and the saleswoman, quite rightly, asked my wife what she was looking for, and whether the Polo was fitting the bill.

And then she did a really neat thing. She asked me what I was interested in.

'Safety,' I replied. 'I quite like my wife and I certainly like my 17 year old and I'm interested in how safe this car is. I won't drive it,' I continued, 'but if I had my way I would have a man with a red flag walking in front of this car to ensure they have a safe journey.'

'It's the only car under £10,000 with side air bags,' Lorna said.

Get in!

She had worked out the implications for me in this sale. She had established my need. She hadn't talked about brake horsepower or how quickly it goes from 0 to 60. Is that turning features into benefits? Well, it is for someone who's interested in that, but it's not for me. That's why just turning features into benefits is horrocks.

So we said we would think about it and we went home to discuss things with Seb.

'Can I get involved in this decision, Dad?' It was, after all, to be 'his' car. And I could see more material for my book looming, so of course he could get involved!

We returned to see Lorna the very next day. A buying signal if ever there was one.

Before we did go it was important to look at other cars. It was important for Seb to *want* another car if we were to get the best deal on the Polo. When we come to look at negotiation, if yours is the only show in town you can hold your price better than when there is a little competition.

'Hello,' said Lorna. 'This must be your son?' gesturing to Seb. 'Hello, Mr Hesketh,' she said as she shook the 17-year-old learner driver's hand. He visibly flexed his shoulders and brought himself to his full height. The thing is, you don't get called 'Mr Hesketh' when you're 17, do you? Well, obviously if your name isn't Hesketh you don't, but you know what I mean. It was lovely for him and made him feel important.

She asked *him* what he would like to look at. He recalled the conversation we had had, and could he now look at the Polo?

And he did that funny thing of sitting in the driver's seat and looking at the dashboard, not really knowing what he was looking for.

She asked him what he was interested in.

'Has it got alloy wheels?'

She looked at me and I looked at her and we both went to look whether or not it had got alloy wheels.

'No it doesn't, but…' (guess what?) 'they are available at extra cost.'

Get in!

And then she got even better. She asked again what he was interested in.

'Does it have a CD player?'

'No it doesn't, but…' (guess what?) 'it is available at extra cost.'

Get in!

She had established his needs. She had asked questions and accepted the answers. We were nearly there.

My wife, my son and I had different needs and different priorities. And the implications of the purchase were different for each of us, too. The implications for me were that my wife and son were happy and safe. The implications for my wife were that the car was economical, easy to run, easy to service and so on. And the implications for my son were what his friends would think. And that's a big implication when you're 17.

In the business-to-business selling situation, how often are you selling to a group of people? Almost always.

Do they have different needs? Yes.

Are there different implications for these people after the sale? Yes.

Can they all buy? No.

Can they all influence, and will they all have a need to feel they have influenced so that, in turn, they think they have been involved? Yes.

And so it was with Seb. Does he have any money? No.

Can he influence? Yes—big style.

I believe that he didn't actually think through or fully understand what went on in his head. I believe that he felt the decision was pretty much made by his mother and me. But he wanted to play his part. He certainly had the power of veto, and if the thought of owning a Polo filled him with dread I wouldn't have gone ahead. But he wanted to feel he could influence the decision. The implications for him of *not* influencing the decision a little (by choosing the alloy wheels and the CD player) would be that he wouldn't feel he owned the car. He wouldn't feel as proud. He wouldn't enjoy it as much. He might even feel a little resentment.

He wanted to be involved.

And so it is in business. There are people in the buying process who have the power to write the cheque but don't feel the need to influence. Enlightened managers allow their people to make decisions. They understand the importance of their people feeling they are involved. When people own a decision they are much more likely to a) make it work and b) enjoy their job more.

There are also people who have huge influence but have little or no buying power. The point is, you have to *plot* the people you are trying to persuade in the business-to-business (B2B) situation: ability to buy on the vertical scale and ability to influence on the horizontal. And you not only have to establish each of their needs by asking questions of each of them, but also establish the implications for each of them in buying your service, product, idea or excuse.

What are the ramifications for the IT guy if this goes wrong?

What are the ramifications for the FD if the terms aren't right?

What are the ramifications for the whole deal if you exclude the MD's PA?

And so on. You need to know the implications for the other people.

I worked on the Wallace Arnold account for a little while. They are coach tour operators who sell coach holidays to the 'older end'. My dad was into his seventies and wouldn't go on a coach holiday because, he said, 'They're for old people, Phil.'

The creative team at the agency wanted to show their prowess by having a lovely shot of the Scottish Highlands (nothing wrong with that); but a large coupon for people to respond ruined the 'look' of the ad. And the creatives weren't for turning despite the client, Gordon Durrans, consistently telling us that the coupon needed to be bigger.

Because the older your target market is, the more likely it is that the respondents will have trouble with their eyesight, have arthritic hands and therefore trouble with writing in small spaces. It was only when I invited a group of people in their late seventies into the agency to look at the creative work, and the creative people could see the difficulties the septuagenarians had with filling in the coupon, that we managed to get bigger coupons in the ad.

Response increased. It was about the implications for the other person.

Often, in what's sometimes known as 'big ticket selling', top management is most interested in the return on investment. They want knowledge and they want improvement and that means money. You've got to talk figures when you're taking to the big cheese.

The department heads are usually interested in a solution to a problem. On occasion, a solution to ease his or her life. Sometimes they don't really want the best price (but may have to be seen to be getting and asking for the best price) and the operators are interested in downtime and ease of working. And so on.

Case study

I've always wanted a Mont Blanc pen. The big fat one.

It's an emotional thing, as all purchases are. But I couldn't bring myself to buy one and spend what is, quite frankly, an obscene amount of money for a fountain pen. At the time they were £250. For a pen!

Nevertheless, a time came when my wife said she would like to buy me a Mont Blanc for Christmas. We went to a store in Harrogate called

Jespers that has a fine range of Mont Blancs, Watermans, Cross, Parker and other quality brands.

As we entered the laboratory (most people call it a shop or a store, but to me it's where I do a lot of my studying) by chance the managing director, Peter Jesper, was serving.

'Can I help you?'

'Yes,' I said, 'I'd like to look at that pen there.' Pointing to the mother and father of all pens that I had not ever handled in my 40+ years.

'Would you like to try it?' I nodded and he carefully laid out a little velvet cloth. (Always treat your product with the utmost care and attention. Watch the way jewellers handle expensive watches. It makes you feel good about the purchase.) He slowly opened a bottle of Mont Blanc ink.

I was enjoying this and so was he.

I handled the pen and unscrewed the top. I dipped the pen into the ink and began to scribble on a piece of paper he had also lovingly prepared for me.

And as I wrote with the Mont Blanc pen for the very first time, it was like writing with an old-fashioned quill pen. It didn't glide, it juddered. It didn't feel like silk, it felt like sandpaper.

Oh no! All these years I've wanted one and it's rubbish!

'Would you like to try the Waterman?' asked Peter Jesper. Now, I was here for the ride. This was the antithesis of the time I was buying cufflinks so, yes, I would try the Waterman. And this time it was like silk. It was like putting on an old, friendly jacket.

But I didn't want the Waterman.

So what would you do now? In my seminars I ask this question and I almost always get remedies. I get solutions. Particularly from men. Problem? Solution. Sorted.

Wrong.

Peter Jesper said a great thing that I suggest you say if you know someone likes the brand you are selling: 'What do you like about the Mont Blanc?'

'I don't know,' I replied with blunt honesty. 'I've always wanted one. I just like the Mont Blanc—the big fat one.'

'What are you thinking of using it for?' Peter asked.

'I've no idea.'

And I hadn't. I just wanted one. Like most people, I sign letters and cheques, fill in forms and write little notes to the milkman (nothing soppy, just a request for an extra pint now and again, that sort of thing).

One of the key issues for persuasion, as you've seen, is to establish the other person's need. But not necessarily the other person's need in terms of what they will do with a product or how they will use a service, but also in terms of how big their emotional need is. In the last chapter we looked at the scenario of establishing how important it was to have delivery of 200 boxes of widgets by the first of the month. In this scenario we are exploring the importance of how high an emotional need there is. When we come to look at negotiation this is absolutely critical.

Back to Jespers.

Case study

Then Peter Jesper said another really neat thing. 'Many of our clients use the Mont Blanc as what they call their "contract pen". You look like the sort of gentleman who might sign big contracts.'

Get in!

Not only did he call me a 'client' (I like that), but he thinks I'm the sort of 'gentleman' who signs big contracts. Prenuptials and the like.

He's making me feel important. And that, in persuasion, is really important.

Make your persuadee feel important. Don't patronize and don't be insincere. Don't be dishonest and cynical. But make the other person feel important: by listening with rapt attention; by focusing on what they are saying because, right now, they are the only person you are interested in. And you are really interested. If you're bored, you're boring.

Case study

Peter Jesper said, 'A lot of our clients find the Mont Blanc scratches a little at first.'

'That's what happened to me,' I said.

He knew that, of course, and continued, 'Can I suggest we try other nibs and that you hold the pen in a slightly different way?'

Only *now* does he start to find solutions. He has found my need and established that the Waterman, good as it is, is not the pen I've come for.

'It comes in an attractive black leather holder, sir. If you wish you could look at the three-pen holder so you could complete the set with a roller ball and a pencil at some stage.'

And that's what I did. Because he established my need—my emotional need—before he started offering solutions.

In this scenario there is little in the way of objections. So often, it's the objections that are the stumbling blocks and we need to address them. And I'll do that later in the book.

So the 'N' in the NAIL is for Need(s); the 'A' is for Ask questions and Accept the Answers; and the 'I' is for Implications, which give you a much better chance of Influencing when you have fully uncovered and explored them with your persuadee.

Time for Chapter 10 and the 'L' in the NAIL.

10

THINKING LONG TERM AND GETTING YOUR OWN WAY

Let me tell you about a Ralph McTell song. It's on one of the 17 albums I have of his. 'Sweet Mystery' is about a young man wanting to do the 'right thing' in courting a young girl, instead of finishing up in the mess he always seems to find himself in. He hopes that one day he will 'do it right' and take her out to dine by candlelight. Even if she asks him to come in when he gets to her door to say goodnight, he'll make himself say 'no' so he can call again.

Because he's thinking Long term. The 'L' in the NAIL persuasion process stands for Long term.

L IS FOR LONG TERM

I was at a client conference recently, and after my talk the sales director got up to speak. At the end of *his* brief talk he said to his sales team, 'And don't forget the ABC—Always Be Closing.'

Horrocks.

Always Be Selling, perhaps, but don't always be closing. That's what old-fashioned salespeople do and it won't do now. It can ruin the sale.

Of course, if you take thinking long term the wrong way, you could end up not closing. And you don't want to do that.

When do you close?

When you know how much the nail hurts and the dog (remember him?) knows what you can do about it.

If you *do* want a formula or process to follow, this is it. This is selling in the NAIL process.

1   Find out the need: how much does it hurt?
2   How deep is the emotional need and can you amplify the need? Ask questions and accept the answers.
3   What are the implications?
4   What are the ramifications for the buyer of buying today or not buying today? Can you build the pain of the nail and help the buyer picture themselves away from the nail? Discovering the requirement is not necessarily an opportunity to sell. You need to know the implications.
5   Influence the buyer.
6   Only talk benefits that are relevant to the buyer. Only talk about matching their needs with your offer.
7   Test close. Test closes are expressions and questions such as: 'How do you feel about that?' 'How does that strike you?' 'Are you happy with everything we've discussed so far?'
8   Think long term but always act short term. Ask whether they are in a position to buy if certain conditions are met. But don't ask a direct question unless you are sure you will get a 'yes', as it's not so easy to regain the ground once you have had a rejection.
9   Ask for the order.
10 Shut up.

How are *you* perceived throughout this process? Many years ago people in advertising talked about the 'USP', the Unique Selling Proposition. And, at the time, brands often had a unique 'thing' to offer. But in today's business environment it is very, very difficult for the majority of companies to have a unique proposition for longer than a Bank Holiday weekend before their competitors have copied their very 'uniqueness'.

So often it's *you* that is the USP. It is you that has the Unique Selling *Persona*. It is you who makes the difference. Remember, people buy people first. Most of my clients sell products and services that you can't buy unless you have a relationship. Again, going back to the world of advertising, the frequency and number of times a typical consumer gets to see a television commercial is measured by the 'OTS' or 'Opportunities To See'. In persuading in a long-term relationship with a client or potential client, you need to talk about Opportunities To Interact (OTI).

OPPORTUNITIES TO INTERACT

Think of the relationships you have with your friends. Apart from some very special relationships—deep relationships forged either over time or under situations of great stress, great enjoyment or a lot of time together—relationships wither on the vine if you don't keep seeing people.

Over the years we have met some fine people on holiday. Friends for a week or two who, if they lived nearby, would undoubtedly become very close friends. The sort of people who would come to our children's weddings. But the distance means that we don't see each other and, as a result, eventually they even drop off the Christmas card list.

So it is with business relationships. You need to find opportunities to interact with your clients. Keep in touch, go and see them, but for goodness' sake have something to say when you do. Because if you don't see your clients your competitors certainly will. And you don't want that.

Closing

Back to closing and step 8.

Closing should be as simple and easy as, 'Will you marry me?'

In my seminars I ask if anyone has asked this question and the other person said 'no'; or if someone has asked the question of them and they have replied in the negative. Rarely does anyone say it's the case. On the handful of occasions it has happened there's a great story!

One guy, Jeremy, put his hand up at a seminar I was running. 'You've asked someone if they would marry you and they said "no"?'

'Four times.'

'Four times?'

'Four times,' he confirmed. 'Four different girls.'

'How well did you know the girls?' I asked.

'Well, perhaps that was the problem; I didn't know them at all well!'

He made my point for me. You don't typically ask someone to marry you until you are both sure. Now, it would be easy to say that the business environment is different; that in the business world there are greater time pressures; that people have to do business with people they wouldn't necessarily socialize with.

But that would be missing the point.

The *principle* is still the same. Find out the needs, the emotional needs, work on the gap between you and the other person, and pop the question when you're confident you will get an affirmative answer because you have already asked the test question. Look for your persuadee saying things such as 'We're thinking of…' or 'We're exploring the possibility of…' and keep saying, 'How would that affect you? Why is that important?'

A friend of mine, Mike Marshall, was getting married on the banks of Loch Lomond and he and Trina kindly invited us to the wedding. As we are wont to do, Mike and I were having breakfast in Betty's, a famous teashop in Harrogate, and I asked him how long it would take to drive from Harrogate to Loch Lomond. 'An easy four hours, Phil.' Not 'four hours', an 'easy' four hours. A simple expression that helps you feel good about the journey. For Mike, any walk seems to be a 'pleasant ten-minute stroll' even if you need stout boots, a flask of hot tea and Kendal Mint Cake.

So improve your language by talking about how much a client would be 'happy to invest' rather than simply asking their budget. Ask people to get involved rather than commit. Talk about fees rather than commission, talk 'form of payment' rather than card or cash. Talk about 'particular issues to address' rather than 'problems'. Say 'I shouldn't tell you this but I will', to engage and give the feeling of rarity.

Shut up

Now back to step 9, when at the end it's all gone quiet.

The theory goes that if you are selling and persuading, and you have closed and asked for commitment, the next person to speak 'loses'. I'm not sure about the word 'lose', but I do agree that shutting up and staying well and truly shut up is the best thing to do. After all, you have nothing else to say and all you want is the client to agree. So give the client time to think and give them the next chance to speak.

No matter how long it takes.

Sometimes people need 'acceptance time'. Ever had a parking ticket? Frustrating, isn't it? And not easy simply to shrug it off. In a year's time you won't remember paying it, but at the time it's annoying. You need 'acceptance time' while you come to terms with it. When sportsmen and women have achieved an unlikely result, journalists often ask them how they feel about their victory. 'It hasn't sunk in yet,' they often reply. Or when people experience great personal tragedy, it often takes time to digest the enormity of the change they are experiencing.

Over the course of one season I recorded all the interviews with the winners of the major knockout football competitions in England. The results were clear and revealing. The expression most often used by professional footballers after they have won a trophy is 'Unbelievable', closely followed by 'Absolutely unbelievable'. Not known for their wide vocabulary, professional footballers. And when asked for the key to their success, the most popular response is 'Belief', closely followed by something along the lines of 'Great set of lads'. So they think it's unbelievable but the key reason they have won is their self-belief. Excuse me? Crazy? Not really: just acceptance time and, of course, a limited vocabulary, which doesn't help.

Often it takes years to accept change. In this book we don't deal with the process of how people react to great trauma, nor to great personal victory and achievement. But interestingly, the process that people go through is bizarrely similar.

There are reasonably clear and systematic changes in self-esteem during a tough or dramatic transition. Often it starts with what might best be described as a feeling of numbness, followed by a denial or unbelievability that this wonderful (or tragic) thing or event could have happened to them. Then it starts to 'sink in'. With particularly bad news it can lead to depression before there is an acceptance. For those who have had good news, this starts them off on a new 'plan'. They have won the League or the Cup, but now the planning starts for next year. For really bad news there is a need to search for meaning and internalizing before testing acceptance and working out how to move on.

We need to accept that people require acceptance time. Later in this chapter we look at the importance of understanding this process; not from the persuader's point of view (you're off onto something else or banking the cheque or delivering the widgets), but from the persuadee's point of view. They are now stuck with the widgets and how you handle that persuasively has a huge bearing on your next interaction with the client.

So shut up. But what happens when you shut up and they do too? For ever!

This happened to me when I was selling to a client the notion of paying a fee for some work we would do to test his ads. I'd worked on the 'Power of One': that in order to reduce the size of the 'gap' between me and him, Pat Chambers of Suite Ideas, I reduced the apparent size of his investment.

Pat and I had agreed in principle that he would pay us a fee to produce ads that he could test against his own ads to see if we could improve the quantity and quality of his response.

'So how much, Phil?' asked Pat.

'Well, you spend £700,000 on advertising, Pat. If you were to spend just 1% of that budget on the test, it would only require you to improve the effectiveness by just over 1% to justify the investment. Would you agree?

'So I propose we work on a fixed budget of just £7,000 for this work and for that we will produce artwork for you to send direct to the publications. We could do all that and have ads ready for the key Easter period if you gave your go-ahead today. Can I assume we can go ahead?'

And I shut up.

Pat, being a good salesman himself and knowing all the techniques, did too.

He smiled.

So did I.

Who would end this deadlock?

Importantly I had nothing else to say, so I stayed silent.

He was partly experiencing acceptance time and partly testing me out, as so often the persuader is put off by silence and starts jabbering about reducing the price.

So if it ever happens to you, say this: 'I read in this book recently that when the buyer is silent it means he wants to go ahead—was he right?'

And the most important thing is to shut up again.

Use it; it works.

Case study

Do you recall the story of my wife and I looking at the house we currently live in, and her saying with her eyes, 'Say nothing—we're buying this house. This is ours'? That was only the start of the story.

My wife hasn't been on my course. Indeed, she's never seen me speak. I can't get a word in edgeways at home. But she used the 'Power of One' that night.

We drove home in silence. The house was everything we could have wished it to be apart from one thing. It was more than we could afford. Well, perhaps one other snag. It needed gutting. There was no plumbing to speak of, the bathrooms and kitchens were as they had been built in 1925 and there was dry rot under the floors. Oh, and it needed a new roof. And to cap it all, we had three children under 5.

'We simply can't afford it,' I said. I accepted that it was the house of our dreams, but at £90,000 and no possibility of the vendor negotiating, it was not possible. I had done all the calculations and even allowed for us selling our own house quickly and at its top price. I had assumed we would live in a caravan on the drive for as long as necessary, with me working in advertising by day and rebuilding the house by night, but I couldn't see a way, at that precise moment, of coming up with £90,000.

'Well, what can we afford?' she asked. I looked at the calculator again. I punched in all the numbers assuming I would make no pension contributions, maximizing on the loan I could get with my current salary and assuming full value for the house we were sitting in.

'£86,500.'

'Pass me the calculator,' she said and held out her hand. She continued, 'If we were to live in that house, how long would we live there?'

'Well, it's a couple of steps up the property ladder for us. And it's very near the school the boys would go to and the youngest is four months old. If he went to the school and went straight through sixth form, then we would still be living in the house in 18 years' time. 18 years minimum, I'd say.'

And then she paused and her expression changed as she looked at the calculator, and with her head down she said, 'So the difference is just £3,500.' She tapped on the calculator. 'That's just £194 a year.' She tapped four more times. 'That's just £3.74 per week.'

There was no sound then from my wife apart from this quiet, but impassioned, plea: 'So it's come to this, has it? I'm living with a man who for £3.74 a week will stop me having the house of my dreams? £3.74 a week.'

We still live in that house. The Power of One.

How did we do it? We found a way...

COGNITIVE DISSONANCE

The final—but key—aspect of thinking long term is all about buyer's regret, or what I learned about when studying psychology as 'cognitive dissonance'. To understand cognitive dissonance better, it's worthwhile defining the meaning of the two words.

A 'cognition' is a belief, and we all have them, remember? Festinger described *cognitions* back in 1957 as 'the things a person knows about himself, about his behaviour and about his surroundings'.

'Dissonance' is the feeling resulting from two *non-fitting* or *contradictory* beliefs or bits of knowledge about the world. In other words, if an individual simultaneously holds two cognitions which are psychologically inconsistent it's an unpleasant feeling, so the subconscious mind sets to work to reduce the dissonance either by adding some 'harmonious' cognitions, or by changing one or both cognitions to make them 'fit' better or be more consistent.

For example, if individuals smoke but also believe that smoking is bad for their health, they experience cognitive dissonance; so they need to stop smoking or work on the belief that we're not here long and they would rather die than get old.

Cognitive dissonance is typically experienced by people making a major investment, such as a new car. They spend the money and know that as they drive away the vehicle has already depreciated in value. They are experiencing cognitive dissonance or 'buyer's regret'. If you have felt it, it's okay—it's normal. This particular 'buyer's regret' explains why car brochures are typically read by people who have just bought the car rather than people who are *thinking* of buying the car.

So as persuaders, what can we do about cognitive dissonance? Earlier in this chapter I touched on how there are reasonably clear and systematic changes in self-esteem during a tough or dramatic transition. If you are in the business of selling, you will no doubt have experienced the feeling of achievement when your buyer has bought. They have committed themselves to your widgets (or whatever) and you feel pretty pleased with yourself. You have been on a roller-coaster of emotions, hoping the buyer will commit to your company, and finally you have reached the top of the loop. The drive home feels like it's all downhill. But where is our buyer on this roller-coaster?

They are now stuck with your widgets and are typically experiencing cognitive dissonance, or buyer's regret (see Figure 10.1). Will they sell them on? Have they paid too much? Have they done the right thing? So while it's a great sale you have made, it's also a great time to help develop the relationship further and differentiate yourself from your competitors.

And this is not just about selling widgets, is it? In professional services I consistently get feedback from buyers that the 'big guns' with the sharp, expensive suits and empathic smiles come in to pitch for the business and are never seen again.

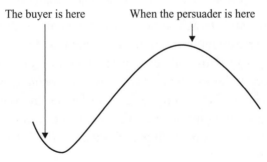

Figure 10.1   Buyer's Regret

It took me a long time to really appreciate this one, as I sold a service too. I couldn't afford (and the company couldn't afford) for me to get involved in actually handling a client's account, so I foolishly, for many years, stayed away once the business was won. It was only in my forties that I fully realized the error of my ways. The client doesn't expect you to be at their beck and call. They don't expect to see you at their offices on a weekly or monthly basis. But they do want to know that you care. They do want you to make that unsolicited phone call to ask how things are. On more occasions than I care to itemize, a phone call to the MD at the client end to check on progress unearthed a 'situation' that could easily be put right. In the past, clients had simply felt unloved and uncared for and voted with their feet.

So, in summary, particularly if you are persuading someone to make a substantial investment, remember buyer's regret. Remember that they are likely to experience cognitive dissonance and keep in touch.

Your response can be as simple as offering them a free sample of something that will be launched soon and you would value their opinion on. Better still, call them a week or two after the purchase and ask them how they feel. Just knowing you care can make a huge difference to them using you again, recommending you, and you yourself feeling like what you are doing is worthwhile. And we all want that, don't we?

Why do hotels treat you better when you arrive than when you leave? Arguably it's more important to treat you well and help you with your bags when you are going, because it reinforces the memory of the stay and encourages you to come back and to recommend it. Delegates at conferences are always telling me stories of how they got more sales and recommendations by calling back satisfied (and dissatisfied) customers and clients.

Both First Direct and Vodafone are excellent at calling me from time to time to check it's me using my credit cards or mobile phone if I'm out of the country for a while. They build up empathy, trust, credibility and, of course, loyalty. And we all want that as well, don't we?

11

THE IMPORTANCE OF PREPARATION IN INFLUENCING

A friend of mine, Barry Smith, was financial director of Shires Bathrooms in the early 1990s. I was always careful to separate my personal relationships from any possible commercial ones, and although as an agency we had targeted bathroom manufacturers as potential new clients, I hadn't mentioned it to Barry. We had done some substantial research into the bathroom market and undertaken group discussions. We had asked over 50 homeowners what they thought of magazine advertisements for the likes of Adamsez, Ideal Standard, Armitage Shanks, Plumb Center, Shires and Twyfords. I had written to the managing directors, marketing directors and marketing managers of these companies and explained that they could have the research for free on three conditions. First, that they had to meet me face-to-face, secondly that they would listen to 15 minutes on my agency's capabilities and thirdly that the meeting would be at our offices rather than theirs.

All but one were happy to comply. It was a simple case of each client understanding the rules. They got free research and we got to meet them, so that if they were to become unhappy with their agency we might be considered. And, on the grounds that we had commissioned the research, we could tell each client about the reactions of consumers not only to their advertising but also to that of their competitors.

The one who didn't want to meet me was Charles—the marketing manager of Shires. I still to this day don't know why, but the irony was that Shires' advertising was universally disliked. It was bottom of the pile. The reasons were easy to see. So I went on a bit of a crusade to get Charles to come to the agency and he eventually, albeit reluctantly, agreed to come one Thursday morning.

By chance I was having a beer with Barry at a Round Table night on the Wednesday evening. He asked how business was and who I was seeing and, frankly, I couldn't help but tell him I was meeting up with his marketing manager the following day. And he told me that the company was mightily unimpressed by the response figures it had been getting in the likes of the *Sunday Times*, the *Daily Telegraph* and the *Mail on Sunday*. He asked me what sort of response figures could be expected in those publications and went on to tell me the response Shires had actually had in the previous week's papers.

So when Charles came in the next day, boy was I prepared! He was very offhand and took our reporting of the feedback to the Shires ads badly. So badly that he became very defensive and said that if I was such an expert, what sort of response did I think last weekend's ads achieved in—you've guessed it—the *Sunday Times*, *Daily Telegraph* and *Mail on Sunday*?

I am not making this up.

So I gave him an 'estimate'. I told him what I thought was a reasonable range, and then delivered the killer blow by 'guessing' (I didn't keep them precise) what response he probably got from the three ads in question. Are you familiar with the expression 'ashen faced'?

Now, we didn't win the account for all sorts of reasons but he was impressed! And although it's a rare opportunity to know that sort of information, that's the ideal preparation for a meeting, isn't it?

BE PREPARED

So what can you do to ensure you are prepared to be persuasive? Well, having covered the essence of the persuasion process, I can more easily talk about preparation.

It's not merely anticipating the persuadee's needs and reading up, but also about thinking things through. It's what I call the 'ball boy factor'.

I had the idea that potential clients who were into football would love to play a game alongside their heroes. I knew the former England captain Trevor Cherry quite well and asked if he could fix up some players. So with Joe Corrigan in goal, Trevor at centre half and Frank Worthington up front, I was to captain a side against an opposition eleven that included former players Eddie Gray, Derek Parlane and Arthur Graham. I wanted to play the game at Accrington Stanley's ground. It had been made famous by a television commercial for milk and it was only an hour's drive away. Keith Hackett agreed to referee the match and so I wrote invitations to a group of clients and potential clients: a bunch of excited businessmen who would be able to have a distinctly memorable time and would then feel a certain obligation to us.

I had already spoken to the people at Accrington Stanley and they had agreed to let us use the pitch, dressing rooms and all the facilities. But in order to complete my preparation I wanted to visit the stadium. The secretary of the club couldn't understand why; we had all the arrangements in force and he saw no need for me to visit in advance. But I knew that to be properly prepared I needed to go. The first reason, which I couldn't share with him, was that I never assumed people would do what they said they were going to do; and the second was the 'ball boy factor'.

The secretary toured me round the dressing rooms and I realized then I hadn't thought about providing tie-ups. As we journeyed round it occurred to me that I should provide shampoo and remind the players to bring their own towels and so on. And it was when we were walking around the pitch that he asked if I wanted ball boys.

Of course! It's a huge ground and would have next to no one in the stands. Without ball boys we would be forever jumping over the barrier and running up the terraces to retrieve the ball. And frankly, I couldn't see Joe Corrigan doing that every time someone skied one over his crossbar. At £5 each, I booked four and it made all the difference. As is always the case, the evening's success relied on the little things being right. Similarly, your ability to persuade in a meeting relies on you preparing fully and getting the little things right.

Top golfers have a routine before they take a putt; professional tennis players bounce the tennis ball two or three times before they serve; footballers place the ball themselves before taking a penalty. Indeed, all the people at the top of their sport have fixed routines that they follow in order to get into the right frame of mind.

Do you?

When you enter the reception area before a meeting, do you prepare mentally? Do you always go to the toilet to check your appearance or just assume your tie is fastened straight? Do you carry shoe-cleaning brushes with you? Do you always use a mouth spray before you meet your client or customer? Do you check you have a spare pen in case the one you have doesn't work? Do you have a small hairbrush in your bag or briefcase or handbag? Do you double-check the names of the people you are seeing before you knock on the proverbial door?

Or is it too much trouble?

Do you know what sort of person you are meeting? Do they want it quick and snappy or do they want to chat?

Decorators, tilers, carpet fitters and tradespeople of all types tell me that preparation is critical. Structural engineers tell me that the size of the hole in the ground dictates how high they can build their buildings. Chefs tell me that preparing the food is the most important aspect of cooking. Motorcyclists tell me that maintaining and preparing the engine and being ready for the ride are critical. Nurses tell me that without cleaning a wound properly, it doesn't heal. Farmers tell me that if they don't sow seeds in the right way at the right time, their harvest isn't maximized. And so on.

Preparation is about doing ordinary things well. Little things like establishing how long the meeting will last and who'll be there, confirming the appointment in writing, gathering all the information you need and letting them know discreetly that you have prepared. It flatters people. It says to the recipient that this is an important meeting. It's about preparing to meet their expectations; it's about doing all you can to avoid being late. It's about knowing all you can about the internal politics and attitudes, competitors and existing supply arrangements, the trading preferences of the prospect, and so on.

Let's talk about chipped cups, scuffed shoes, and Bobby Charlton-style comb-overs. Stay with me on this one, there's a point.

It could be argued that there are only two types of people you know—and are going to know—in your lifetime: those who think everything matters and those who don't. If you offer someone a refreshing brew from a cup with more chips than Tiger Woods, it's not a good start. Because if you're not bothered about presenting a potential client with a possible bacterial infection, it doesn't bode well for the care you'll take when working with them. Similarly, whenever I'm in a shoe shop I can't help observing the state of the assistant's footwear. If they look scruffy, worn, scuffed or like the laces have been chewed by a small dog, I'm likely to turn on my heels. And finally, does your hairdresser sport a Bobby Charlton-style comb-over? No, neither does mine.

The bottom line is that the look of an environment suggests a certain standard of behaviour. And it's the small things that matter. Back in the 1980s, researchers in America demonstrated how a litter-strewn, graffiti-spattered environment suffers more petty crime than a neat and tidy one. It's called the 'broken windows theory'. A team of behavioural scientists supported this more recently with experiments on Dutch streets that showed how people misbehave and care less about the environment when other people do the same. One experiment compared the amount of litter cyclists dropped in an alley that was spotlessly clean, with the amount of litter they discarded when there was graffiti on the walls. The result showed that twice as many cyclists were 'encouraged' to litter the environment when it was already a mess.

The second experiment involved a supermarket car park and four carelessly 'abandoned' shopping trolleys. Again, researchers discovered that in the car park with the trolleys stacked neatly in their stations, fewer customers were tempted to litter the floor with the flyers that had been placed on their windscreens. But in the car park where the trolleys were all over the place, shoppers were more likely to add to the chaos by discarding the flyer on the floor. Incidentally, they made sure that nobody moved the strategically placed 'abandoned' trolleys by smearing the handles with petroleum jelly; a practice which staff at my local supermarket employ just for a laugh.

So be aware of your behaviour and carefree attitude to detail. Because when times are tough it's the ones with the metaphorical tidy car park that survive.

Four hundred years ago in *As You Like It*, the Bard wrote:

> All the world's a stage,
> And all the men and women merely players:
> They have their exits and their entrances;
> And one man in his time plays many parts.

We all play a part and we want people to think well of us. We want to project a certain image and so often that is not consistent with the life we are really living, with the real world we inhabit.

So when we 'act' in a social situation we create a certain impression of ourselves. And that takes preparation.

Everything matters.

12

DIFFERENT STROKES FOR DIFFERENT FOLKS

My old Uncle John used to say, 'All the world's queer save thee and me—and even thee's a little queer.' People are funny, aren't they? They're different.

I am a fan of Myers-Briggs and a whole host of personality profiling systems. I have a passing interest in astrology. I read books where people are segmented into animals such as sharks, tigers, puppies and bears. NLP practitioners talk about auditory, visual and kinaesthetic types. You can segment people as either positive or negative versus active and passive, and neatly put everyone on the planet into one of four 'types'. Positive and active people have a dynamic effect on you. Positive and passive people are good at detail and are hard working, whereas negative and active folk are trouble. They're disruptive and not constructive. Keep away from them, particularly the ones who stay in their pyjamas all day. And finally there are the 'negative and passives', who suck the life out of you slowly. They're the 'anti-cyclones' of misery.

I haven't finished yet. There is a 'system' of establishing whether people are 'activists, reflectors, theorists or pragmatists'. Another whereby people are either technical expert/ analytical, bottom liners, friendly supporter/amiable or extrovert. Then there's left and right brain dominance. Left brain equals learning such as language and logical mathematical processes, while right brain equals rhyme, rhythm and pictures. And let's not forget a long time favourite: the socio-economic groupings A, B, C1, C2, D and E.

And all this is without touching on some of the neat acronyms that advertising agencies have come up with such as Glams (grey, leisured, affluent and married), Yuppies (young urban professionals), Oilkies (one income, loads of kids) and Dinkies (double income, no kids).

According to one anthropologist you can make judgements on people by the size of the peel in their marmalade. I can quite believe it.

These categorizations all have a role, but none of them has the answer. The real answer is that we are all different. Now, if the key to persuasion is seeing things from the other person's point of view, there has to be more to it than simply saying someone is an ENTJ (Extended iNtuitive Thinking Judger; a Myers-Briggs personality type term), left brain dominant, 'B', extrovert, negative Libra who prefers shredless marmalade.

People's propensity to be persuaded is influenced not only by their need for what it is you are offering but also their childhood, their experience in similar situations and what their peers and bosses expect of them. People buy emotionally and justify logically. And what you offer typically has what might be described as hard differentiators (logic) and soft differentiators (emotion).

Logic (hard differentiators) is the tip of the iceberg. Logic is what you appear to want and what you say you want: cost, speed, size, compatibility, reliability, specification etc.

Emotion is ego, kudos, power, politics, chemistry, security, CV building, effect on other people, how it will reflect on your management, your own 'brand reputation', image, relationships and so on. And most of this stuff your buyer either doesn't know (it's in their subconscious) or doesn't want to know.

And there isn't one buying 'process' we all follow, is there? Sometimes we start with a basic need for a product or service. We then decide what we want and the process can be reasonably logical at this point. But then we get into our higher needs—our emotional needs. Sometimes we buy things we don't need. Sometimes we buy things we didn't know we needed until we saw them.

In addition to all that, if you are selling in a business-to-business (B2B) area, you have more than one person involved. Why do people buy in B2B? Well, once a need has been established (and over and above their need to be certain that the new product or service will be sustainable, reliable and good value), there are typically four reasons to buy:

1 It saves or makes them money
2 It saves time
3 It improves efficiency or their ability to compete
4 It makes life easier and allows them to do other things

Within this, the top managers typically are most interested in the return on investment. They want knowledge and they want numbers. They want improvement and that means money. As I said earlier, don't talk to the big cheese until you can talk numbers.

But the department head is often more focused on the solution to a problem. When I got potential clients away from their office and asked them what they really wanted from an agency, they would confide in me that what they often wanted—their real, emotional need—was a solution for an easier life. They didn't necessarily want the best price. They had to be seen to be getting and asking for the best price, but the main focus was on protecting their job and allowing them to do what they wanted to do.

What of the technical people? They need technical evidence; they want reassurance not only on the technical ability but also on back-up. They sometimes want the latest 'toy' and who cares about the money—that's someone else's department.

How 'big' is the purchase? If words are the language of the relatively low-cost items you buy in a retail shop, numbers are the language of the B2B large-ticket sale. So if you are selling to a group of people, I recommend that you plot them on the scale in Figure 12.1.

The horizontal axis is the individual's ability to influence the decision and the vertical scale the ability to actually buy.

Do you recall in Chapter 9 Sebastian and I buying the VW Polo? We examined who could influence and who could buy. My wife had a big influence and could also buy. I could buy as I was ultimately the one with the chequebook, but

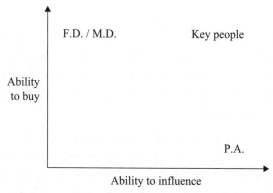

Figure 12.1 Plotting the Influencers and Buyers

Seb could influence enormously. He had power of veto. No money; loads of power. And although he didn't see his power of veto, it was important for me (the 'managing director' in this case) not only to have him along in the decision, but also to allow him to influence part of the decision so that he would be more interested in looking after and maintaining the car. It wasn't a decision foisted on him. In the Victorian era that's how decisions were made. In the twenty-first century we need to be more conciliatory.

So plot the people you are seeing. By all means plot them as activists or pragmatists, ENTJs and left brainers. But more importantly, don't miss out on who can make decisions and who can influence. And establish their individual needs if you want to be successful.

I shared an office with my PA for 20 years. My relationship with her was important to me because the success of that relationship had a huge bearing on my ability to do the thing that I was best at: getting in front of potential clients. And if anyone who wished to sell to me was rude to her, I found out about it pretty much instantly. That then made their job very difficult indeed, partly because she was my gatekeeper and partly because I didn't want to put broken glass into all the layers of tissue paper I was laying down between her and me. Could she 'buy'? No. Could she influence my relationship and thereby willingness to buy from that rude supplier? You bet.

So plot the people you're seeing, establish and list their different emotional needs. Reinforce the things you can do better than your competitors, work on the issues you're struggling with and remember these five things:

1　People buy to solve a pain or fulfil a desire (carrot and stick). The key to getting the sale is to move the prospect's pain (their NAIL) to the top of their list.

And to do that you need to be persistent. You need them to experience or at least see the pain of not making a decision.

2 People buy emotionally and justify logically.

3 All the people who can influence and/or buy have different needs. Different strokes for different folks.

4 The conversation is the relationship, so the depth of your questioning and the depth of your conversation is the depth of the relationship.

5 You need to ask good questions of each individual. You have to feel how they are feeling about what's important to them. Ask the hard questions and deal with the responses.

PART 3

OVERCOMING OBJECTIONS AND NEGOTIATION

Techniques to Handle All Objections

The First Four Steps to Negotiation

The Final Four Steps to Negotiation

Getting People to Do What They Have Agreed to Do

13

TECHNIQUES TO HANDLE ALL OBJECTIONS

A book on persuasion and influence could not be complete without addressing the issue of the 'cold call'. Telephoning an unknown prospect to sell an idea, product or service—or indeed, just to make an appointment—is one of the toughest things to do. People object to doing it. It can be the biggest objection to getting a new customer. And it's your objection, not theirs!

I know. I've done the cold calls and have several T-shirts to show for it. It can be an extremely costly and deflating business, and if it can be avoided by judicious use of SEO (search engine optimization), mailings, advertising, leaflet drops and other marketing means then these routes should be pursued. But if you are looking for a recommendation on overcoming the reluctance to pick up the phone to make that call, here is my advice.

Create a 'pain gap' of time and give yourself an incentive at the end of it. I tend to allocate one and a half hours in my day in advance. During those 90 minutes I don't take calls, I don't take interruptions, I don't drink coffee and I don't gaze out of the window or check my e-mails. I plan my calls but, importantly, I don't start with the easy ones first. I put myself in a mindset of going to the dentist and do nothing else but cold calls for the 90 minutes. At the end I reward myself with a coffee and a biscuit and, if necessary, extend the time frame if I'm not achieving as much as I set out to do with my cold calls.

When I was working with new salespeople, I would have us all sit in a room together. Typically there would be four of us and I would effectively 'lock' us all in the room. With four phones there is literally nothing else to do. That factor, coupled with hearing others calling and having a degree of success, had a marvellous effect on the others. I would go so far as to tell *other* colleagues exactly what we were doing so that we were really committing ourselves to doing it.

It worked. Create your own 'pain gap' and go for it.

Better still, do it regularly. I used to have 'Ten before ten on Tuesday' and allocate the first hour of each Tuesday to nothing else but unsolicited calls and I made sure I completed at least ten calls.

OBJECTION MANAGEMENT

Let's get on to handling objections, then. What are the first three things you should do with any objection?

1 **Let the other party clearly state their objection in full.** The more heated they are, the more you need to listen with rapt attention until they have finished. The more agitated they are, the more they will not hear anything you say in reply until they have said what they need to say.

2 **Agree with the person objecting.** Empathize and let them know that you can see the situation from their point of view. And remember, avoid using the word 'but'. People see it as an objection, so you need

to create empathy first by appreciating the validity of their objection. You have to see it from their point of view just to get on the dance floor.

3 **Ask if there's more.** Make sure that you hear their whole objection out.

Let's take a simple objection first. Suppose you want someone's time to discuss an issue and they say, 'I'm far too busy.' The key is to repeat what the other person says. So your response should be, 'I can see that you are very busy.' They will often go on to explain more: 'You've come at a bad time. I've got all this work to do, a deadline I can't shift and there's no way I can see you now.'

Again, reflect back what they say: 'I can see this is not a good time for you and you've got a lot on.' And remember to let them know you understand how they must *feel* about it. You are making emotional investments in the other person. Most people don't do this, so if you display genuine empathy it makes you different. You are building up their obligation to see you. Importantly, you're also building trust. Often the other person then asks you what you want and sees you as an ally, someone who appreciates their issues and how hard they are working.

Do it. But be absolutely sincere.

I was running a seminar recently when a delegate asked me, 'Can you teach me how to fake sincerity?' I thought he was joking but it turned out he was asking me in all sincerity. Or as much as he could manage, anyway. I suggested he get another job.

As far as making a sale goes, I believe that objections are great opportunities rather than barriers. But how do you turn an objection into an opportunity?

Let's look at it step by step.

Step 1: Prevent the objections from arising in the first place

For example, if you know that your product or service is more expensive than your competitor's, address that early in the meeting. You can't run away from it because the prospect is bound to find out eventually. Then concentrate on the positives, like why you are more expensive. Why is it better? How is it stronger? What can you do that the competition can't? And *most importantly*, what are the *intangible, emotional* benefits that you can offer over and above your competition? 'Peace of mind' is a superb example of an intangible benefit. Make sure you have some impressive answers already worked out before you start persuading.

Indeed, if you know that the prospect has a major objection and it's not easily resolved, you have to *dissolve* it. If you keep presenting knowing the 'bomb' is going to go off at some point, your prospect isn't listening anyway. His subconscious is focused on the problem. So raise it very early on.

For example, distance between you and your prospective client might be a big issue:

Salesperson: 'I'd like to think that our service is relevant but we are 200 miles from your head office. Do you see that as an issue?'

Buyer: 'Yes, I do.'

Salesperson: 'Should we address the issue now?'

The buyer is bound to answer in the affirmative—in fact they will be pleased that you have brought it up. Once they've agreed the 'issue' (not a 'problem', remember) needs to be 'aired', it's important that you ask them to start. If you break the issue down into several smaller issues, you can often dissolve it by showing that the ramifications are not as bad as they thought.

Step 2: When you know what the objection is, the next thing to do is agree with the persuadee

You're not agreeing that they are right, you're agreeing that there is an issue that needs to be addressed. Phrases like 'I can understand that', 'I'm glad that you raised this point' or 'Some of our best customers thought that at first' will avoid conflict and reduce the importance of the objection in the prospect's mind.

Step 3: Discover the real objection

Often people raise price as an objection when really something more fundamental is stopping them moving forward with you. The first and most important thing to do is to get to the heart of the objection. To do this, ask some searching questions. If it's a price objection, find out just what the problem is. Is it outside the company budget? Is it more than they can authorize? More than they expected? Dearer than the competition? Questions such as 'Compared with what?', 'What would that mean to you?', 'Why is this important to you?' or 'How much did you have in mind?' can start to get to the heart of the objection.

But at the same time, don't assume that everything is an objection. I was in Harrods recently and asked the salesman what kind of person spent £6,500 on a pen. Instead of telling me (and flattering me that it was people like me), he simply went on to show me Mont Blancs at the very bottom of the range. Why assume it's an objection?

If the objection is that they need a response very quickly, explore the need by saying things like 'We *could* get back that quickly, but it won't be very good', or 'We couldn't possibly do it the justice it deserves without spending some time exploring the answers to these questions'. I always use this tack and, on more occasions than not, more time is often made available if it means the difference between a good, measured response and a knee-jerk reaction. I say, 'There is a quick and easy, ready-made solution to every problem.' And then pause before adding, 'Unfortunately it's usually wrong.'

Often you get more time because the first objection turns out not to be the main one, once the client has thought through the implications of getting a quick response. And anyway, you never talk to 'the Big Cheese' until you know your maths; they want numbers.

Often it's politics that create objections. People like to haggle for control of money, resources, decisions and, of course, other people. In short, they like to score one over their rival in the company. Getting to the heart of that little topic is not just a completely new subject, it's a whole new book by itself.

Step 4: What is the expectation?

A friend of mine, Mike Baxandall, invited my wife and me to his wedding 'fest' a few years ago. He and Liz had known each other for many years and both were entering their second marriage. We were delighted to be invited, but had no real idea of what a wedding 'fest' was. All we knew was that the evening affair was to be in a marquee in the grounds of their house and that there was to be a jazz band. So the nature of the venue, the invitation itself and Mike and Liz's light-hearted attitude to the whole wedding 'thing' led us to believe it was to be a reasonably low-key affair. They had actually married the week before with only immediate family present. So, in our *perception*, this was a summer barbecue type of event. As we were preparing to go, my wife commented that she would probably not know many people and that she would drive.

It turned out to be the best night out of the year! We knew a lot of people there, the jazz band was sensational, the marquee, the food, the ambience, the gospel singers, the wine—everything was first class. And one of the key elements in enjoying ourselves so much (we abandoned the car and got a taxi home in the wee, small hours) was that we were not *expecting* it to be that special. You see silver medallists unhappy with their gong because they came to win while bronze medallists are delighted, because their expectation was just to get to the final. Newly promoted teams to the FA Premiership are happy with fourth from bottom, while fourth from top is a disaster for a big club. It's all about expectation. That's why one of the five keys to persuasion is to manage expectation.

EXPECTATION AND THE 'PYGMALION FACTOR'

In Greek legend, the story goes that a brash young sculptor in Cyprus called Pygmalion thought that all the women on the island were terribly flawed in one way or another. So he took it upon himself to carve a statue of his ideal woman, embodying every feminine grace and virtue. For months on end he toiled away with all his apparently prodigious skill until he had fashioned the most exquisite figure ever conceived by art. The story goes that he did such a good job that Pygmalion fell passionately in love with the statue, and could be seen in his studio kissing its marble lips, fingering its marble hands and generally dressing and grooming the figure as if he were looking after a doll. However, in spite of the work's undoubted loveliness, Pygmalion was desperately unhappy, for the lifeless statue could not respond to his warmth and love. He had set out to shape his perfect woman, but had succeeded only in creating frustration and despair for himself.

It would be a pretty sad story if the tale ended there, but it doesn't. According to the scribe who wrote all this down, the goddess Venus took pity on Pygmalion and brought his statue to life, and —da daa —he and Galatea (as he named her) blushed, embraced and married with the goddess's blessing. All lived happily ever after.

A load of old horrocks? Maybe, but after an excellent study by Robert Rosenthal and Lenore Jacobson in 1968, the 'Pygmalion factor' became part of the lexicon. These American academics had become increasingly concerned that teachers' expectations of lower-class and minority children were contributing to the high rates of failure among these types of students. It's what my English teacher wife calls 'teacher expectation'.

So they carried out an experiment in a state school in a predominantly lower-class, but not impoverished, community. At the beginning of the school year, the researchers gave the students an intelligence test they called the 'Harvard Test of Inflected Acquisition' to give it a bit of gravitas. They told the teachers that this test could determine IQs and also identify those students who would make rapid, above-average intellectual progress in the coming year, whether or not they were currently 'good' students.

Before the next school year began, teachers received the names of those students who, on the basis of the test, could be expected to perform well. Unbeknown to the teachers, Rosenthal and Jacobson had actually picked the names from the class list at random, so any differences between these children and the rest of the class existed only in the heads of the teachers. The Inflected Acquisition test from

Harvard was of no value except to give the researchers a baseline reading of IQ for later comparison.

When the second intelligence test was administered at the end of the year, those students who had been identified as 'academic spurters' (sorry, this is American research) showed, on average, an increase of more than 12 points on their IQ scores, compared with an increase of 8 points among the rest of the students. The differences were even larger in the early grades, with almost half of first and second grade 'spurters' showing an increase in IQ of 20 points or more.

Teachers' subjective assessments, such as reading grades, showed similar differences. The teachers also indicated that these 'special' students were better behaved, were more intellectually curious, had greater chances for future success and were friendlier than their 'non-special' counterparts.

In essence, a self-fulfilling prophecy was at work. The teachers had *unconsciously* encouraged the performance they *expected* to see. Not only did they spend more time with these students, they were also more enthusiastic about teaching them and unintentionally showed more warmth to them than to the other students. As a result, the special students felt more capable and intelligent. And they performed accordingly.

It wouldn't be allowed now, would it? Fact is, this is going on all the time. Your people will achieve more if you expect them to achieve more. Your own children are more likely to achieve more and do more if you gently expect more and tell them there are no limits to what they can achieve.

It's the same for you. Don't raise the buyer's expectation more than you need to. And certainly don't allow it to rise inadvertently by letting your buyer assume that you can deliver on Friday or have the product in a choice of colours if you're unlikely to be able to fulfil your promise. When new starters joined our company I used to give them a piece of advice on day one. I would say, 'Just do what you say you are going to do and you have a career here. If you don't remember anything else from your first day in this company take this away. Do what you say you are going to do.'

FEEL, FELT, FOUND

So in entering the field of 'objections' we are effectively talking about expectation and negotiation: managing expectation, understanding negotiation, knowing when the other party is using 'tricks' and when they are just looking for a reasonable resolution.

There is a neat, ready-made solution to every problem. Unfortunately, it's usually wrong.

And so there is not a ready-made way of handing every objection. But one way of doing it comes close. It effectively uses the 'third person': someone who is just like you and has experienced the same objection. It can often be a pretty neat way of handling all objections but one. I'd like to attribute this to the original author but my research suggests it's lost in the ether. However, the principle has stood the test of time and I offer no apology for repeating it here if you haven't come across it before.

Many situations can be eased by 'feel, felt, found'. Imagine someone is shocked at what you are asking them to do or commit to. They react and wait for a response. It's important to choose your own set of words, but just as important to use 'feel', 'felt' and 'found' in that order. So, for example, 'I can understand how you *feel*. A lot of our satisfied customers *felt* just like that when they first saw the investment. But what they *found* was that the durability and the 24-hour service [etc.] made it worth every penny.' Insert your own response in each situation: 'I understand how you feel. Many people felt that way, but they found that...'

For example, nurses can use it when talking to patients who don't want to be treated because the medicine or operation seems more painful in the short term than the illness: 'I can understand how you feel, a lot of our patients have felt the same way. However what we've found is that in the long term it cures the problem.'

And the one objection it doesn't work for? 'I don't like you.'

Think it through.

14

THE FIRST FOUR STEPS TO NEGOTIATION

Negotiation starts the moment you begin the persuasion process. Negotiation isn't a stage that you get to; it's not a milepost or a hurdle, it's built into the whole process. If you take that on board you begin to see the importance of building your own value, the persuadee's perception of you and your value proposition right from the start. Clean shoes, being on time and all that. Negotiation is the journey, so enjoy the journey but, most importantly, make sure you're always walking.

Negotiation is about people. Just as companies don't appoint ad agencies, companies don't negotiate with companies. For the most part, people meet people.

Arguably, negotiation starts when the persuader and the persuadee are conditionally committed to the 'sale'; and negotiation generally results in a compromise between persuader and the persuadee. Typically, sellers reduce something (often what they charge) and buyers increase their offer from their starting position. But that's only part of the story.

The relationship is critical. *Relationship negotiating* is the ideal if you want to get the most out of the 'deal'.

Imagine you have seen a house with your significant other. Suppose you have a budget of £800,000 and as you are viewing the house you think it's perfect. Everything on your 'wish list' is here in this house. It's the right location, near to the amenities you need, it has the right number of bedrooms and bathrooms, the garden is just the right size and so on. And the more you look around the more you are looking at each other and saying (without speaking!) that it's a bargain. It's everything you want it be and you just don't see why the seller is asking only £800,000. You have been looking at houses in the area for some weeks and this is the one for you. You are emotionally involved and you want to buy. You feel like bursting into song. What do you do?

Well, not bursting into song is a good start.

Do you tell the buyer it's perfect? Do you let them know you think it's a bargain? Do you rush in with an offer at the asking price?

No.

Why not?

Because you already know that the key is to let the other person think they're 'winning'. And this, if you know what you're doing and can control all the urges of your subconscious (which is controlling you 95% of the time, remember), is what you do:

1 Don't let your body do what it wants to do.
2 Don't give away how keen you are or they will think they can get more than £800,000.
3 Create empathy.
4 People sell to people they like, just as people buy from people they like. But you don't want to add value to the house, so compliment the buyer on the internal décor. In effect, tell them what you like about it without saying you think the house is priced too low.
5 Don't agree quickly.

6   If you rush in with the full price they aren't going to think they've 'won', are they?

7   Let them think it's a struggle.

8   Give the distinct impression that £800,000 is absolutely at the top end of the range. Maybe put an offer in? Better still, ask them what they would be prepared to accept. Because you don't know their position. They might be even more desperate to sell than you are to buy. Putting to one side the issue of surveying the property and so on, does this make sense?

Arguably, you would be willing to pay more than £800,000 so in effect they've 'lost'. But what if they would be delighted to take £750,000 for a quick sale because of their circumstances? Now you've 'lost'. It's about finding out the other person's perspective.

In most negotiations there's a power differential, in that one person wants to buy more than the seller wants to sell or needs to sell more than the buyer wants to buy. Your power is defined by how much you need the 'deal', so you need to improve the other person's perception of you. And of course, the more you understand about the other side, the better your chance of getting the right deal for you. Everyone has a minimum and a maximum and most of the negotiation takes place in the zone in between. You may well also have 'deal-breakers' and you sometimes have to remind yourself of their importance to you.

It's time for another acronym: NEAT negotiation. Here's the first NEAT.

N IS FOR NEVER PUT A MARKER DOWN FIRST

When I worked in advertising I used to run a number of interesting events for clients and potential clients. I did that because all the research (qualitative, quantitative and anecdotal) said that clients hired and fired advertising agencies for two key reasons: creativity and relationships. If the agency was creative (in the broadest sense of the word) and if it had a good relationship with the key people, the client stayed on board. Put either or both of those things in jeopardy and the client started to look around. So I wrote what I hoped were creative communications and invited clients to 'creative' events in order to meet them and form relationships.

We went land yachting and water painting, did fly fishing and archery, and also held a number of seminars on body language, goal setting and so on. I was in conversation with John Foster at Dunlop Slazenger one day when he mentioned he knew a golf psychologist. Now this interested me. Other people did golf days and one of my criteria for organizing an event was that I wasn't willing to do something someone else did. But the idea of getting together a dozen or so clients and potential clients with a golf psychologist held an immediate appeal.

So I got the golf psychologist's details and called him. He had impressive credentials and worked with some big names. I asked him what would be involved in a Golf Psychology Day if I provided 12 players, the golf course and paid for the course fees, the meals and so on.

He explained that he would arrive at 8 a.m. and suggested the clients arrive at 8.30 a.m. for breakfast. Over breakfast he would talk for about 30 minutes on the psychology of golf. After that we would go on to the putting green, with a putter and a ball each, and he would explain the psychology of putting. Following coffee we would go onto the practice ground and, starting with the lofted clubs and working up to the longer irons, we would practise chipping on to the practice green while he told us what we should be thinking about.

After a break for lunch we would stand on the tee for a full 20 minutes while he would share with us the ideal thoughts for standing on the tee. And then we would play a round of golf while he accompanied different groups talking to us about our mental state. And believe me, we would be in a mental state by this time.

At this point in the conversation I'm like one of Pavlov's dogs. It sounded perfect. The clients I had in mind (indeed, the clients who came along) would between them spend over £50m on advertising. And most of it wasn't with us, I can tell you.

So I asked him the price. I'm picking up the bill for the golf course, the food and the drinks. Everything apart from him.

I was thinking he might be in the range of £2000–3000, but I didn't know. He might well be out of my price range and over £5000 a day. I ask this question at my seminars and almost always have one or two who are expecting the price to be in excess of £10,000. I'm willing to pay over £1000, but if it gets over £3000 I'll have to think hard.

'So how much do you charge for the day?'

'£400.'

£400! Like me at the time, you may now be experiencing two knee-jerk reactions. First, marvellous! It's well within my budget and is only £30 a head. The green fees are more than that; in fact, so is the catering for the day. It's a bargain.

But there's another thought going on inside my subconscious and I'm certainly not in control of the fear gripping me at this point. Is he any good? Can he possibly be the best in the business if he charges only £400 a day?

Two key issues here. He put his marker down first, so what's the most I'm going to pay? £400. And perception of value and price are inextricably linked. So if you can avoid it, don't put your marker down first. What is important to the other person?

Whether you are buying or selling, find out the other person's need. Do you remember the discussion on buying 200 boxes of widgets in Chapter 7? Explore their need if you can before you put your marker down. And if there is flexibility and you have to put your 'offer' in first, go as high as you possibly can if you're selling and ridiculously low if you're buying. Find out what the other person needs, including personal and emotional aspects.

And remember, some people cheat! I have often had a client say, 'Well, wxy has already offered me £z' when no such offer has been made. If you suspect the client is cheating you need to explore and test whether it's a true offer by asking for more detail. I've also known clients to 'plant' a letter on their desk that appears to be a bid from someone else so I get a false impression of the competition.

And in case you're wondering about the value of the golf psychologist: yes, he was good. Worth £400 of any corporate budget, I'd say.

E IS FOR EMPATHY

People buy from people they like and sell to people they like. So listen intently; see it from their point of view but separate the people from the issue.

Why is the relationship so important? Because unless your product offer is itself unique, you're the only part of the deal that is. You can create a unique position for your product or service, as we said in Chapter 10, by becoming the

Unique Selling Persona. That's about building trust, rapport and empathy with the other person. And while establishing an impression of uniqueness is a very effective technique when you are selling, denying uniqueness is a really neat ploy when you're buying.

Let the buyer think they've 'won'. The key benefit of not putting your marker down first, or going for your highest or lowest plausible offer, is that it is more likely to mean that when you move they think they've done well.

The Mexicans have a saying that 'every cock crows on his own dunghill'. Buyers, in particular, tend to like the power that their ability to buy gives them. Some abuse it, which is a shame, and some are intoxicated by it. That's a tragedy for them when they leave the job and find that their friends were just suppliers. Indeed, to throw another quote in within four sentences, Henry Kissinger paraphrased Lord Acton who, in turn, paraphrased the British Prime Minister of 1770, William Pitt, by saying 'Power corrupts. Absolute power corrupts absolutely.'

Accept that your persuadee will enjoy being powerful and let them have their power. Accept their power but then move into your area of expertise. You could perhaps even buy the other party a small present—well before the real negotiation starts. It builds empathy and obligation. Last, a great thing to say when you are unhappy with someone's price offer and you want to retain empathy is 'I think I might need your help here...' instead of 'Can you reduce the price?'

Avoid deadlock to help with empathy. There are obviously times when you accept a stalemate. However, if you have developed the relationship in the right way and you both know that you would like to progress, then don't shut the door.

A IS FOR ASK ABOUT THEIR INTERESTS

Of course, the ideal situation is to know exactly what your buyer (or seller) wants before you talk figures. Often your persuadee's personal and political needs are important too. The bigger the deal, the more significant these factors become.

Salespeople tend to forget that when you sell to someone in a large organization, the buyer is staking their reputation on you, so you need to understand all of their needs and concerns by asking questions. Ask them how they *feel* about the situation. Ask what the implications are and what will happen after the transaction. Ask what the downside might be of using a competitor. Ask about their interests. Only then can you begin to understand what the implications, costs and perceived values are.

And if you really want to buy that £800,000 house, why not have a friend put in a bid to see whether the vendor will negotiate with them?

If necessary, ask the other negotiants what is important to them away from their office. A café, a restaurant or a golf course will often elicit a different (and real) answer compared with the one you might get when they're sitting on their own dunghill.

When I worked in advertising, we pitched for the Spam account. The marketing manager, Rob Lucas, had asked us and five other agencies to do so. We had an 80% chance of failure until I spent an evening on board the cruise liner SS *Canberra* during a marketing conference and found out the real needs and desires of Rob and his colleagues. Once I had asked all these questions away from the office, listened with rapt attention and knew the bigger picture, we were probably in with an 80% chance of success.

We won the account. What a marvellous advertising account to win it was as well. The PR value was completely out of proportion to the advertising spend, but we loved it and benefited from it. I was interviewed on BBC Radio 5 and quoted in the *Sunday Times* and the *Wall Street Journal*. Happy days.

One of the best things about handling the Spam account was going to their golf day run by Newforge Foods. Spam for breakfast, Spam for lunch, Spam for dinner, Spam golf balls, Spam umbrellas and Spam tees. The only thing missing was the cast of *Monty Python* performing their Spam sketch. Of course, this was before the days of the internet, when Spam wasn't an expression for unsolicited e-mail, but rather filled you with nostalgia—not to mention pressed meat.

Ask about the persuadee's interests and find out what's important to them.

T IS FOR THINK : 'THE OTHER PARTY NEEDS TO THINK THEY'VE DONE WELL'

A lot of buyers don't want win–win. They want win–lose. They don't care about your position as long as they win. It might well be short-sighted, immoral, unethical and unfair, but the buyer is paid to get the best price. The lowest price they can. And in many circumstances in today's environment (thankfully not everyone) they don't care if you go to the wall.

Do you remember the film *Pretty Woman*? In the movie, Edward (Richard Gere) picks up a prostitute, Vivian (Julia Roberts). He's from the East Coast but in LA for the week. He has picked her up by accident and agreed a fee for an hour, but as far he is concerned she is far too preoccupied by time. He wants to relax and chat.

'How much for the entire night, Vivian?'

'To stay here? You couldn't afford it.'

'Try me.'

'$300.'

'Done.'

He has certainly raised her expectation of how much she can charge by agreeing quickly. In the morning, as Vivian enjoys a relaxing soak in the suite's magnificent bathtub, he has what he describes as 'a business proposition' for her.

'Vivian, I'm going to be in town until Sunday; I will pay you to be at my beck and call 24 hours a day for the rest of the week.'

She thinks about it and says, 'If you're talking 24 hours a day it's going to cost you', working out that $300 × 2 × 6 is just under $4000.

Vivian: '$4000.'

Edward: '$2000.'

Vivian: '$3000.'

Edward: 'Done.'

At this point, arguably we have a win–win. She has got more than he offered to pay and he is paying less than she first asked. A reasonable compromise. But then she can't help herself. She thinks that even $3000 is an obscene amount of money. She's delighted.

As he turns to leave for work she blurts out triumphantly, 'I would have stayed for $2000.'

'I'd have paid $4000,' he replies.

What's that? Lose–lose!

In the *relationship*, no one's happy. Because what matters is what the other person *thinks* they've got. It's their perception of the negotiation that matters. It's managing their expectation. It's allowing them to think they have a got a good deal in the broadest sense of the word 'deal'.

So what matters is not whether *you* 'won' or *they* 'won', but rather whether the deal you have struck is acceptable to *you*—regardless of whether or not the other person *thinks* that the deal is acceptable to *them*. And remember, this isn't just about money. Let's use the word 'OK' to describe an acceptable deal.

Companies are forever charging different prices for the same thing. So in theory anyone who hasn't got the best price has 'lost'. But that doesn't take into account all the other factors such as time of booking, need, knowledge and so on and so on.

So let's not always think only win–win. That's naïve. Instead, let's focus on ensuring that you have achieved a deal that you are happy with in the circumstances and, most importantly, you have allowed the other party to *think* they have got a deal that is OK for them. That is, think either 'I know I've "won" and you *think* you've done OK', or 'I'm OK and you *think* you've done OK'.

Bit more wordy than win–win, I agree, but more realistic. The key is that the other person needs to *believe* they have done well.

There are a number of interesting things that emanate from the negotiation in *Pretty Woman*. Vivian didn't fully understand that $1000 either way didn't make as much difference to Edward as it did to her. She put down a remarkably high marker for her, but it still didn't faze him. He was willing to pay the $4000 but negotiated just for fun.

Once she asked for $4000, that was the most he was going to pay. It never crossed her mind that he would pay more. And once Edward offered $2000, that became effectively the minimum he would pay. She would have gladly settled for $1000!

So some of the time win–win is horrocks, but it's important for you to know at what point you will walk away; to know what is the least you will settle for. Look for aspects of your offer that are of low cost to you and high benefit to the other person, and don't give these away lightly.

Summary? The other party needs to think they have done well.

IS THAT YOUR BEST PRICE?

Let's further explore the question: 'Is that your best price?' The value of this book for you personally—not just the money you paid for it but the time you have invested in reading it—is in the next few paragraphs. I absolutely guarantee you will save money and make money both in your personal and business life if you use this question regularly and at the right time.

Case study

We are in a furniture store. It is only two days before we go on a four-week holiday and it has been decided that we are definitely buying a new three-piece suite today. It is the time of the summer sales and bargains are to be had. We are definitely buying today, from this very shop. Indeed, we are definitely buying the three-piece suite we are sitting on.

The 'marked' price is over £6000 but today the price is a little under £4500. We are giving the salesperson, Sue Taylor, all the buying signals. Not only empathy but also sizes, formats, colours and textures are pretty much agreed. We go to Sue's workstation and she inputs these into the computer. With the protective coating and delivery the total cost is £4678.

Would we like to go ahead with a 10% deposit?

At this point a salesperson (particularly if they are on any sort of commission) is feeling that this particular fish is hooked and is being reeled in. And it's at this point—when the salesperson is calculating the commission in their subconscious (they're not in control of that, remember)—that you change your body language.

I pull back in the chair. I grimace. I am having second thoughts and say so to my wife. I say to her that it's a big investment and that perhaps we should go on holiday and think it over. Sue gives away her feelings by her expression. The fish is wriggling off the hook.

Then, and only then, as I make to stand up and walk away, do I say the words I am asking you to say that will guarantee you will save money:

'Is that your best price?'

She says, 'Let me see what I can do...'

Get in!

She taps away on the calculator as my wife stands impassively by. 'My absolute bottom price is £4500, Mr. Hesketh. I know it's only a gesture, but it's the best I can do.'

£178 is a gesture? I can buy a new guitar with that! Relative to £4500 it might seem like a gesture, but I've just saved myself £178 because we were happy to buy at £4678.

I puff and blow (so she thinks she's done OK) and, with a few looks between my wife and me, we agree.

As she recalculates the deposit and tells us about delivery times, I ask her for her calculator. Just for my own interest I time myself pulling back, grimacing and saying 'Is that your best price?' It takes 15 seconds and I make £178. I tap the numbers into the calculator. At this rate I am earning over £42,000 an hour.

Result!

And when the sofas were delivered I learned another valuable lesson by phoning Sue.

So by all means leave room for negotiation, but focus on the other person feeling they have done well. We recently had a bathroom salesperson come to the house, and after he had measured up he gave us a quote of just over £20,000. I hadn't even had time to raise my eyebrows and begin the intake of breath before he said, 'But we have an offer on at the moment and I can do it for £10,000.' He certainly needed to leave room for negotiation, but to drop so quickly by so much took away all the credibility.

Now on to the second NEAT.

15

THE FINAL FOUR STEPS TO NEGOTIATION

N IS FOR NEUTRALIZE YOUR BODY

Or to put it another way, 'Don't let your body do what it wants to do.' If you really, really want 'it', don't let the other side know. Never give the impression of wanting anything too badly.

That brings me to the 'intake of breath syndrome'. You're doubtless familiar with it. The seller gives their price and the buyer has a sudden intake of breath or grimaces. It could be a painful bout of wind, but the chances are they're going for the simple and low-key approach: 'That's more than we had in mind.' Alternatively, they may opt for the more extravagant approach, typified by a sharper, more audible intake of breath followed by a theatrical puffing of the cheeks and an exasperated exhalation.

How often is this genuine and how often is it a ploy? Well, who knows? What I do know is that if you use the intake of breath regardless of what you think of the price, you will save money—a lot of money—over the course of a lifetime. I have trained myself when buying always to use the intake of breath.

Remember our golf psychologist? Despite my surprise that he wanted just £400 I still used the intake of breath. Do you know what he did? He said, 'Well, I won't charge you travel expenses if you think it's too expensive.' It was a tempting offer, but I would still be wracked with guilt if I hadn't paid his bus fare. He was a good guy and he deserved to be rewarded accordingly.

So if you think the price you are being offered is a bargain, don't act like a springer spaniel and wag your metaphorical tail. Brace yourself to act like it's too much or don't react at all. If you are selling and you believe you are asking for a premium, don't allow your perception of price to affect the buyer's view.

One of the key issues for retailers I work with who sell a premium product is with their own salespeople in the stores not believing anyone is willing to pay such a premium. When you are being paid less than £10 an hour it's hard to accept that someone is willing to pay £100 for a pair of shoes, £250 for a pen or £5000 for a work of art. But you have to see it from the other person's point of view and not react.

Don't let your body do what it wants to do. You are not in control. Remember, 95% of your thoughts and actions are controlled by your subconscious, so unless you tell your horse what to do, the other person's horse will work out your reaction and neither of you knows what you're doing.

As a persuadee you can read the degree of interest in the other party by how they move. A chin stroke is a positive sign and someone pushing forward while their hands are under their seat is another. Remember that the closer people are, or want to be, the closer their patterns of behaviour. If you are persuading, mirror the body language; if you are buying or feeling uncomfortable, don't let your body do what it wants to do.

But back to the intake of breath. What if someone uses the intake of breath on you? Well, they might think it's a 'big ask'; or maybe they've been on a course! Here are five things to do if someone uses the intake of breath syndrome on you:

1 Become more extreme: 'Hey, that's my price now, it'll be more in six months' time.'
2 Repeat the price: 'That's right!'
3 Intentionally misinterpret: 'I know, it's a great price, isn't it, when you think of xyz?'
4 Do nothing.
5 Use 'feel, felt, found'.

E IS FOR EQUATE EVERYTHING IN THE DEAL

Professional, well-trained buyers tend to break up and separate your offer and negotiate what appears to be the whole, but then ask for other things once the price is agreed. They can erode your position piece by piece, so it's important to keep the whole package in mind at all times.

In the early 1990s Maastricht, a small town in the Netherlands, became forever famous, as it was there that members of the European Union went through some hard bargaining to ensure that monetary union was secured before the year 2000. Many were not keen to allow any member states to have exemptions. Where exemptions were allowed, the French argued that dates should be agreed when these countries would join the monetary union. There were also disputes over the future of the Social Chapter, which would allow for certain rights to be given to workers in the workplace. The French said they would block the Treaty if these measures were not included. The British, on the other hand, were adamant that they should not be included, and would therefore block the Treaty if the measures were included. At the negotiating table, John Major said, 'Some colleagues won't sign without the Social Chapter; I won't sign with it.'

The result of the negotiations was that Britain was granted two major opt-outs: one from the Social Chapter and one from monetary union. *The Times* said, 'Major wins all he asked for at Maastricht'. *The Daily Telegraph* led with 'Out of the summit and into the light' and *The Economist* wrote, 'The deal Tory ministers and most backbenchers had been praying for'.

I recall John Major having what was almost a mantra during the negotiation of the Maastricht Treaty: 'Nothing's agreed until it's all agreed.'

Nothing's agreed until it's all agreed.

Don't give things away that have a value to your buyer (or seller) without recognition for it and don't agree until it's all agreed. Get the other person's full 'shopping list' before you start to negotiate.

You are not a mind reader. And although the other person may not be totally open and may need some prompting, they may not even have thought through all the possible variables that are of interest. So keep exploring and looking for them. The more variables you find, the less you will have to give on price, and the more added value you can build into the deal.

Keep accurate notes and show that you are doing so. At some point say, 'Does that include everything?' and draw a horizontal line across the page to suggest in the strongest terms that there is nothing else to bring into the negotiation.

I've known buyers conveniently to forget things that I thought were agreed, so taking notes is very important. Keeping notes shows that you are professional and allows you to summarize at any point.

Don't assume that everything in legal gobbledygook is not negotiable. We all believe the written word.

Beware the devaluing of services over time and don't say, 'We can tie that up later.'

Don't agree, then look at little concessions afterwards.

A IS FOR AGREE ONLY WITH A STRUGGLE

Let's go back to 'I'm OK—you *think* you've done OK'. The key issue is that the other person needs to feel or believe that they have got a good deal in the broadest sense of the word. Clearly you know what is acceptable to you (and remember, it's important for you to know the point at which you will walk away from the situation if you can); and you need to let the other person think they have got a good deal. If they don't, they may wish to renegotiate then or later. If they're not happy, they may take some other action that doesn't meet with your approval.

So only agree with a struggle. Lead the other person to believe that you have gone as far as you can go.

Do you recall in Chapter 9, when my youngest son and I went to the VW dealer and were interested in buying a Polo? I wanted to get the best price and it was important to find out the salesperson's lowest price. It was also important to give the impression that we could walk away. This is what happened.

On the drive to the VW dealer I said to Seb that he needed to be really keen on another car. 'But I'm happy with a Polo, Dad. Why should I want to be keen on another car?'

'If you're the only show in town you charge the top price. If you don't have an alternative, how can you agree with a struggle?' So he decided that the Renault Clio was his choice.

'What do you like about the Clio? What colour do you prefer? What will your friends think of the Clio? What do you like about the drive?'

'Why do I need the detail, Dad?'

'Because if Lorna's been on a course she will have been taught to "test" the objection and she will ask you what you like about the Clio to see if it's a negotiation ploy or a genuine preference.'

'OK.'

So after we had been through the shenanigans of CD players and alloy wheels, we sat down to talk numbers. Lorna made an offer for the part-exchange and worked out the difference I needed to pay and I did the old intake of breath. She asked me what sort of figure I had in mind, which already meant that she had to reduce her demand. I asked if that was her best price and suggested a particularly low figure, which meant that we were heading for stalemate.

And then, good as gold, Seb pipes up, 'Perhaps we should go back and look at the Clio, Dad?'

Get in!

Lorna visibly recoiled. 'Oh. I thought you were keen on the Polo. What do you like about the Clio, Seb?'

And he told her, missing out the bit about it being a fabulous bargaining tool. At 17 you get to be interested in cars and he was able to talk detail.

If someone says something along the lines of 'I like your presentation and your offer but this is all I have in the budget', you have to test whether it's a genuine budget issue or a ploy. You test it by taking something out of your offer to bring the price down. If they are not interested in the cheaper alternative, it's likely they can afford the full package.

Eventually we agreed a compromise figure and Lorna asked me what I did for a living. I had asked far too many questions during the two days. And I asked her if I had really got a good deal. 'Yes. You got such a good deal that the sales director said he hopes we don't lose money on it.'

I like that a lot. Now, I don't know if it's the truth, but she gave me the impression that I had 'won'—that I had done OK. She gave the impression (and so had I) that I had only agreed with a struggle. So if it's an important negotiation, crawl through the process towards the end, don't just walk.

And don't just 'split the difference' to achieve an 'I'm OK—you think you've done OK' result. Let's imagine you want £100,000 for a product and the other person offers £80,000. Let's also assume that you would be happy with £90,000. You would be satisfied to split the difference. First, don't jump in with the suggestion. You are not agreeing with a struggle and as soon as you have gone to £90,000 there is little or no chance of you getting any more. Wait for them to suggest splitting the difference. Next, dwell on the fact that they're willing to pay £90,000. Get a clean sheet of paper and write the two figures down. 'So you are suggesting £90,000 and I was asking for £100,000. We're not too far away now, are we?' *Then*, after an acceptable waiting period, suggest splitting the difference at £95,000.

Throughout the negotiation reduce the size of your 'giving-in', and don't let your last concession be a big one or they'll think there's more to be had. It's all about closing the gap and letting them believe they have got a good deal.

It's all about creating a climate for them to really value what you offer. For example, the phrase 'What you are asking for is exactly what we specialize in. We are ideally suited to your needs' would create such a climate. It's important to create a climate for them to think they've done well in the negotiation. And the key to doing that is to raise the perceived value of what you do. Aim high if you're selling and justify the premium via intangible benefits. If you are a buyer, aim low so that you reduce the perceived value of the service or product to you.

So let's summarize the key issues before we move on:

✦ Establish at the start of the meeting how much time the other person has. If you are selling, don't tell your buyer you have a plane to catch. If you're buying you might want to consider it, but beware dishonesty and the ramifications for the long-term relationship.

✦ Find out what they want first (remember the NAIL) and establish how much they want it.

✦ If someone says what you offer is expensive, agree with them. Say, 'Yes it is. But look at what you get.' And then talk about the emotional, intangible benefits to that particular client.

✦ Towards the very end of the negotiation say, 'Is that your best price?'

✦ When someone says, 'I want to think about it', you say, 'I agree you should think about it. Often when our clients say that it's because there's a particular issue they need to address. Is that the case with you?'

✦ Use the intake of breath syndrome if you are buying and ignore it if you are selling. Or use one of the other four techniques.

✦ Don't just 'Split the difference.'

✦ Sell value, not price.

- ✦ Know what your bottom line is.
- ✦ If you are selling, empathize and understand that it's the beginning of the process for the buyer and not the end, as it is for you. As you close the deal don't just get bored, walk away and think about your next 'conquest'.
- ✦ After you have completed the deal say, 'Thank you for your faith in me (us).' It shows the buyer that you appreciate that it's a bit of a gamble for them and creates greater empathy.
- ✦ Call your buyer after the sale and ask how things are. But be honest, sincere and genuine and truly care. Or don't bother. The best thing a salesperson can have is a hot referral. And the best way of getting a great referral is to have a great relationship with the buyer.

T IS FOR TIE UP ALL THE DETAILS

When you feel that the deal is done but you're walking on ice, it's very tempting to leave all the details till later. Perhaps you don't want to mention that mileage costs will be added on, or to remind them that VAT is payable, or that there's a delivery charge and so on. But if your buyer isn't expecting additional costs it may make all the difference between using you again or not. The customer who pays the bill and doesn't come back often is the one who doesn't give you the feedback.

Beware the buyer who reluctantly pays but says nothing at all. And months down the line it's just too late to recover. All my service industry clients tell me similar stories. They win a client, they have a relationship, they take the relationship for granted and the client has started a new relationship and worked with someone else on a project before they find out. And they all tell me it's usually too late to recover the situation at that point. They didn't point out all the details at the time of buying and they created the direct opposite of a 'special deal'. (More of that in Chapter 21.)

In many respects it's a shame that there is a need for lawyers. It strikes me that they came into being because what people thought they had agreed wasn't what they had actually agreed. Or at least the aggrieved party had a different interpretation of the agreement.

So the final step in negotiation has to be to tie up all the details. Write things down and ensure that all the little add-ons are not left to assumptions. Remember, your reputation is a result of people's experience of you minus what they expected of you. That's why you need to tie up the details.

Here is a summary of NEAT-NEAT negotiation:

+ Never put a marker down first
+ Empathize
+ Ask about their interests
+ Think 'The other party needs to think they've done well'
+ Neutralize your body
+ Equate everything in the deal
+ Agree only with a struggle
+ Tie up all the details

16

GETTING PEOPLE TO DO WHAT THEY HAVE AGREED TO DO

In Chapter 10 we talked about getting people to commit to what you want them to do being as easy as asking 'Will you marry me?' There are three important issues with this analogy:

1 Without exception, all the women I surveyed when doing my research for this book told me that they *wanted* to be asked the question, 'Will you marry me?' They did not want their potential husband to just assume that marriage was a foregone conclusion. So asking for commitment is a good thing.

2 Good closing comes from good influence rather than persuasion. And that means understanding the process.

3 Good persuasion comes from people who have developed a good relationship.

In Chapter 6 we looked at the five keys to persuasion and influence. You establish the other person's emotional needs by building the relationship. You ask questions, understand the implications, get to grips with the other person's point of view and always think long term. You talk about emotional value and not price. You make it easy for the other person to buy into your idea, product or service.

So far so good, but if you *only* do that you may finish up being seen as a nice guy (or girl). And nice guys, as Leo Duracher famously observed, 'come last'. The risk of being seen merely as a nice guy is that you don't get the commitment. Selling (or persuading) without closing is like lathering without shaving.

A qualified prospect is like a good throw from a goalkeeper. Getting an appointment is like a good pass to a winger. An effective presentation is like a good cross. But if you don't put the ball in the onion bag, you don't score. It's just been nice to watch. There are no bonuses for nice football.

If you attempt to gain commitment or close too early, you run the risk of not establishing enough value for you or your product. Instead, you may appear to have 'crashed' into the deal, much as a Neanderthal would club an entire animal to death whenever he felt a little peckish. And sometimes you create irreparable damage, just as our caveman did. Let's extend this Neanderthal analogy. In those days, there were two ways to get your food. You either went out hunter-gatherer style and clubbed the nearest prey without any thoughts about herd preservation or the ramifications for the animal; alternatively, you grew and harvested it at the time that nature allowed you to.

Nowadays there are arguably two ways of persuading. You either go out and club away by closing too early, or you grow and nurture the relationship much as a farmer sows seeds, waters carefully and regularly, and waits for harvest time. The first approach can work and we'll look at how and when in a moment. The second also works so long as you can afford to wait. The analogy fails here because the skill of the salesperson is to know when to 'club' and when to 'grow'—when to close and when to keep building the

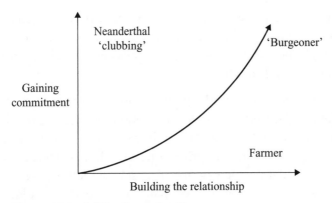

Figure 16.1   Building the relationship

relationship and continue asking questions to establish the real needs. The emotional needs.

In this third millennium people are more knowledge-able, more cynical and have more choice than ever before. So what you need to be is what I call a 'burgeoner' (see Figure 16.1), someone who can grow rapidly and flourish. Someone who can establish when to grow and when to close. Someone who knows how and why you need to develop the relationship, but, just as importantly, when to ask for the commitment.

A 'no' from your prospect can mean one of four things:

1 You haven't developed the relationship enough
2 You haven't developed the need
3 The buyer just isn't sure yet; they don't have enough information
4 No

So a key lesson is not to confuse your situation with the buyer's. 'No' doesn't necessarily mean 'no'. You may have caught the person in the wrong mood and circumstance.

And mood and circumstance do matter. If people need to spend money to cheer themselves up, it follows that they're at their most vulnerable to sales pitches when feeling a trifle melancholy. But why?

According to research by psychologist Jennifer Lerner from Harvard University, people whose mood is best described as 'sad' are not only more likely to buy something, they are also willing to pay a higher price. Interestingly, her research also revealed that people who felt disgust at something are more likely to sell at a lower price than they otherwise would.

Lerner asked three sample groups to watch a different movie clip and recorded their emotional state before, during and after the viewing. A third of the sample watched a clip from the 1970s weepie *The Champ*, where the young hero loses his father. Naturally enough, this brought a lump to the throat. The second group watched a clip of a heroin addict's attempt to quit by going cold turkey. This group described feelings of disgust on viewing the clip. The third group—the control group—watched a fairly neutral clip of tropical fish on the Great Barrier Reef. This would have excited me beyond measure, but apparently it produced no emotional reaction in them at all.

The participants were then shown a set of highlighter pens. Some were asked to set the price if the pens were theirs to sell, while others were asked what price they would be willing to pay for the pens. Lerner's research found that the 'sad' group were consistently willing to pay far more for the pens than those who had watched the fish and were feeling no particular emotion. And as for the group with feelings of disgust, when given the choice to keep the pens or sell them, they consistently chose to get shot at just about any price.

So, why is this? Lerner concluded that sadness sparks a need in us to change and expand our world. And one way to do this is to buy stuff. However, when we feel disgust at something we get the urge to expel what we have rather than to acquire even more.

Here's the bottom line. If you're selling, it's best to pick out the potential buyers who look down in the dumps because their mood is telling them to buy at any cost. And if you're a consumer, you'll most likely get a better deal if you can elicit some kind of disgust from the salesperson...

Fact is, you need to build the relationship, and as you do so, look for when the time is right to ask for the commitment.

WHEN IS THE RIGHT TIME?

I am often asked 'When do I close?' and the answer, as outlined in Chapter 10, is: 'When you are ready and have closed the gap between you and them.' But that is very different for different industries, isn't it?

If you have a straightforward, relatively low-cost sale and the buyer is in 'distress' (e.g. buying a new exhaust to get the car back on the road quickly), you can develop the relationship quickly and close quickly. Frankly, our Neanderthal friend could do the job. At least in the short term. If you are buying a washing machine when the old one has reached the end of its life and the washing is piling up, you can establish the needs quickly and often the buyer will close the sale them-selves. Our friendly receptionist in the hotel in Birmingham was doing a reasonable imitation of a Neanderthal club-man. And although he got the sale, he could have had more money and more chance of me returning if he had justified the price and shown a little more enthusiasm.

To continue the analogy, if we replace the expression 'gaining commitment' with a sliding scale of 'easy sale' to 'complex sale', and substitute 'building the relationship' with

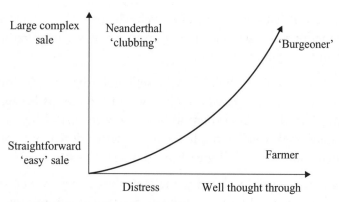

Figure 16.2   Building the relationship

a distress purchase at the low end and a complicated, well thought-through buying decision at the high end of the scale, it looks like Figure 16.2.

Most of the people reading this book will want to persuade in the top right-hand segment of the last two matrices. And the more you are endeavouring to persuade someone to buy a product or service that is important to them—that is, one that has repercussions well after you have gone and needs to be thought through—the more important the relationship. But also important is knowing when to close and when to ask for the commitment.

Things have moved on in business. People have wised up and buyers know more and more about 'closes'. The hoi polloi know about marketing and 'positioning statements'. We recognize unsolicited mail, spam and free offers for trips abroad. Or at least we should. Scams still exist, but we're a lot wiser. And an inappropriate closing technique can do more harm than good. The best close these days is something like, 'Are you happy that we've covered every-thing and would you like to go ahead?' Or simply, 'Would you like to go ahead?'

Basically, if you have developed the relationship in the right way and have established rapport, then the simple 'summary and shut up' will gain you the respect of the buyer and get you the commitment. You need to have your own words so it doesn't sound like you've learned a script. However, a simple, professional statement and question should be all that's needed if you have done the right things up to that point: 'So we have a product that meets your needs, is competitively priced, will help your efficiency and we can deliver with a full guarantee. Shall we go ahead and progress things straightaway?'

Importantly, I don't suggest '*Can* I go ahead and progress things?' This is about us, together, having worked as a team, deciding that this is the best thing to do. Say 'Shall we?', not 'Can I?'

The best closes come not only from developing the relationship and knowing when the gap is just about closed, but also after you have used a 'conditional close' or two. Expressions such as 'If I do this, can I assume we can go ahead?' or 'If I were able to respond to these three points to your satisfaction, can I assume we can go ahead?' should establish just how near you are to closing the gap.

CLOSING

When I work with buyers they often want to know the different types of closes—as though they might be 'tricked' into buying. So if you are a student of closes, here are my top ten in alphabetical order:

1 **The Alternative Close.** 'Would you like it delivered Tuesday or Friday?' or 'We can do the XL model in silver or we have the XLS in midnight blue, which one would you prefer?'

2 **The Ego Close.** 'We usually find that only the people who appreciate quality and are prepared to pay for the best service like this option. How do you feel about it?' 'Presumably cost wouldn't stop you from buying today... would it?'

3 **The Elimination Close.** You list all the benefits and put a tick against all the issues you have addressed to the buyer's satisfaction. When you get to the one (or two) that is the reason for not going ahead, you highlight it and explain how you can overcome it and say, 'So we agree that if we can solve this one small issue we can go ahead? I know how we can do that, so if I can use your phone and get clearance we can get started.'

4 **The '50 Pence a Night' Close.** This is a variant on the 'Power of One' we looked at earlier. For example, 'I appreciate it's a lot of money for a bed, but on average people have a bed for 12 years. Although it's just over £2000, that's only 50 pence per night. Wouldn't you pay 50 pence a night for a good night's sleep for the next 12 years?'

5 **The 'Look at What You Could Have Had' Close (or 'Non-Buyer's Regret').** For example, 'You don't want to be sitting at home knowing you could be watching the game on this big-screen television, do you?' In selling upgrades on airlines you could say, 'I wouldn't want you to be in economy not enjoying a night's sleep when you know that just 50 metres further up the plane they will be relaxing on those big seats.'

6 **The 'Price Goes Up on Monday' Close.** If you are offering a special deal and can justify going back to the original price the following week, this is a good one to use but many people are wised up on it. It's old-fashioned and not one I suggest using unless it's

a real situation. Where is your credibility when they can buy for the same price next week?

7   **The Puppy Dog Close.** Or, 'Let me leave it with you and you see how you get on with it.' If you work in retail, let people handle your product. Let them sit on it, try it on, feel it, hold it and stroke it. Imagine taking a puppy dog home and then the pet shop asking for it back a week later. Let your persuadee have the experience. It's why test drives work.

8   **The Question Close.** For example, if the persuading has been focused on saving money, use a straight-forward question such as, 'If you were ever going to start saving money, when would be the best time to start?'

9   **The 'Treat Yourself' Close.** Let's take the example of a stair lift. The elderly person is infirm, the product is within their price range and the stair lift will appreciably improve their standard of living. They are reluctant to buy only because they feel they are being decadent. They have had a lifetime of scrimping and saving and doing the best for their children, and to get them to commit the best close in this situation is to say, 'Treat yourself'. And shut up.

10   **The Twenty Pound Note Close.** When we worked with Leeds United the managing director was considering whether or not to spend money on advertising season tickets. In the previous years the case had been clear: basically, every £1 spent produced an extra £2 in income over and above renewals and what would have happened without advertising. I saw Bill in the Flying Pizza restaurant in north Leeds and went over to him. 'Hi Bill, can you give me £10?' I waited, he smiled and handed over a £10 note. I then took a £20 note from my pocket and gave it to him. 'That's what you're doing

when you spend money with us, Bill.' And walked away. As we were having our cappuccinos he came over and gave us the go-ahead for the advertising. I didn't get the other £10 back, but it was worth the investment.

I'd also like to make reference to the 'just before I go' technique, which can be used when you feel you have had a pretty definite 'no' and it's time to go. You begin to put your jacket on and say something like, 'I accept you're not going to buy from me today, but just before I go can you tell me where I went wrong? Was it price? Was it quality? Was it something else?' Often when buyers feel the pressure is off they will then tell you the real objection and you're back in business.

WOULD YOU LIKE *SOMETHING* WITH THAT?

My research on this began when I ordered a latte at the Starbuck's franchise within a book store. After establishing I wanted a regular size and skinny variety, the fresh-faced barista asked me if I was drinking it in. I assumed she meant the latte rather than the general ambience and said 'yes'. Then she added the magic phrase, 'Would you like something with that?' I considered replying wittily, 'A discount would be nice', but to be fair to her, she'd already gestured in the direction of the cakes and croissants with a raised eyebrow.

I asked her if she was trained to ask that question and she said 'yes' and enquired if I was a mystery shopper. I told her I'm not allowed to reveal that information but that she was doing well. We then began to discuss the sales benefits of asking 'Would you like something with that?' I have since turned this simple conversation into a worldwide study programme that includes the US, New Zealand, Australia, Dubai and Singapore; indeed, anywhere I've got a few hours to kill through turning up ridiculously early to speak at a gig. Having interviewed over 50 baristas on the subject, they all tell me that simply saying 'Would you like something with that?' increases sales by around 50%. An interesting footnote to this extensive research programme is that I can now go for days on end without sleep and still remain perfectly alert.

How often in business do we ask that question of our clients to get more sales? Hardly ever. We've got a sale and research tells us that the time people are most likely to buy is when they have just bought. That's because they are in a buying mode, the mood and circumstance are right and their wallet is already open. On that occasion I bought a biscuit that upsold the initial sale by 67%. As the Americans say, with a Starbucks on every corner around the globe, 'Do the math on that.'

LOYALTY AND ONGOING COMMITMENT

Finally, what can you do to generate loyalty and get ongoing commitment from both your customers and your team? This is the goal of every business. It's a very serious matter for airlines, hotel chains, credit-card companies and other organizations that offer loyalty programmes to customers. You want salespeople to sell more and customers to buy more. Traditionally, this means providing them with incentives, targets and rewards. But which work best?

When I studied psychology, we spent a good deal of time observing rats running towards food. This was obviously before the advent of Sky Sports and all-day opening hours, otherwise we would have knocked off a lot sooner. However, we were rewarded with the discovery that rats ran faster the closer they got to the food.

Interestingly, humans behave in much the same way. That is to say, the closer we get to a goal, the more effort we put into achieving it. That's why football teams find an extra gear when they've just scored, and marathon runners sprint for the line when five miles ago they were ready to collapse.

Two academics, Joseph Nunes from the University of Southern California and Xavier Dreze from Wharton, translated this theory to business with a study of two different loyalty card incentive schemes at a car wash. One required eight stamps of the card to claim a free car wash, while the other needed ten visits but had two 'free' stamps already affixed to the card. So in effect they were the same offer: buy eight, get one free.

The result? Nearly twice as many people with the ten-stamp card went on to claim their free car wash. What is more, in both cases the time between visits shortened with each additional wash purchased. Why? Because the closer they got towards earning the reward, the more effort they put into going.

McDonald's experienced a similar effect when it did a joint promotion with Sony's online music store. It found that five free songs after five Big Macs was vastly preferable to ten free songs after ten Big Macs. Personally, I can only manage three at one sitting and then I have to go and lie down and listen to Fleetwood Mac.

However, for many people everything is a trial. They are much more likely to climb their mountain if they feel they are not alone. If you point out how well they've done so far, they'll be encouraged to continue working towards the goal. How are you more likely to get that ongoing commitment? How do you best incentivize? The answer is obvious. The more someone feels they're making progress, the more effort they will put in. Or, as my sons would often say on a long journey, 'Are we there yet, Daddy?'

So how do you get people to do what they say they are going to do? You have to get them to tell you, very clearly, what they have committed to. Exactly what they are going to do as the first step and when they will make the first step. You need to get them to tell you when they will do it by, how they will do it, how they will know it will be done and exactly who will help them. And they need to know the implications for you and for them if they don't do it.

PART 4

THE REASONS PEOPLE BUY WHAT THEY BUY

17

THE PSYCHOLOGY BEHIND WHY PEOPLE BUY WHAT THEY BUY

People buy because they have a need. But why do they buy one brand over another? Why do they prefer one colour or a particular retailer to another? And what about impulse purchases? What goes on there?

Why do we spend more than we have to? Your decision to buy everything you buy is influenced by the thoughts impressed on your subconscious mind through a set of beliefs that you have developed. When you set out to buy your conscious mind is the starter, but after that it's the subconscious mind that is the motor, the driver. Just as you don't consciously decide what you think of someone when you first meet them, you are not in full control when you are deciding what to buy.

People are more likely to buy when they are in an 'emotional' state; that is to say, the 'right frame of mind'. People buy when they are in a state of 'trouble' or tremendous opportunity. 'Emotion', mood and circumstance are all factors in how we buy what we buy and in this chapter we look at this from a psychological point of view. Consumers in a good mood will be more aware of the positive attributes of a product or service than those who are sad, angry or resentful at the time you are trying to persuade them. Indeed, attempting to get closure from someone in the wrong frame of mind can irritate.

I was working with a sales representative called Margaret in Cheshire one day. We were going to see a vet and, as we waited in the reception, we could hear the raised voice of a man who was unhappy—extremely unhappy—about the bill he had received for treating his Rottweiler. The Rottweiler was there. And he was getting upset too.

What a noise! I was frightened of what might happen to Margaret and me should the dog get even more agitated. When the angry man left, I asked myself if there was any point at all in talking about a new drug to a vet who had been through such an ordeal. Margaret did absolutely the right thing in making tea and biscuits and sympathizing with the vet in that situation.

The result? No sale then (there wasn't going to be one anyway unless the vet's need was desperate), but the relationship had been built for next time. Tissue paper well and truly in the box. No room for the Neanderthal at that point.

Dickson and Sawyer, in the *Price Knowledge and Search of Supermarket Shoppers* (1990) concluded that although shoppers said they looked at competitive brands and made price comparisons, observational techniques clearly illustrated that:

+ They did not check prices
+ More than half did not know what they had paid
+ Regular buyers did not even know that their preferred product was on special offer

The conclusion? We don't know what we're doing!

Why did we buy into that cultural thing that happened in the 1960s, when artists such as Bob Dylan, John Lennon,

Joan Baez and Mick Jagger made a difference to us? Why did we believe in the Age of Aquarius, Che Guevara and Flower Power? What was the mystique that was right for that time and not for now?

Why do respectable middle-aged men buy Harley-Davidsons and drive through sleepy villages on a Sunday morning looking 'hard'? Or is that the reason?

Why do people go fishing? Is it the fish they're really after or is the peace and quiet and the mental challenge?

After winning one particular account in the advertising agency I asked the client, Geoff Thompson, why he had chosen us over and above the competition. 'You were all pretty much the same. We just thought we'd have more fun with you guys.'

A young woman working for the Children's Society stopped me in the street in Knightsbridge recently. It was 5 p.m. on a warm spring evening and I had just finished the first day of a two-day course. She had such a passion for what she was doing. Her eyes glowed as she told me what good work the Society was undertaking to help children who were being abused 'as we speak'. There was no intention before I met her of committing myself to £10 a month to play my small part, but that's what happened.

Why did I buy? Did I have a need? Well, if I did, I didn't know about it before she approached me. Do I still pay the £10 a month? Yes.

In Chapter 10 we looked at buyer's regret and cognitive dissonance; the very fact that these exist tells us that we don't simply buy what we need when we need it. We can be persuaded: sometimes by others in the case of this excellent young woman in London, and sometimes by ourselves or friends and relatives we are with. In this chapter we look at peer pressure and at all the various reasons people buy: why they buy people, products, services, even excuses.

BUYERS IN THE CIRCLE OF RELATIONSHIPS

In Chapter 5 we looked at the 'circle of relationships' and how we move on from ritual and cliché. The relationships we have all around us sit in this circle. We have a small number of very close friends with whom we have a 'peak' relationship and a limited number of people with whom we discuss our feelings. The number of people with whom we have a 'ritual and cliché' relationship is literally too many to count.

Now let's relate that circle to how we buy jewellery as a gift. Let's assume that a man is buying jewellery for a woman. Why he is buying is going to influence how and what he buys, and a good jeweller establishes the 'why' before the 'what'.

Here are five possible 'positionings' for our buyer:

1 He is coming from the outside of the circle and trying to impress a new girlfriend.
2 He is in a developing relationship and looking to move towards the centre of the circle.
3 He is attempting to get out of the dog house—he has been kicked out of the circle—and back into the relationship.
4 He is having an illicit and short-term affair and therefore attempting to go right into the middle of the circle and back out again.
5 He is looking for a solution to a problem: Christmas, birthday, anniversary etc.

For our persuadee, isn't it so much better to know the real need before we start to provide solutions? The fact is that when you have behaved your way into a problem, you need to behave your way out of it. Life stage has a huge bearing on persuasion too.

HIERARCHY OF NEEDS

If you don't know about Maslow, let me précis his life and work. Abraham Harold Maslow was born on 1st April 1908 in New York. He was the first of seven children born to Jewish immigrant parents from Russia. Maslow created the now famous 'hierarchy of needs'. The essence of his hierarchy is that you cannot focus on other issues if your physiological needs are not catered for. At its most basic level these include oxygen, water and food, as well as the need to sleep, avoid pain and so on.

If those basic needs are catered for, you can begin to focus on safety and security needs. You naturally become increasingly interested in stability and protection for you and your immediate family: living in a safe neighbourhood, having job security and a retirement plan, that sort of thing.

Once you feel comfortable that you can provide for your family and feel secure, then you feel a greater need for friends and sound relationships; what Maslow called 'love and belonging'. It was interesting to see how many people became more interested in rugby when England won the World Cup; in the same way people in Britain play more tennis during the Wimbledon Championships than in any other two-week period. A great sense of belonging can only be there if you share the interest. During World and European football tournaments 'white van man' everywhere has his little flag of St George fluttering from his aerial and window.

And then we look for self-esteem. At one level, the respect of others: status, fame, recognition, reputation and so on. At another level, the need for self-respect, confidence, competence, achievement, independence and freedom.

If your aspiring career is under threat, you slip down the 'greasy pole' and want attention. If your partner announces they are having an affair and are leaving you, it seems again that love is all you ever wanted. And it works for nations too. When society itself struggles, people look for a strong leader.

Maslow died in 1970 at the age of 62 and, as you would expect, others have developed his work. After all, things have moved on since his original idea was published in 1954. And it's that development that is useful to help us understand why people buy certain things in today's economic climate. In the UK in the early 1950s there was still rationing after the war, there were few brands and relatively little advertising, and life was lived at a slower pace than today. Indeed, some of the priorities of today's youth look rather fanciful to those born before the mid-1950s with money to spend and still having the values of being brought up in the 1960s.

Maslow importantly pointed out the need for air, food, water, shelter and so on. But there's another important aspect in retail. Showing people how much you care isn't just something you say, something you feel, but also something you do. As a married man who sometimes has to accompany his wife on shopping trips that include looking at dresses, what I really, really, really want is a chair.

A chair in a retail shop says that they care about me. Most men tell me that after about 45 minutes of looking at dresses they begin to lose the will to live, but a chair and a newspaper can extend that period substantially. So why don't dress shops quite get it?

Of course, Maslow failed to touch on one or two other things apart from the seating arrangements in dress shops. It strikes me that not only do blokes out shopping with their wives want to sit down a lot, the degree of indebtedness they feel towards their partner is directly linked to the length of their relationship. Naturally, when this is at an early stage both are keen to please the other, particularly in the bedroom. However, as the relationship matures, sex is often reserved for special occasions such as to celebrate a British gold medal at the Olympics or the installation of a new Pope. The conclusion? The longer the relationship, the less interested and indebted the person and the greater the need to sit down in dress shops.

Right; got that off my chest. Back to Maslow.

It is clear that 'esteem needs' are greater for today's youth than ever before and that brands matter. As we get older we search for knowledge and meaning; what Maslow calls 'cognitive needs'. Importantly, as we become more wealthy, it is an appreciation of (and search for) beauty and balance that means we pay for works of art and look for just the right dress for the occasion—'aesthetic needs'.

When Bono wants to help play his part in reducing Third World debt, or when Sting wants to help stop the destruction of rain forests in South America, they are both seeking to realize their personal potential and find true fulfilment. They are looking for personal growth and peak experiences.

'Self-actualization needs' are about helping others to achieve self-actualization. And on that warm spring day on Knightsbridge, I was giving money to charity because of a deep feeling of needing to 'do my bit'.

MOTIVATION

So what motivates us? Allow me to make reference to another American academic, David McClelland.

David Clarence McClelland was born in 1917 and died in 1998. He achieved his doctorate in psychology at Yale in 1941 and became professor at Wesleyan University. He then taught and lectured, including a spell at Harvard from 1956, where he studied motivation and the need people have for achievement. He pioneered workplace motivational thinking and talked about three quite different 'needs': achievement, authority and affiliation.

He argued that some people are 'achievement motivated' and therefore seek achievement, attainment of realistic but challenging goals, and advancement in the job. They have a strong need for feedback relating to achievement and progress, and a need for a sense of accomplishment.

Others feel the need for authority and power. These people are 'authority motivated' and need to be influential, effective and to make an impact. There is a strong need to lead and for their ideas to prevail. There is also motivation and a need to increase personal status and prestige. The point is, if you manage one of these people and don't give them enough 'rope', they become frustrated and disruptive, and may even leave.

And a third section (there are more) consists of the 'affiliation motivated'. These people have a need for friendly relationships and are motivated towards interaction with other people. The affiliation driver produces motivation and the need to be liked and held in popular regard. These people are team players. They're great to have around and be around, but don't isolate them or they won't be at their best.

As with all the other classifications we discussed in Chapter 12, most people possess and exhibit a combination of these characteristics. So why do some people buy into your ideas and others not? Why do people buy things? Well, not only do we have all these factors in play, we also need to consider mood and circumstance and the fact that we're not in control of 95% of our thoughts!

Many men don't know the size of their own underpants. As one of my sons once said to me, 'They're funny blokes, women.' This book is not dedicated to the difference between men and women, but if you can explain it all to everyone, please send up a flare.

We are enormously influenced by touching things. We often need to talk to a friend, colleague or sales assistant just to allow ourselves to vocalize and rationalize the need to buy. Particularly towels, bed linen, carpets, children's pushchairs and, of course, hammers. It's a bloke thing.

Frankly, buying, shopping and committing to a decision is something we need to know more about. There are seven psychological reasons for why we buy anything and everything. You rarely need all of them but you always need at least one of them. REASONS is an acronym that spells out those key psychological triggers, which I discuss in the following chapters: **R**arity, **E**mpathy and **E**go, **A**uthority, **S**pecial **D**eal, **O**bligation, **N**ervousness and **S**ocial pressure.

18

RARITY

About six or seven months after we set up Advertising Principles, I decided it would be a neat idea to provide free bacon sandwiches for all the staff on pay day. No money, just a bacon buttie. Only kidding. People were paid by bank transfer on the last Thursday of the month so there was no pay cheque or cash to count. And for no other reason than I thought it was a nice thing to do, I asked my PA to buy 27 bacon sandwiches, and we put a tannoy announcement out that at 10 a.m. on pay day there would be a free bacon sandwich for everyone. The gesture went down well.

After a couple of months my PA started getting a call or two on the day before pay day with requests: 'Can I have sausage and tomato and can David have his bacon well done?' 'Can we have two egg sandwiches and one plain toast?' That was fine.

After six months had passed, it became something of a chore for my PA. Few people simply settled for the bacon sandwich and they were putting in their orders. Slips of paper and phone calls built up to the point that there were more 'specials' than bacon butties.

One pay day I went down to reception and found one of the young female account executives in what can only be referred to as a 'right state'. 'Not again!' she was saying. 'You can't get anything done round here. I ask for egg and there's never any egg left—it's terrible.'

I stopped the bacon sandwiches then. It wasn't 'special'. And once that happened and it became a 'given', the whole psychology changed.

Dr Terry Pettijohn, a social psychologist at Mercyhurst College in Pennsylvania, carried out a study involving examining photographs of actresses and poring over issues of *Playboy* magazine to see whether there was a correlation between attraction and national prosperity. 'Boom or bust' took on a whole new meaning. The clear conclusion from studying the faces and figures of 'Playmates of the Year' from 1960 to 2000 was that men prefer stronger-looking women in hard times and softer, more vulnerable types when things are buoyant. In essence, we want someone to have fun with when times are good, and we want someone to take care of us—and themselves—when times are bad. Pettijohn created an annual 'hard times measure' by tracking changes in US statistics on unemployment, marriage, homicide and other factors for the years 1960 to 2000.

Then, using clear, front-on photographs of *Playboy* Playmates of the Year for each of those 40 years, his researchers made precise measurements of key face and body dimensions. Comparing models over the years, the researchers discovered that, in hard times, Playmates tended to be slightly older, heavier and taller, with larger waists and bigger waist-to-hip ratios. Smaller eyes—a feature linked to 'stronger' faces— were also predominant.

The boom years of the early 1960s, for example, produced both the youngest-ever Playmate of the Year (18-year-old Donna Michelle, 1964) and the lightest (102-lb June Cochran, 1963), according to Pettijohn.

It was also in the 'Swinging Sixties' that Audrey Hepburn and Twiggy were at the height of their popularity, whereas in the early 1990s, when the economic picture was relatively gloomy, it was the heavyweight actresses such as Emma Thompson and Kate Winslet that were getting the meatier roles. If Dawn French ever makes it big in Hollywood, my advice is to liquidate your assets fast.

In summary, when times are good and there is plenty of food around, an attractive woman is a slim one. When times are bad in poor countries, an attractive woman is a plump one.

Basically, we want what we can't have. We want something that's special. It's what I call the 'tiramisu factor'. I like tiramisu. It's very tasty. But if I had it every night I would tire of it and eventually grow to dislike it. That's called satiation.

It was while doing research on food and people's attitudes to it that I began to realize that we are all looking for the perfect food: great tasting and good for you. Does it exist? Can we have chocolate lager that doesn't pile on the pounds? It seems that foods are on a sliding scale, shown in Figure 18.1.

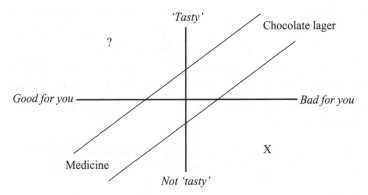

Figure 18.1 Food Glorious Food

Essentially, if it tastes great it's not good for you and if it's good for you it tastes like cod liver oil. There are some mid-ground products that sit in the middle of 'life's food plan', such as milk, orange juice and fish, but food manufacturers are all looking for the Holy Grail: really tasty and no guilt. Hence the success of a whole range of products that offer the consumer the opportunity to buy in the top left-hand corner of the matrix.

We are drawn to things that are rare. The more difficult things are to have—indeed, the more we are told we can't have them—the more we want them; the forbidden fruit. The expression 'play hard to get' summarizes it.

As a family going to Disneyland in Florida, we originally planned to have seven days there, but opted to stay longer to see more of the park and experience more of the rides. I clearly remember my youngest son on the tenth day saying with a weary expression, 'I'm all Disneyed out, Dad.' He had had too much of a good thing.

Think of paintings that are signed by the artist, 1 of 100 or 13 of 500. They are worth more. Why? Because they are rare and special.

I was buying a small sculpture recently and asked the owner of the gallery why one piece, which looked very much like another, was appreciably more expensive. 'Ah,' he said, turning each, in turn, upside down so I could see the detail on the bottom of the sculptures, 'this one is one of only 20 the sculptor made, whereas this one is one of 40.' And that was all the explanation he felt he needed to make: one was rarer than the other!

Do you recall the Joni Mitchell song 'Big Yellow Taxi'? In it she sings, 'You don't know what you got till it's gone'.

Rarity.

It was around the same time that the song 'Je T'aime' was banned by the BBC. Needless to say it then went to number one! Children under 18 want to go to movies with an '18' classification. Under-age drinkers want to do just that. Philatelists tell me that postage stamps with errors are appreciably more valuable. And the Penny Black is worth a lot more than a Penny Red. Why? It's rarer. People want more of what they can have less of and less of what they can have a lot of.

So how can you use this?

I did some work for a very good restaurant in town. A friend of mine, Bob Fern, owned it. Bob needed more people in his restaurant and we put together a special deal that offered a great menu and a free half-bottle of wine. We organized an insert in the local paper and bookings started coming in. I had already said there needed to be an 'end date' on the offer as part of the rarity factor. ('Closing-down sale', 'Only one left', 'We're running out of stock' and 'I can squeeze you in' are all exploiting this psychological need.)

In a matter of days Bob was full on Friday and Saturday nights.

He called me. 'What should I do, Phil? I'm full every Friday and Saturday. Shall I extend the offer?'

I suggested he tell people he was full on Friday and Saturday but he could offer them a table mid-week.

'But people want to go out at the weekend, not mid-week.'

I asked him if he wanted to be part of an experiment and he agreed. We would hold our nerve and tell people we were full; the offer was too good to extend but he had availability mid-week. He started filling up mid-week.

People want more of what they can have less of and less of what they can have a lot of.

EXCLUSIVITY

I worked for a guy called Jerome Hirst in the mid-1980s. He was chairman of a now-defunct advertising agency, the AB Group. I was with him one day when he got a phone call from a client. Could they have lunch? Jerome opened his diary and said to the client, 'Let's see what I can do that particular week. I've got a diary like the Paris Metro.' It was empty save for the hand-written note, 'Pay rates bill'.

He gave the impression to the client that to have lunch with such a busy man was almost a privilege. One of the ironies of the way I now make a living is that clients want to be able to book me on the date of their choice, but would be horrified if I were always available as that would mean I had no bookings. Work that one out.

If in 2007 someone had offered you an unbelievable experience on the all-new A380 in return for £50,000, you'd probably have told them to take a hike. However, the A380 in question wasn't the infamous trunk road in Devon, but rather the new jumbo aircraft formally introduced by Singapore Airlines on 25th October 2007. It was not only the biggest passenger aircraft in the world at the time but also the most lavish. Advertised as 'a class beyond first', it featured seats so wide you could fit two of the Roly Polys in them. There was your own personal cabin space, a 32-inch widescreen television, plus a full-sized bed. Food was strictly gourmet, entertainment non-stop. In short, we're talking outrageous luxury.

And one man who decided that all this was worth £50,000 for two tickets on its maiden flight from Singapore to Sydney was Australian-based Briton, Julian Hayward. His successful bid bought him the 'Suite Class Package' and the honour of being the first one up the steps. For that kind of money, I'd want to be guaranteed the first one down the emergency chute too. With my shoes on.

An Australian, Tony Elwood, paid a measly £25,000 for his two tickets but supplied the most valuable quote for the marketing people. As he digested his lunch of marinated lobster, sipped Dom Perignon from a crystal glass, and reclined lazily on the double bed with his wife, Julie, he said, 'I've never been in anything like this in the air before in my life.' Elwood then neatly summed up what is the real trial for everyone who works in marketing by adding, 'It's going to make everything else after this seem simply awful.'

I travel Singapore Airlines every year and once you've experienced its Business Class it's very difficult to go to the back of a plane. When it comes to luxury travel, the airline has raised the bar another notch for all its rivals. And it's the same whatever product people are marketing. The expression 'If you always do what you have always done you will always get what you have always got' should be confined to history and the dustbin.

If utopia for marketing professionals is to get people to queue up to spend obscene amounts of money, then there are great lessons to be learned from the A380. Rarity and exclusivity sell. And people are willing to pay a premium price for rarity.

USING RARITY TO YOUR ADVANTAGE

The question for you is, can you make your product or service seem rarer and more special? Toy manufacturers often get this down to a fine art at Christmas. We caring parents want to buy that special toy for our youngster, and the more difficult it is to buy, the more the child wants it. Have you ever seen children who want to play with the same toy over and over, despite the fact there are plenty of other toys to play with?

And rarity comes in different guises. Chippendale can only have made so many pieces, so their cost increases if popularity remains high.

Often, singers and songwriters are far more popular after their death, particularly if it was untimely, than they ever were before. Think Buddy Holly, Eva Cassidy, Eddie Cochrane, Janis Joplin, Marc Bolan, Jimi Hendrix, Jim Morrison, Tim Hardin, Steely Dan's and The Beach Boys' drummers, half of the Grateful Dead (very grateful I should imagine), Patsy Kline, Sam Cooke, Brian Jones, Sid Vicious and, of course, John Lennon and Elvis. Even The Carpenters weren't safe. The most popular methods of premature death in the glory days of rock 'n' roll were drugs, suicide and plane crashes. A fair number died in their own swimming pools and even more died in their own vomit. Picking up a guitar or a drum kit in the early 1970s was more risky that going to Lenin Square with a sawn-off shotgun and letting everyone know what you thought of Karl Marx. Why Sam Cooke didn't just stay in his motel room and why John Denver isn't revered I don't know.

Fawlty Towers might not have proved quite so popular if there had been 130 episodes rather than 12. Even *Friends* knew that you could only have so much of a good thing. The very last episode was watched by a huge audience because it had become suddenly rare. Enoch Powell said, 'All political lives, unless they are cut off in midstream at a happy juncture, end in failure because that is the nature of politics and human affairs.' Familiarity eventually breeds contempt and people tire of anything that is too familiar.

Car manufacturers also use rarity very well. Often they hold back stock so that a model can hold its top price, as the new car is exclusive, prestigious and 'rare'. We are told by the salespeople that they are 'difficult to get hold of'. Cars are released in line with demand but, importantly, just lagging behind it.

I was running an open course in London recently and we were talking about the use of rarity. A head teacher of a well-known public school was a delegate and he told me that the most effective advertisement he had ever run in a national newspaper was one done by mistake. The school was fully subscribed and there was a waiting list for some years. He had a small but steady stream of people calling and asking if their son or daughter could apply, and it was proving an irritant, as there were no spaces. So he decided to run an advertisement in a national newspaper simply to say that the school was full. Effectively, 'Please don't call us, the answer is no.' He was then, to use his own expression, 'inundated' with responses! People want what they can't have. They also want what everybody else has got if it's the best; we'll come to that later.

Think ticket touts at major sporting events. Think invitations to the Queen's garden parties. Indeed, think of our own Honours' List. Many people are desperately keen to have an MBE or OBE because relatively few people have them—and they can't be bought. If I were advising parents of teenage children I would suggest they be cautious about completely forbidding their children to drink, smoke and see friends they themselves regard as unsavoury. Weren't Adam and Eve banished from the Garden of Eden because they craved the one thing that God said they couldn't have: the forbidden fruit?

LESSONS ON RARITY

The lesson for you? Can you highlight unique benefits and exclusive information? Can you make you, your product or service seem more 'rare' and 'special'?

19

EMPATHY AND EGO

Some people buy things they don't need with money they haven't got to impress people they don't like. We're complicated creatures, aren't we?

As I mentioned in Chapter 3, I've spent a few happy Saturdays and Sundays in autumn taking my sons to university. Without planning it, I wear pretty much what every other dad is wearing. As the dads walk past each other we all acknowledge with a nod of the head and the briefest of 'hellos' that we are 'alike'. We are doing the same thing and therefore we have empathy. The students grunt acknowledgement too, but mums and dads don't greet students and vice versa.

People buy brands because of their emotional appeal. People buy emotionally and justify logically, remember? It explains the passion of a sports fan rooting for 'their' team; the importance of having a common goal and why we buy on impulse.

We have empathy.

In the 1960s there were mods and rockers and hippies. I was a bit too young to fully appreciate the Sixties, but I caught the back end of them. In the summer of '69 I got a part-time job and bought myself some brogues, a pair of

Stay Press trousers, a Ben Sherman button-down shirt and a corduroy Wrangler jacket. Brown it was, and I only ever fastened the one button near the top. With a short haircut I was a mod. But I also had a motorbike, because I saw Peter Fonda in *Easy Rider* and thought he was the coolest dude on the planet. I had a 250cc Ariel Arrow. I painted stars and stripes on the petrol tank, fitted ape hanger handle bars and completed the ensemble with a chrome back rest and a bit of fur on the top.

I must have looked a right wazzock.

I also learned that I couldn't wear the mod gear with the bike. Fellow mods didn't like the bike and rockers couldn't get the gear I was wearing. No empathy with anyone.

I was in Bantry Bay in south-west Ireland a few years ago at a music festival. A relatively unknown artist was playing and in introducing the next singer-songwriter, he said, 'And please welcome a West County Cork boy...' The crowd went wild. He was one of them. They had common ground. If you are to be persuasive, the more common ground you have—or appear to have—the more likely you are to persuade.

When we were producing advertisements targeted at women over 60 who wear size 20 dresses and bigger, did we find that the best ads were the ones with models who were over 60 and size 26? Of course not. Did the ads work best with a very young, slim model? No. What worked was a model we used to describe as being of 'indeterminate age, attractive but not beautiful'. Large, mature women found empathy with women who were how they *wanted* to be—how they *wanted* to see themselves—not how they actually were.

Bottled water. What's that all about? There are roughly 17 brands of bottled water in the average supermarket. Save the difference between still and sparking, you can't tell the difference between one brand and another. Indeed, you would struggle to tell the difference between what my grandad called 'Corporation Pop', the stuff that comes out of the tap, and any brand of water. Some labels make reference to the fact that this water has been in the mountains and fjords since time began and then they put a 'Use by month and year' label on it!

Why do people buy brands? Familiarity breeds acceptance and we buy what we are familiar with. Does Persil really wash whiter? Have you ever tested one shirt versus another with different detergents? I thought not.

Welcome to empathy.

LESSONS ON EMPATHY

The lesson for you? Can you create greater empathy with the people you want to persuade? Undoubtedly so. 'Mirror' them and do what they do, be genuinely interested in their interests and, most importantly, tell them what you think they're good at. And don't buy an Ariel Arrow.

20

AUTHORITY

We like to buy from people who know what they are doing, don't we? If I have a problem with my knee, I don't want to see a general practitioner, I want to see a knee specialist. We believe in specialists and what they say. If someone is positioned as an 'expert', what they say must be true, mustn't it?

I am a qualified football referee. I took up refereeing because all my sons play, and at junior football level it's not easy to get a referee. So I started refereeing, enjoyed it, and decided I would take the exams and qualify. That then positioned me as an authority. I am now authorized to make the most awful decisions on a football field.

Linking this with 'rarity', the effect I have wouldn't work at the highest level of adult football because they *always* have a qualified referee. But at junior level, where it's often a 'tracksuit dad', I turn up with the full kit and the FA badge on my black referee's shirt. I check I have my yellow and red cards in full view of the players and allow them to see my preparation (two pencils, a coin and so on). The boys see the referee and often comment to each other, 'Proper ref this week.' The match is easier to referee because they see me as an authority—a qualified authority—and take my decisions much better than they would if I were not *perceived* to be a specialist, qualified individual.

Adrian Furnham is a friend of mine. Adrian is Professor of Psychology at University College London and is the second most productive psychologist in the world. I had occasion to introduce him at a conference in London and, in common with all speakers, he has a standard introduction. And as a fellow speaker I know the rules when introducing another speaker. You say what they want you to say. You don't ad lib or try a funny line, because often the introduction itself is something the speaker works from.

So I was reading this intro and it said, 'Adrian Furnham is the second most productive psychologist in the world...' And my subconscious was immediately doing what yours is probably doing now. Second! Who's first? I don't want to hear from number two, I want the best! Now, Adrian is an excellent speaker and quite possibly more entertaining and educational than the first-placed American who has written more papers and books, but we want *the* authority, don't we?

I'm sure people join the armed forces for a wide variety of reasons. Members of the emergency services and security guards very often have a great passion for the work they do and for many it is a true vocation. But a key aspect for some of these individuals is that they get to wear a uniform.

And that makes them an instant authority. It means they command respect. Unless the uniform is that of a traffic warden, when the normal rules don't seem to apply. The bottom line is that we all see people differently when we see them as an authority and it's a key reason why we buy.

LESSONS ON AUTHORITY

The lesson? Can you position yourself as more of an authority in the market that you're in? Can you qualify your product or service in some way? Have you won awards or been given formal recognition that positions you as the authority? If you can, it helps you to be persuasive.

21

SPECIAL DEAL

When I was at university Professor Hammerton asked us to perform an experiment. He had three buckets of water. One contained extremely hot water, uncomfortably hot, one was at room temperature and the third was extremely cold, as it contained ice. The buckets were lined up together on a table with the lukewarm water bucket in the middle of the three. He had each of us put one hand in the hot water and one in the cold water and hold it there for a few seconds. Then he asked us to put both hands quickly in the lukewarm water. We then had to concentrate on what each hand felt like and describe it. Clearly, the warm water felt cold to the hand that had been in the hot water, and felt warm to the hand that had been in the ice-cold water.

The temperature we felt—relevant to what each hand experienced—was different. We've talked about the issue of expectation and your ability to persuade is, to a large extent, influenced in turn by what the persuadee's expectation is. Managing expectation is critical and in this chapter we examine that.

People don't want cheap brands, but they do want brands cheap. Everybody wants a special price, a special 'deal'. Your ability to position your offer as a special deal is at the very fulcrum of the seven psychological reasons.

'Good cop/bad cop' works on this very principle. Let's summarize what 'good cop/bad cop' is about. Our 'accused' is in jail. 'Bad cop' reads the riot act to him. He tells him how bad the whole situation is. He even exaggerates how much evidence they have on the accused. If 'bad cop' has his way, our frightened individual will go down for a long time. No mirroring of body language, no sharing an experience. Just bad, bad news.

And then he leaves and 'good cop' enters the room. He mirrors the individual's body language, he offers him a drink and they share that experience. He talks in a kinder tone and asks him to chat. He is a friend. Compared with the bad guy, this guy seems downright friendly. So the accused tells his story. It's become a special deal because relative to 'bad cop' this guy doesn't seem so bad at all.

There are three key aspects to special deal:

+ We all want to think we've done well
+ It's relative to something else
+ It's not just about money

A good salesperson can create empathy with a customer and then go along the lines of, 'I'll see if I can get my boss to agree to this.' The unseen boss is the 'bad cop' and the salesperson, the 'good cop'. It's a case of 'Me and you, Mr Customer, against the boss'.

My retail clients tell me it's so much easier to sell an expensive item first (for example a suit), then sell smaller, less expensive items such as a shirt and tie. The cost of a CD player or alloy wheels seemed relatively small once I had committed myself to nearly £10,000 worth of Volkswagen. Optional extras in kitchens usually put the price up appreciably, but once you have bought into that kitchen with that installer it's easier because, relative to the main cost, it doesn't seem a great deal. When there is a choice of three sizes (and costs associated with those sizes), inevitably the most popular size will be the middle one. The largest seems expensive and the cheapest seems small. And our beliefs and stereotypes come out here too. 'Expensive equals good.' (Remember our golf psychologist and my fear that if he's not very expensive he can't be very good?)

Everyone selling anything has within their armoury a variety of components in the offer that has a higher perceived value to the customer or client than the actual costs to themselves. It could be free delivery, insurance/warranty, gift wrapping, time consultancy, quick turnaround, installation or whatever. Make sure you understand the value to your prospect and you can offer a great, special deal without too much cost to yourself.

Some very good friends of ours have two daughters. The youngest one went to university in Exeter, which is a long drive from Harrogate. Anyway, after they had dropped her off at the hall of residence they didn't hear from her for quite a while. She must be the only 19 year old I know without a mobile phone. Understandably, her mum and dad were really beginning to worry when, in November, they still hadn't heard from her. Indeed, our friends were going to drive down to Exeter for the weekend when they received this letter:

Dear Mum and Dad,

As you know, I've been at university for almost three months now and I would first like to apologize for not writing to you sooner. I am truly sorry for my thoughtlessness but things have been a bit hectic on campus to say the least.

Before I bring you up to speed with what's been happening it might be a good idea if you sit down. If you are already sitting down, you may even want to lie down. Either way, it is important that you do this before reading on. OK, I'll begin.

The good news is that, just like you said, the Fresher's Ball was an unforgettable experience and I got to meet a lot of new people. Paramedics, policemen and of course so many wonderful doctors who tell me that my skull fracture is now well on the way to healing. I don't actually remember jumping from my bedroom window, although when he visited me at hospital, the Chief Fire Officer did praise my presence of mind and said that he'd never seen a Halls of Residence go up quite so quickly—even with 30 little Christmas lights arranged so close to the curtains.

Fortunately, my fall was broken by Ben, the night watchman. He said I wasn't at all heavy in just my underwear and even carried me to his room in the Gate House to wait for the ambulance. Would you believe it took nearly an hour for them to arrive? Luckily Ben's a qualified First Aider and was able to give me the kiss of life and also massaged my heart several times to keep the blood circulating.

Anyway, until they rebuild the Halls, Ben has kindly invited me to share his flat with him. Some of the other girls have been a little horrid to me recently, but I put this down to the shock of the fire and the fact that they're living in tents in the car park. Ben is a lot younger in outlook than he appears in real life and we've fallen deeply in love with each other and plan to marry. We haven't set a date yet, but it will have to be soon if I don't want to walk down the aisle with my bump showing.

Oh, yes, by the way, I'm pregnant. Isn't it marvellous news! I know how much both of you are looking forward to being grandparents because you talk about nothing else to my elder sister, Louise. Has she told you yet that she can't have children? It's so sad but, as they say, every cloud has a silver lining and I know you will welcome my baby and give it the love, devotion and tender care you gave to me when I was a child.

Now that I have brought you up to date, I want to tell you that there was no fire at the Halls, I did not fracture my skull, I am not engaged or even pregnant. There is no man in my life and as far as I know Louise can have children. However, I am getting a Third in History and a Fail in Philosophy and I wanted you to see those marks in the proper perspective.

Your loving daughter,
Janie

What a great way of using the 'hot and cold contrast'. Compared with what they were *beginning* to think, a poor result is nothing at all.

'Buy one get one free' (often known as BOGOF) is the staple diet of all sales promotion. Buy product A and get product B free is also at the heart of many sales promotional ideas. The key for all marketing people is to have a high perceived value for product B but at a low real cost.

When the BSE crisis became a big PR issue in Britain in the 1990s, I remember Chris Jacks at Asda telling me that in his experience, he had never seen such a marked decline in sales of a product as what happened to red meat. Overnight, people quite simply stopped buying it. But he said he also had never seen such a high dramatic increase in sales as when the store reduced all red meat to half price. He said, 'Phil, I can only conclude that people are willing to die for half price!'

And why do retailers continue to price items at £9.99 rather than £10? Because it helps the feeling of 'special deal'. We're at the point where we want to buy and we're beginning to look for evidence to support our belief that this product is good value, that it's a good 'deal'. The fact that it's less than £10 or less than £100 helps to support our view that it's good value. There certainly can't be a logical explanation, can there?

Many of the studies I have done testing 99 endings with 00 endings suggest that you sell more units with 99 endings. Indeed, in one famous study I did with a major UK retailer we proved that adding 99p to rounded-up prices actually increased unit sales. More sales and more profit.

But you have to be careful with 'special deal' and, as I said about negotiation, it needs to appear to be a struggle.

Case study

I worked in a large electrical retailers for the day. It was one of our advertising clients and I took the opportunity to don a white jacket and an 'I'm Philip and I'm here to help you' badge to see how people bought electrical appliances. The manager was keen to share his more than 20 years' experience with me and I listened with great interest as he told me his 'research' on how he developed the skill to sell television sets. It's perhaps important to point out here that in a typical electrical retailer commission on sales forms a significant percentage of salary, so this was more than mere academic interest in how and why people bought televisions.

He told me that his preferred technique was initially not to establish the individual's needs and budget, but rather, especially if it was a man, to ask if the buyer would like to see the 'latest thing'? Invariably, the manager told me, men are interested in televisions and they would gladly follow his enthusiastic walk to the top-of-the-range television. In case you haven't been to an electrical retailer recently, let me explain how it works. The televisions are typically stacked up against one wall with the highest-priced TVs at one end and the cheapest at the other. They are typically graded by price rather than size, type and features.

So the manager leads the potential buyer to the most expensive television and explains all the features. He turns the features into benefits and the buyer becomes engaged. Only at this point does he appear to chastise himself for not asking about the customer's needs and says, 'I'm sorry I should have asked you: what sort of budget did you have in mind?'

Now, a top-of-the-range television set can cost over £3000, but an average budget for someone coming into a store is £500. So our buyer explains to the manager that his budget is £500 and the manager says, 'I'm sorry. I should have taken you to those first. Let me show you the televisions at £500.'

He guides the potential buyer down the line, but before he's arrived at the £500 televisions, the buyer is looking longingly over his shoulder at the most expensive television. This is a superb combination of the first impressions we talked about in Chapter 3 and also a great use of 'special deal'. The televisions at £500 seem rather disappointing compared with the new, top-of-the-range product at over six times the price. The manager of the store explained to me that although it's rare for someone with a budget of £500 to spend over £3000, they invariably spend more to get some of the features they liked.

He then went on to explain that he'd carried out an 'experiment' for two weeks. 'It cost me a lot of money,' said the manager. For a fortnight, he told me, when someone said they were interested in televisions he took them to the bottom of the range. He explained that for around £99 you could have a good-quality colour television with remote control, 12 months' guarantee and a reputable brand name. Again, he learned to almost chastise himself for appearing not to listen to the customer and then say, 'I'm sorry. I should have asked: what sort of budget did you have in mind for a television?'

On virtually every occasion, the manager told me, the prospective buyer would explain that he had a budget of £500 in mind although he was wondering if he needed to spend that much. He would be steered up to the £500 televisions, but the chance of him spending more than £500 was almost non-existent. Indeed, on the vast majority of occasions he would spend less than £500 and hence the manager lost commission.

What a great way of using 'special deal'.

Everything's relative: it's the hot and cold contrast.

It's the psychology of 'special deal' that goes some way to explaining spoilt brats. Children brought up knowing that they get what they want and being spoilt means they don't fully appreciate things when they come along. If you get used to always having your own way and pushing people around, it becomes difficult for anybody to tell you differently. You can't play golf in Hanmer Springs and Banff and Gullane without the pain of air travel. No pain, no gain. Or what goes up must come down. The tide goes in, the tide goes out. Yin and yang, Zig and Zag.

LESSONS ON SPECIAL DEAL

And the lesson for you? Can you make it appear that right now is a great time to buy? Can you use the hot and cold contrast to make people 'feel' like they're getting a special deal? If you run a restaurant, can you keep the prices where they are but have more expensive-looking menus and better design? Create an aura of it being special so that the prices are a pleasant surprise.

I was working with a group of CEOs not long ago and working through 'special deal'. I asked them to think whether there was an aspect of their service that had a high perceived value for the client but a low cost to them. Or to consider whether they gave something away for free that a client would actually value. One MD told me that he always sent one of his well-qualified engineers out to do a survey of the client's needs whenever they were tendering for a big contract. It had a real value for the client (free consultancy, basically), but he was happy to do it because without the survey he would risk putting in a tender that didn't necessarily reflect the client's needs fully and it could cost the company.

He decided to put a price on the 'survey' and have it available as a service. He called me a couple of months later and gave me the feedback. He had printed an A4 flyer that outlined in detail what was involved in the survey and costed it at £1500 + VAT. It was quite legitimately available for sale (and he would happily take business from it), but that wasn't the point. He had started using the flyer to explain to prospective clients what he was willing to do before they tendered and the client would see the cost. He said he actually enjoyed letting the client build up the belief that this was to be paid for before saying that, on this occasion, he was willing to do it for free.

This is another great example of 'special deal' at work and also he found that the clients then felt obliged to him.

It's time for Chapter 22.

22

OBLIGATION

In Galatians 6:7 it says, 'Be not deceived; God is not mocked: for whatsoever a man soweth, that shall he also reap.'

If you are invited to someone's house for a dinner party and you eat their food and drink their wine, do you feel obliged to have them back to your own home? Even if you don't like them? If you receive a Christmas card from someone who wasn't on your list, do you find a spare card and send them one back? If a friend says, 'Are you coming for a beer?' do you only have one beer or do you have two? If he buys the first beer, isn't it then your 'turn'?

Lindsey Chinar is someone I have known from birth. Her parents and my parents were very good friends and we saw a lot of each other. Indeed, her family were very good to me when I was growing up. When she married Andy Oultram, my wife and I saw Lindsey and Andy socially as we lived in the same area for a while. But they moved to Oxford and had three delightful children, and we moved to Yorkshire and, by coincidence, also had three of our own. And, as a consequence, we didn't see very much of each other but would keep in touch as best we could. When Lindsey heard I was changing careers she said to me, 'Any time you're in Oxfordshire, Phil, you must come and stay.'

An occasion came when I had to be in London one day and Cheltenham the next. So I called Lindsey and Andy and they very kindly invited me to dinner and to stay overnight. I was more than happy to accept, we had a most delightful evening and they said, 'Any time, Phil. You must come again.' But despite the closeness of our relationship, I feel rather guilty at going again until either Andy or Lindsey, or both of them, has come to stay at our home. I feel obliged.

Lindsey will, of course, be horrified that I feel this way, but it's a natural psychological reaction, isn't it? It's what the hospitality industry relies on, after all. The seller wants the buyer to feel a little obliged.

Of course, there's plenty of logical justification about the ability to improve the relationship and discuss issues and there's nothing wrong with that. However, the deep psychological root is that people are building up obligations. Sellers are happy to build the buyer's conscience level.

I mentioned Bob Fern and his restaurant in Chapter 18. He told me that the percentage of people who simply didn't turn up after they had made a reservation was at a consistently higher level than he would like. I recommended he did two things: first, ask them for their telephone number; second, ask them if they would let him know if they had to change their plans. And people did.

The 'no show' percentage dropped dramatically as people either felt duty bound to turn up because they thought Bob might call, or called to tell Bob they had changed their plans. They had made a commitment and they then felt obliged.

Ever stopped at traffic lights and some guy jumps out and washes your windscreen even though you never asked? Find it hard not to open the window and pay something?

My wife goes to the extent of buying two or three small Christmas presents, wrapping them and keeping them to one side over the festive period just in case…

And how not to do it? My father was a professional buyer for a company called Paterson Zochonis. It's a Greek-owned company and, among other things, owns Cussons, hence its parent company name, PZ Cussons. Dad was a buyer for the chain of retail stores in West Africa and bought all manner of products. I recall just before Christmas each year he would hire a van to bring home all the products, gifts, bottles and give-aways he was given in the run-up to Christmas. For me it was a real treasure trove and a day to look forward to.

I remember asking him who'd given him particular things. He had no idea. He was given so much that it became ordinary, and there was no obligation because he couldn't even remember who had given him what. The point is that, if you are going to work on obligation as a psychological reason, you have to make sure that what you do is memorable and highly relevant to the individual.

By far and away the most memorable (and commercially successful) hospitality I ever got involved in was running 'Father and Child Weekends'. I would invite clients and potential clients to bring their son or daughter, typically aged between 8 and 14, to spend a weekend in the Yorkshire Dales. We would climb, abseil, orienteer, canoe, pothole and generally have a challenging, educational and rewarding weekend. Even now, clients whose children are themselves married with children tell me it remains one of the great highlights of their childhood.

But you can't *make* people feel obliged, can you? I also wouldn't suggest that you try to do it in some false way. If you are honest, sincere and genuine and want to be as helpful as you can towards your clients, you'll find that they naturally become a little obliged to you.

I always thought the most valuable information I could ever have about a particular client was their birthday. I didn't need to know how old they were, just the day and month of their birthday. I would send them a birthday card and small token on that date. I recall one client writing back to me and saying, 'In an ever-changing world it's a wonderfully reassuring thing to know that Phil Hesketh never forgets your birthday!' Did he feel obliged? I'll leave that to your own judgement.

Trust is the glue that holds relationships together, so every-thing must be done sincerely. But if you want to build a long-term relationship with your client, get them to feel a little indebted to you. Build their conscience level and give what you want to receive.

One of the most successful direct mail programmes I ran in the agency to help develop relationships with potential clients was what I called 'Playback'. In essence, I offered a choice of three CDs (one pop, one classical and whatever was top of the album charts at the time) if they would reply on an easy-to-fill-in postcard and give me information that was pretty much easily available and public knowledge: advertising spend, areas of interest, company size and so on. Importantly, when they received their free CD there was another card to fill in and another choice of three CDs. This time I wanted more detailed information, and typically over 80% who had responded to the first mailing replied again. The third and final mailing was another choice of three CDs, a chance to win two tickets to a concert and, of course, I wanted even more information. Birthdays, personal interests, favourite sports and so on. Again, over 80% hung on in there.

I did it to gain information and allow me to move up the triangle of relationships, but what I also got was a feeling of indebtedness. Given the CDs were less than £30 for three and I only targeted companies who spent over £1 million on advertising, it worked very well.

But to quote Samuel Butler, who wrote these words over 300 years ago: 'He that complies against his will, is of his own opinion still. Which he may adhere to, yet disown, for reasons to himself best known.'

Welcome to obligation.

LESSONS ON OBLIGATION

And the lesson for you? Can you build up the conscience level with your client or customer so they feel a little indebted? Can you get your buyer to make a commitment to you so that they feel obliged? What can you give or say or do that would build up indebtedness?

If you own or run a dress shop and a woman is with her significant other, make a fuss of the man. The older and wealthier he is, the bigger the fuss. Find him a seat, offer him a coffee and the day's newspaper. Make him feel important. First, because he is; second, because you'll make him feel obliged; third, because he'll have empathy with you; and finally, because it might be me.

If you want someone to do something for you, ask them to write down their commitment and e-mail it to you. They'll feel much more obliged to carry out the action if they themselves have made the commitment.

But be careful about giving a gift right out of the blue, as alarm bells may start ringing in their head. Not literally, of course, that would be terrible. But, metaphorically, they become suspicious of this unexplained act of kindness.

For instance, when presented with a lovely bouquet of flowers, my wife always asks me what I've done. Or where I am about to jet off to. Or whether the car is still in one piece. What is more, research conducted by Tim Wilson of the University of Virginia supports the theory that it's sometimes better to be kept in the dark. And he's never even met my wife.

What the research showed was that mystery increases pleasure. To prove it, Wilson had people distribute two types of greeting card, both with a $1 coin attached. The design was identical: a big smiley face at the top and the words 'This is for you!' Underneath this was written 'The Smile Society, A Student/Community Secular Alliance. We like to promote Random Acts of Kindness! Have a nice day!' The only difference between the two cards was that half of them also carried the words 'Who are we?' and 'Why do we do this?'

People who received the cards with the added questions could see a logical explanation for the unexpected gift, whereas without the questions the gift was more mysterious. Then, under the guise of carrying out a different study a short time later, the researchers got a measure of their mood. What they found was that those who didn't know why they'd been given a gift remained happier than those who were more certain, proving that mystery prolongs the pleasure.

Why is this? Well, we normally associate uncertainty with worry and anxiety. We don't like surprises. When people are exposed to traumatic events, the sooner they 'make sense' of what has happened, the sooner the negative emotion is reduced and they recover. And the same process seems to operate for positive emotions. We try to reduce our uncertainty by explaining positive events and thereby reducing the amount of positive emotion we feel.

So consider giving a little gift to someone who matters to you. It is effectively the gift of far exceeding their expectations of you. No explanation. We don't like surprises; unless they are nice ones.

Can you do that and build those layers of tissue paper? Can you do it with honesty, sincerity and a happy heart?

23

NERVOUSNESS

Coming up with acronyms takes ages. I don't mean the likes of BSE, USP and OTI. I mean the ones I've created, like BLUFF, NAIL and NEAT-NEAT. Acronyms that are created with the intention of helping people remember steps or a process. You probably think I knocked off REASONS on a wet weekend in Yorkshire, but in truth it took me nearly 12 months. And when I say 'nervousness', what I really mean is *fear*. It's just that Fear wouldn't fit in the acronym.

Sometimes we buy things because we're frightened. Sometimes we buy because we're running away from the pain. It's a psychological fact that the fear of loss is a greater motivator than the desire to gain. And sometimes people will do things because they're frightened of what will happen if they don't. A remarkably high percentage of people buy a home security system within a few days of being burgled. They didn't have the need before, but now they're frightened.

Some people tell me they buy private education for their children because they're frightened of what the end product will be if they send them to the local state school. All we would need is the government of the country to say there's an extremely high risk of chemical warfare attack in Britain, and people would start buying gas masks, chemical suits and long-life torches. Petrol must be one of the few products that we all rush out and buy more of when the price goes up rather than down.

If there's a sugar shortage, people start stockpiling. A day or two before Christmas, panic sets in and all manner of festive products will sell because people are frightened. Even toilet rolls sell way above the average for the month. Old England Sherry becomes the brand leader for three weeks partly because people are frightened of what people will think if they call by and there's no sherry in the house.

Insurance companies, banks and building societies are going to great lengths to explain the ramifications of the low-growth forecast for low-cost endowment policies. Most holders of these policies are going to have a shortfall, but are putting their heads in the sand and doing nothing. It's only by using scare tactics that they can get people to buy. Indeed, arguably all insurance is sold, to a greater or lesser extent, using this reason.

In advertising we found that selling a security alarm system for elderly people who lived on their own didn't work when we used the 'peace of mind' tactic. And the ad with the octogenarian sitting with her 55-year-old daughter, sharing a cup of tea and talking about how much comfort they had because the alarm system was in place, didn't work half as well as a photograph of the old dear on her own, lying face down and in distress. Indeed, the ad improved as we closed in on the elderly woman's face and had her grimacing a little more. You have to be careful using fear as a motivator to sell, but the fact is, it is one of the seven REASONS.

Welcome to N-n-nervousness.

LESSONS FOR NERVOUSNESS

And the lesson for you? Well, of all the psychological reasons this is the one to be most careful about using. Is it the first time the customer is buying? What will happen if they don't buy now? Is it fair for you to point that out? Can you do it in a way that is persuasive?

Fear can be a great motivator and persuades us to do many things that we wouldn't do otherwise. But instil too much fear and you paralyse people. Certainly, too much 'false fear' triggers stern resistance.

24

SOCIAL PRESSURE

I learned to play the guitar because I had a girlfriend when I was seventeen who could play very well and, indeed, performed in folk clubs in the area regularly. She was called Stasia Cwenar. Frankly, my burgeoning ego struggled with people buying me free drinks simply because I was attached to her and I resolved to play the guitar myself.

I went out the morning after one particularly embarrassing session while she was playing and bought Bert Weedon's *Play With Yourself in a Day* (or at least that's what I think it was called) and taught myself 'The Boxer' by Paul Simon. It was pretty soon after that I latched on to Ralph McTell's music and it became a burning passion. I still have the holes in my pockets to prove it.

I had a regular spot in the Broadoak Hotel in Ashton under Lyne playing three or four numbers in the interval every other Wednesday when a quite well-known band called The Fivepenny Piece was playing.

Flushed with my moderate success and not, at that early stage, realizing that I was never good enough to make it, I started busking. What I'd failed to spot was that other buskers always put coins in their cap or guitar case before they even started to play. It took another busker to tell me that people don't put money in an *empty* cap. They need to see that other people have also put money in. We like to do what other people are doing.

In the 1970s, supermarkets briefly stocked tins of Heinz baked beans in an impressive pyramid shape that caught the shopper's eye. The trouble was, no one wanted to be first to take a tin and spoil the effect. Learning their lesson, supermarkets now leave one or two gaps on the shelves when stocking product to encourage people to take one. And have you noticed how press ads and television commercials use expressions such as 'Everybody's buying'? It explains why you never see a successful busker with no money in their cap.

In Chapter 3 we talked about how to be more liked by more people, and the importance of doing what other people are doing. And that's the root of social pressure: we like to do what other people are doing.

Do you want to sit in an empty restaurant or one that's really popular? That's the reason waiters fill the window tables first. It looks popular and attracts people in. Personally, I want to have lunch at The Ivy. Everybody tells me 'everybody goes there', so I want to go. I don't care what the food's like, nor the service. They could serve me a lettuce leaf in a dog bowl and I'd be happy. I just want to do what everybody else is doing.

It's always interesting to stand in a lift and observe people's body language change. Everyone stares at the numbers on the lift and we act and behave in the way that people act and behave when they are in a lift. We do what everybody else is doing.

I was approached by a woman selling for Barnardo's recently. We got chatting because she was on the high street with her brochures and forms to sign people up. I noticed that there were three other representatives on the same street and I asked her if it was a particular technique or tactic. She told me that it wasn't something that they had been advised to do, but she said that she had much more chance of getting someone to sign up to a standing order when they can see that someone else is also signing up.

This is how testimonials work. Testimonials work best when the prospective customer can see that a client in their industry (who is like them) has also found the person to be satisfactory. On a personal level, TDG Logistics was interested in me because of the work I'd done for Exel Logistics. One big accountancy firm wanted to use me because it saw two of its competitors using me. FMCG clients want to see testimonials from other FMCG clients and so on.

My wife is an English teacher. She has taught for many years at what she describes as 'a nice school with nice children with nice, caring parents'. While she has the highest possible opinion of the school and its staff, she wanted to work in a poorly performing school in a deprived area. And that could be easily arranged!

What she found in terms of disciplining these badly behaved children from underprivileged areas was that she had to get the 'chief whinge' on her side. It was not enough for her to talk to the students and get them to behave in a better way and be more interested in the subject. She had to get the ringleaders to be on side. Because people do what other people are doing. Or, at least, they do what their peers and the people they respect are doing. So often, she would tell me, the students with real potential would develop bad habits and fall in with a bad crowd because of what she described as 'peer pressure'.

As mentioned in Chapter 16, Professor David McClelland spent a lifetime (mainly at Harvard) concluding that the biggest single factor in stopping people being successful when it seemed like all the ingredients were there was hanging out with the wrong crowd. I adopted and adapted my wife's expression, 'peer pressure' and called this psychological reason 'social pressure'.

If you are looking for charity sponsors because you are running a marathon or being silent for 24 hours—or whatever—make sure the first three or four people put down big amounts. Ask the people with money first and after that other people will feel they 'should' sponsor you for £10 (if that's what the first sponsors did) rather than 50p.

THE DOWNSIDE OF SOCIAL PRESSURE

There is a downside to our desire to behave like the people around us. If everyone around you is zig-zagging you may have to zag-zig to make a difference. In the advertising industry it's widely acknowledged that the more creative you are, the more successful your campaign will be. And exactly the same is true when it comes to developing yourself in business. If you can be more creative in your thinking it will pay dividends in the long term.

The problem is that people are scared of new ideas. They like the tried and trusted, the well-worn and familiar, particularly when trading in a tough economic climate. But my advice is to resist the boring and be bold. And above all, avoid the thinktank scenario. Here's why.

Rather than generating lots of great new ideas, thinktanks actually tend to come up with the obvious and safe. That's because they are shaped by powerful 'group norms'. That's not a person in the group called Norman, but rather the unwritten rules that influence how people behave. You see, rather than encourage free thinking and creativity, they kill it. Stone dead. And with really big stones too. Sometimes the size of boulders.

Psychological studies on group norms reveal that they spread like wildfire. People conform to what they perceive to be 'normal behaviour' as a basic psychological trait. That's because we like to conform and be liked and to fit into the way things are. Creativity within groups isn't impossible, it's just that it has to fight all the harder to get out. Coming up with something truly new often means having to steer a path away from the herd, towards new horizons.

So what's the alternative? Well, to start with get out of your office environment, which subconsciously reminds you of how to behave. Go for a walk instead. Maybe take two or three colleagues and agree that there are no rules on the conversation. Then start to think outside the box and rule out nothing. Great ideas can be reined in later if they're too far out. And that's all there is to it.

I'm writing this in Williamsburg, Virginia. Seeing how the English settlers arrived here in the early part of the seventeenth century has been a real eye opener. People had to die before they recognized that their behaviour at home didn't suit the environment here. But then they started being creative. And 400 years on, they have arguably the most advanced and most powerful nation on earth. The good news is that you don't have to cross an ocean to be creative. Just far enough away from your normal environment. But take a map. It'd be a shame to have a bunch of ideas and then never get home to execute them.

25

HOW PEOPLE CHOOSE

Ever wondered why teenagers spend so much time and energy revolting against their parents and 'the system'? It's not because they want to be awkward; it's because they want choice. They want to choose what they do and don't do. It's a basic human desire to want to influence one's own destiny. People who have been in prison tell me that the worst thing is getting used to not being in control. That and the rough toilet paper. As a prisoner, they're told when to eat, when to sleep, when to get up and when to exercise. They have no role in those decisions whatsoever. They no longer have choice.

The dilemma when making a choice is not knowing what would have happened if you had chosen differently. What about the other opportunities you missed out on? So often we choose an old familiar holiday haunt, breakfast cereal or brand of beer. There are around 100 dishes on the average Indian restaurant menu, but you still plump for the chicken korma. Why is that? Because although we crave what's rare and special, we're also fearful it might be different. Of course, when it comes to chicken korma you don't want it rare at all, ideally.

It's the same in petrol stations or at supermarket check-outs. As you wait to pay you're confronted by over 100 lines of sweets and chocolates, yet most people typically choose from a repertoire of just seven.

Back in 1956 the psychologist George Miller described himself as being 'persecuted by an integer': the number seven. Most of us can identify about one out of only five or six musical pitches before we begin to get confused. When dots of light are flashed on a blank screen for a fraction of a second and people are asked how many they've seen, they're able to give correct answers for up to six dots or so. After that, it's guesswork. If we try to store more than seven numbers or words in our short-term memory we struggle. More than seven is simply one too many.

Psychologists and marketing people often use seven-point rating scales as intuitively it seems that more clearly defined opinion adds little to our understanding. Their intuition is probably right.

INFLUENCING HOW PEOPLE CHOOSE

So given that our goal in this book is to learn how to get people to do what you want them to, how do you influence them to choose the option you want them to?

Dr Sheena Iyengar of Columbia University has been studying the impact that culture can have on the process of decision making; not to mention how people choose such diverse products as pensions, preserves, cars, pizzas, ice creams and colour of nail varnish. Studying the consequences of the reunification of Germany in 1990, she found that most former East Germans resented all the choices they were suddenly afforded when the Berlin Wall came down. Some found the new society, with its abundance of options, to be far less personal, as family doctors and small-town shops were replaced by healthcare programmes and shopping malls.

She has also evaluated the habits of people in Asian countries like Taiwan and the Philippines. There she found that many people prefer to have a trusted figure in their life to make the decisions for them. People in these cultures often consider choice a burden; a responsibility they would happily avoid.

I've had the privilege of meeting Sheena. Although based at Columbia University, she was on secondment to London Business School for six months. I was speaking to a group of people at Carbon Trust in central London and she was keen to come and listen to me talk about her studies. She is arguably the world's leading specialist on choice research and she wanted to know what I said about her work.

Sheena's view is that people like choice. Given an option of visiting a store with over 50 brands of televisions or one with just three, the majority of people will go for the one that offers more choice. We like choice. We like to consider our options and choose the best one for us. Indeed, Kitchenaid found that sales of its white kitchen mixers increased when it introduced more colours. The colour options attracted more customers to the display, but they still chose the white one in the end. Importantly, it's not the number of options that influences a customer's satisfaction with the decision-making process, but rather their perceptions of having been provided with the opportunity to choose.

Sheena wanted to learn whether people became happier with their choices if choosing was made easier. So she did what all good academics do: she conducted an experiment. Her 'laboratory' was a magazine rack. On it were displayed more than 100 different magazines, including titles both familiar and unfamiliar to the experiment's subjects. Sometimes the magazines were displayed and labelled in three broad categories, and at other times they were grouped into 18 categories. Sometimes she asked people to pick a magazine they read regularly; sometimes she asked them to choose one they did not read regularly.

Subjects were then asked to rate how satisfied they were with their choices and how much variety they perceived. Those who had to 'create' a preference by choosing from unfamiliar titles—rather imaginatively entitled 'Preference Constructors'—were much happier with their choices and perceived more variety when they chose from 18 categories than when they chose from only three. However, the 'Preference Matchers', those who were choosing a magazine they were already familiar with, did not experience the impressions of variety or satisfaction with their choices to the same degree.

This confirmed Iyengar's hypothesis: namely, that categorization leads to greater satisfaction on the part of the buyer. But it also suggested that choosing from more categories, rather than fewer, would make choosing easier and contribute to satisfaction. When identical products are assigned different labels, buyer satisfaction is related to what they think they are choosing based on its label, not the product's actual contents.

Sheena then turned her laboratory into a coffee shop. A rather elaborate exercise, you might think, in order to take a small break. But as so often when professors and research directors are concerned, there was method in her madness. It was all part of her next experiment. This time, her subjects were tasked with ordering coffee. However, some were given menus with no categories, while others were presented with a menu that featured one of the following:

- ✦ Informative categories such as spicy, nutty or mild
- ✦ Somewhat uninformative categories that used fictitious retailer names such as Coffee Time, The Living Room or The Gathering
- ✦ Wholly uninformative categories labelled simply A, B or C

Once again, she found that 'Preference Constructors' required the kind of help in decision making that categorization seems to provide. They were more satisfied with their choices when they got that kind of help. They were also more satisfied with their coffee choices than 'Preference Matchers' when the choices were categorized. The 'Preference Constructors' also perceived more variety when choosing from any of the categorized menus and far less variety when choosing from the menus without categories.

It's a paradox. We want choice, but more choice is not always better. If customers aren't immediately sure what they want and they see a greater number of categories, they perceive a greater variety of choice, and that increases the feeling of self-determination. And the greater the feeling of self-determination, the happier the customer.

So 'categorization' doesn't interfere with Preference Matchers, but it does benefit Preference Constructors. And since most people in marketing don't know which is which, it's better to provide some sort of categorization scheme in order to make people happier with their choices.

Sheena's conclusion that it's not the number of options that contributes to customer satisfaction with their choices, but rather their *perceptions* of having been provided with the opportunity to choose. This all began with two displays of jams in an upscale grocery store in California. Here she observed very different customer jam-buying behaviour when presented with a vastly different choice. First, 24 varieties of jam were arranged on a display table and although 60% of customers were attracted to it, only 3% actually made a purchase. However, when there were just six jars on display, 40% of the people entering the store were attracted to it, and a massive 30% actually bought. So a 75% reduction in product achieved ten times more sales.

Sheena then went on to do a survey using Godiva chocolates. I know what you're thinking. How come I never get invited to those kind of research groups? Anyway, the result was just as predictable. Not only did more people buy when there was less choice, but those people also indicated greater satisfaction and were more likely to purchase the chocolates again.

Let's leave chocolate and move on to pensions. No really, we must. In terms of the likelihood of people choosing pension plans, Sheena looked at employees' participation in the 401(k) retirement benefit plan in the US. As part of her study, she looked at the buying behaviour of 899,631 employess of 647 plans in 69 industries. She is thorough.

What she found was that when people had a choice of three or four funds, about 75% of them participated. The number dropped to 70% when there were a dozen and to a low of 60% for plans where people had 59 options to choose from. So the more choice there is, the less people buy. Procrastination? Overwhelming? Probably. And did the people who did make their choice from the larger selection make better decisions? I'm afraid not.

Also, the greater the choice, the more likely it is that the first one shown will be bought. Unfortunately there's no data available to indicate how many people would choose chocolate for life over an income.

Have you ever said, 'I knew I should have turned left'? Well, actually, you had both thoughts so you would say that regardless. As humans we are used to making a decision from two options: wink an eye, hold out a hand, shake a leg. Which leg do you put in your trousers first?

Do you remember Lorna talking to Seb about the VW Polo? She asked him what he was interested in. 'Has it got alloy wheels?' We spent longer looking at the alloy wheels than we did looking at the rest of the car. You see, when faced with a choice of 17 alloy wheels Seb has to make 16 decisions. That's because—although we don't realize it—we choose things by a process of elimination. And Lorna helped us eliminate options.

The same thing happens when you're preference constructing. When I work with salespeople whose customers need to construct a preference from a number of choices, I get them to ask the customer to *eliminate* what they don't want rather than persuading them to choose; to influence their behaviour rather than persuading them to buy one.

And if you want a 'can-try-tomorrow' tip, offer people *three* choices. If they have time, don't always take people to the one that best suits their needs. Show them a couple that aren't quite right which you can both eliminate before you present 'the one'. That way the choice is much simpler for them. They've already discounted two options and now only have to decide between staying with what they currently own and buying the lovely new shiny one they are touching, sitting on or experiencing.

I work with furniture retailers and they tell me that the last thing they want to hear from a customer they've just spent an hour or so with is 'We'll take colour swatches home and have a think about it.' That's the ideal time to help them to eliminate, one by one, what is less suitable. When the choice is down to two, then ask them which one they prefer. If they still want to take the swatches home, have a chocolate bar.

When my old employer Procter and Gamble reduced its 26 varieties of Head & Shoulders shampoo to 15 by simply taking out the least popular lines, overall sales increased by 10% and profitability improved too, as it made the logistics easier. The same happened when a major producer of cat litter products simply eliminated its ten worst-selling small bag cat litters: a 12% increase in sales and distribution costs halved.

What Sheena's work appears to conclude is that given a choice of up to about seven (rather than a large number of over 20), not only are we more *likely* to choose, we actually make better decisions and are happier with what we choose. A triple whammy.

Needless to say, it's not that simple. You can probably easily think of a situation in your own experience where you benefited from plenty of choice.

But what we *can* conclude is that people can be faced with too much choice, to the extent that they don't buy. So how *do* people choose, and what can you do to help them choose what you want them to?

It all depends on whether people are trying to match a preference they already have or are actually constructing a preference from scratch. In the chocolate example, people who know their favourite chocolate is Vanilla Caramel simply locate the Vanilla Caramel. Having 30 options will neither help nor hurt such choosers to fulfil their choice-making goal, as long as Vanilla Caramel is available. Preference Matchers are therefore less susceptible to choice overload.

On the other hand, the choice-making goal for choosers without previous experience is to determine their preference from the chocolates available. For these decision makers, 30 options can be overwhelming. However, if the chocolates are categorized into groups such as Caramels, Truffles, Solids and Fruit Creams, even these uninformed decision makers will be better able to distinguish between the options, and will more easily identify their preferences.

ELIMINATING CHOICES

In summary, if you are face to face with a customer, you have to help them to eliminate choices. Don't ask what they prefer; ask what they like the least. Ask their reason, agree with them and eliminate it. Then do it all over again until there's a choice of just two and you can ask them which one they prefer.

Choosing is not merely an issue of maths. That's why people need to articulate the reason. They feel that if there is plenty of choice available to them they really should make the best of it. They can't 'excuse' themselves that they didn't have a choice. Choice begins to make demands on them to make a better decision.

And remember, most people feel more comfortable choosing from three options. If it's necessary to have as many as 27 options, do what many companies that are aware of all the studies on choice do: use the 3×3 technique, whereby the client first chooses from among three choices, which leads to another set of three choices and culminates in a final third set of three options. One of these the customer can reject and then they can choose between two.

Don't forget that if you want to influence a person's choice, you need to remind them of all the negatives associated with the option you don't want them to choose. You don't have to make it up, just feedback to them all the things they've told you about why the non-preferred option is not ideal.

I used this technique in advertising when I presented three ideas. I would only ever present the preferred route first or last and use expressions like 'as you said in the brief' and 'given your reservations about' when discussing the two options we didn't want the client to buy. It didn't always work, mind.

26

PUTTING THE REASONS TOGETHER

On our first night in Auckland, just before I started to write this book, my wife and I went to a restaurant by the harbour called Cin Cin. It was 7 p.m. so we thought we would be able to get a table reasonably easily. What we didn't appreciate was that New Zealanders tend to eat a little earlier than we do in Britain, and the maître d' came over and asked if we had a reservation. I explained that we didn't and could we have a table for two? He grimaced a little and said he would see what he could do.

I thought, 'This is excellent.'

He's already using 'rarity' (difficult to get a table) and 'social pressure' (everybody eats here) and he came back and said he could 'squeeze us in'.

Fantastic.

He was using 'special deal' as well. Would we like to have a drink at the bar while they sorted the table for us?

As we approached the bar I asked my wife, as I have done for 30 years now, what she would like to drink. And, as she has done since we met in the 1970s, she couldn't make up her mind. Eventually she settled on the same choice she's had for over 30 years and I was about to order, when the maître d' said our table was ready. I said could we just have a drink at the bar, but he was keen to get us to the table. What a waste!

He then asked if we wanted water, but by that stage our mouths were salivating for alcohol, thanks very much, and could we have a drink? He said, 'Let me get you some water first.' What a lost opportunity.

In the end we had a delightful meal, but he missed out on the sale of an extra couple of drinks, and instantly ruined the obligation he'd built up by being what *he* thought was helpful, but left us feeling like just another couple of punters.

This is going on all the time.

One of the pharmaceutical companies I work with sells products to farmers and vets. And in the past, they've had marketing people from head office making presentations on new drugs to these people. Wrong.

When we asked ourselves the question, 'Who does the farmer have greater empathy with, a vet or a drugs company executive, suited and booted?', the answer was clear. When we asked, 'Who is the authority for the farmer? A vet, another farmer who has used the product, or the city slicker from head office?', again it is a straightforward answer.

So now the company does things differently. Instead of the suited marketing person, they get working vets who have used the new drug to make the presentation. Ideally, they also have a farmer present who also has experience of the drug and found it to be easy to use, effective and good value.

Car salespeople use 'special deal' (relative price) by not adding on the extras such as CD players and so on until you're committed to the main price. My wife spent more than £300 on designer clothes recently and I felt no guilt in buying an item for £50 while she continued to browse. *Relatively* it wasn't a lot. Fashion is interesting, because most fashion items move from 'rarity' when a new fashion comes in, to 'social pressure' as a style becomes popular, to 'special deal' when it's put on sale because it's gone the way of the shell suit. What goes around comes around.

Sometimes on aeroplanes I sit in economy class. Sometimes the client pays for me to go business class. Selling that premium service effectively uses a combination of 'rarity', 'ego' and 'social pressure'. First, there are fewer business-class seats than there are in economy. It takes a certain ego to want to travel and pay that level of premium, but you want to be the sort of person who's seen to be the sort of person who travels in business class. You do pay quite a premium, and people upgrade and pay more because of an emotional desire. They then justify the decision with logic, but they have already made the decision.

People have to make up their own mind on whether the premium is worth it. I do understand why people want to do it. There's something about the curtains, isn't there? It's separating the Joneses from the hoi polloi that makes the difference. What I don't understand is why business class isn't at the back of the plane rather than the front. Surely it's safer there. After all, you never hear of a plane *reversing* into a mountain, do you?

And I never understood the Post Office's distinction between first- and second-class stamps. Are the second-class stamps put at the back of the train with curtains between them and the first-class stamps so that they can't see the fun those privileged envelopes are having? Answers on a postcard.

Whatever you sell, it isn't a case of 'choosing' which one of the psychological reasons you can best employ. You almost certainly use several. The key is to recognize that, to explore what you can develop and, perhaps, to establish one of the reasons you are not exploiting as much as you might.

THE REASONS FOR LIFE

And the seven psychological REASONS offer us help with life itself. The 'S' of 'Special deal' in the middle tells us that everything is relative. In Britain we appreciate the sunshine in summer because our autumns and winters are cold, dark and too long. Well, they are in Ashton. A hot bath and clean bed linen are such delights when you have been camping in a hot, sticky climate. But then it becomes ordinary. Remember the bacon sandwiches?

The 'S' in the middle (see Figure 26.1) is also the fulcrum of a seesaw.

Life has its ups and downs, and the highs are only appreciated by the fact that there are lows. And at one end of the seesaw we have 'Rarity'. We all need special treats. We all need some surprises and, by definition, some uncertainty.

At the other end of the seesaw there is 'Social pressure'. We all need to belong. We want to feel comfortable. We need certainty in our lives. We need to feel that what we are doing is normal. There is a rhythm to winter, spring, summer and

Figure 26.1   REASONS SEESAW

autumn. A rhythm to the passing of the months that make the year, as Ralph McTell puts it.

If you remember, I had set myself a number of goals in deciding to become a professional speaker. One of them was to play live, my second son Daniel and I, with Ralph McTell.

Why? I don't really know. And when we come to look at motivation, you'll see that my personal view is that you don't need to know why you want to do a certain thing. The key is whether you know what it is and whether you have the emotional desire to do it. So how can I use the psychological reasons to get Ralph McTell to want to play live with me? What will his motivation be? Will he do it because he will enjoy it, because he feels in someway obliged? Should I simply pay him?

Well, on every professional speaking engagement I have, I make reference to Ralph McTell. I have, as a prop, a guitar that I never play. I play his CDs at courses, conventions, conferences, seminars and workshops all around the world and the intention is that I introduce Ralph McTell to a whole new audience. Basically, I am Ralph McTell's one-man marketing machine. For free.

Why am I doing this? Because Ralph McTell will get to hear about me if, as planned, I become the best speaker on the planet. And then one day we'll meet. He'll make reference to the fact that it's a very rare thing for someone to go to such trouble (Rarity). He'll tell me that he likes me doing what I do and, therefore, that he likes me (Empathy).

I'll be able to tell him that I'm the authority on Ralph McTell music and can talk about the 17 albums I have of his (Authority). He'll recognize that this is a great deal for him and may even offer to refund my money. Just a thought. He'll realize that I'm doing all this promoting and hopefully making him more money and giving him a bigger audience and there's no charge (Special deal). And, importantly, he'll tell me that he feels obliged (Obligation). He'll ask me how he can ever repay me.

I shall say that there is one thing he can do for me. He can appear live with my son Daniel and me at the Royal Albert Hall. And we can play 'Nana's Song'.

I don't want to persuade him to play with Dan and me. I want to *influence* him so he wants to. I want him to *choose* to.

At seminars I always asked the audience if anybody knew Ralph McTell. They often laughed. But I always pointed out, as I did in Chapter 8, that 'Shy bairns get nowt'. I told them that if I kept asking eventually I'd meet Ralph McTell's new neighbour.

And one day I did. He's called Tim Skipper.

Nana is Norwegian. My son Daniel lives in Norway and is a full-time musician. You couldn't make this up, could you? Well, at least I've got a plan.

PART 5

HOW MEMORY, LEARNING AND COMMUNICATION WORK

How to Get People to Remember What You Have Said

How Learning Works and Why PowerPoint Doesn't

How to be a More Effective Communicator

27

HOW TO GET PEOPLE TO REMEMBER WHAT YOU HAVE SAID

Why do we remember certain things and not others?

I recall a recent survey of events both within and outside the UK that British people most remembered. The shocking events of September 11th 2001 and the untimely death of the Princess of Wales were very clearly the most remembered events. Depending on the age of those asked, the death of JFK in 1963 and England winning the World Cup in 1966 were also well remembered. Why? Because they are distinctly different, they are relevant and of high interest to a wide audience; and, of course, they are endlessly recalled in various ways in the media. I still remember where I was when John F. Kennedy was shot in Dallas. Perhaps you do too, if you have the requisite seniority. You remember where you were on the morning of 9/11, but you would have to think hard to recall what you had for lunch last Tuesday.

Certain experiences get lodged immovably in our memory, while others are forgotten. We process memory in order to solve problems or improve, whether it's having a lesson at bridge or learning a new skill at work. We learn from things that are particularly important to us or that have strong emotional ties for us.

But what if you want your 'audience' to remember what you have said when they can't see the relevance to them? Well, in simple terms you have to make it relevant to them. I believe there are four simple criteria for events, people, occasions—indeed, anything—to be remembered and lodged in the subconscious.

First, it needs to be distinctly different or outstanding, which in turn makes it easier to remember. If the essence of selling is to make it easy to buy, then the essence of recall is making it easy to remember. Secondly, it needs to be relevant or of high interest. And thirdly, it needs to be repeated. But it's the fourth that really has the impact:

+ Distinctly different
+ Relevant
+ Repeated
+ Emotional appeal

EMOTIONAL APPEAL

Within the brain's structure is an area called the amygdala. It gets activated when we experience strong emotions, particularly negative emotions, and it has a big influence on our memory systems; in particular, a structure known as the hippocampus. The hippocampus sits deep in the temporal lobe of the brain, near the amygdala. It's effectively the gatekeeper of sensory information. Whether it's the smell of a bacon sandwich, the view of the Indian Ocean or a phone number you need to remember; they all must pass through the hippocampus. Only if information gets in to the hippocampus in the first place can it be moved to the prefrontal cortex, where it will be held briefly in what is called 'working' or 'short-term' memory. When you repeat the phone number in your head for a short time, dial it and forget it within a matter of minutes, that's your prefrontal cortex working in tandem with your hippocampus on working memory.

Things that are emotionally charged are more likely to be remembered, talked about and therefore accessed and used more easily. And most of the people you want to remember what you have said have not gone on a memory course or read a book on memory. Let's go back to the telephone number you typically forget after 10 minutes. What if you still can recall it 10 months later? Why? Because that bit of information has gone through a chemical process called long-term potentiation (LTP) that strengthens the synapses. You need LTP to form long-term memories. And LTP takes place in the hippocampus.

The purpose of this section of the book is not about improving your memory. There are many good books for that. If you want to follow the research on that then have a good diet, take regular exercise, don't have too much glucose and eat blueberries.

And no, I am not making that up.

The purpose of this section of the book is to improve your chances of being remembered. So be different, make sure you are making your points relevant to your audience, repeat what you want them to remember and have some sort of emotional appeal.

Emotional appeal is best done through humour. Importantly, emotional content does not necessarily mean that events are remembered more accurately. Indeed, there is scientific evidence that the more emotional a memory is, the more likely it is not to be remembered accurately. In fact, we're continually taking our experiences and revising them as we speak, even twisting them to our own benefit.

28

HOW LEARNING WORKS AND WHY POWERPOINT DOESN'T

One night when my youngest was doing his home-work, I went upstairs to see if I could help. Normally this involves me going back downstairs again very quickly.

'I'm looking for the lowest common denominator,' he said as I entered the room.

'Haven't they found that yet?' I quipped. 'They were looking for it when I was your age."

Laugh? I thought we'd never start.

Then he said, 'Actually, Dad, there is something you can help me with. In Geography tomorrow I have to explain the relationship between the earth, the moon and the sun. I've got ten minutes to talk to the class about how it all works and how big they are in relation to each other and how far apart they are.'

He had all the information, which I would like to share with you now. The figures are rounded up or down for simplicity. The distance from the earth to the sun is 93,000,000 miles and the earth is 240,000 miles from the moon. The earth's circumference is 25,000 miles and its diameter is 8000 miles. The sun's diameter is 865,000 miles and the moon's diameter is 2160 miles.

The moon travels around the earth every 28 days or so at a speed of 2288 miles per hour. That's 6 miles per second. Pretty fast, huh? As I'm sure you know, the earth rotates roughly every 24 hours. Therefore, if you were to hang above the surface of the earth at the equator without moving, you would see 25,000 miles pass by in 24 hours. That's over 1000 miles per hour. There's more. The earth is also moving around the sun at 67,000 miles per hour. As you read this book the earth is travelling at a speed of 18 miles per second as it goes round the sun. I repeat, 18 miles a second! And you step outside today and there's hardly a breath of wind...

Finally, the sun moves through space at a speed of over 100 miles per second in the direction of the star Vega, following its orbital path referred to as the Solar Apex. Still with me?

If you'd drifted off into your own subconscious thoughts when I was on about skip hire a while back, I'll forgive you for wandering off into your own little world just now. Actually, it's a very big world when you consider all the distances and speeds involved. But the point is that the information alone doesn't mean a great deal. What does 240,000 miles mean? You have no idea. To give it some meaning, you need to connect it with something you do know. For example, if you were to fly from England to New Zealand in a decent jumbo you would be up in the sky for around 24 hours and travelling at an average speed of 630 miles per hour. So to go to the moon on Singapore Airline's A380 would take more than a fortnight. That puts it into perspective a little. You are beginning to connect unknown information (240,000 miles) with known information (a very long time on an aircraft). Imagine what it would be like to be stuck on a plane for over two weeks? That's an awful lot of movies and warm

Chardonnay. Even Tony Elwood and Julian Hayward in the Suite Class Package would tire of the marinated lobster and Dom Perignon.

Seb had a football in his room and so I took his ruler and measured it. Just as I thought, exactly 12 inches. Then I measured the football. As luck would have it, the football was 8 inches in diameter. And the earth's diameter is 8000 miles. We had ourselves a scale.

So on a scale where 1000 miles equals 1 inch, you can imagine the earth as a known size: a football. On the same scale, the moon is about the size of a tennis ball and just over 6 yards away. Now imagine a regular-size football pitch. In your mind's eye, picture a football on the goal line and a tennis ball just outside the six-yard box. That's the earth and the moon sorted; the right sort of relative size and the right kind of distance apart.

Here come's the tricky bit: the sun. Imagine a car park one and a half miles away from the football pitch. That's where the sun is. And it's big: 24 yards in diameter, which is roughly twice the height of the average house. It's huge! And it's just one of the reasons why it's so hard to park on match days.

Let me give you another example. Imagine that the time from Christ's birth to now was one day. So, in other words, around 2000 years of history is crammed into 24 hours. What a television show that would be. Suppose you were asleep as the clock struck midnight and Christ was born. There's a bit of a kerfuffle out in the street involving some passing youths and your neighbour's fairy lights, but nothing that disturbs your slumber. Before you wake up in the morning the Roman Empire has both risen and fallen. By noon, the battle of Hastings has taken place and there's little mention of it on the news. By teatime Edward III has ascended the throne and the Black Death has reduced the population of Britain to a little over three million people. You go for a paper and the streets are eerily quiet. By 6 p.m. Henry VIII is king and he's already sharpening his axe.

The interesting thing about this particular connecting of unknown to known information is that the industrial revolution and the invention of the internal combustion engine don't happen until the last few hours of the day. How they got anything done, I don't know.

On the same scale, I bought my first mobile phone at ten to midnight and purchased a laptop, satellite navigation system and sundry other high-tech items just a few minutes before midnight. I'm dreading the credit card bill arriving next month. No such problem for Bill Gates, though. He became the wealthiest man the world has ever known in the final 20 minutes of the day.

Things start to make sense now, right? We've connected unknown information with known information. It's both how and why analogies work. It's also how jokes work. All jokes follow broadly the same pattern of set-up, surprise and connection. And it's when you make the connection that you laugh. In a way, you're rewarding yourself for being bright enough to get the joke. But it only works once. So if you've heard a joke before, it's never as funny the second time because you've already made the connection. Similarly, if someone has to have a joke explained to them they won't fall about the floor in fits of laughter however funny it is. That's because a vital ingredient is missing: they didn't make the connection for themself.

How do you kill a circus? Go for the juggler.

Venison's dear, isn't it?

I went to the south of France to finish my last book. I'm a very slow reader.

I have kleptomania but when it gets bad, I take something for it.

Get it? You have to make the connection otherwise it's just not funny. I think the best one-liner of all time was delivered by the late comedian, Bob Monkhouse, when he said, 'They laughed when I said I was going to be a comedian. They're not laughing now.'

Lecturers and trainers use a similar technique to teach better time management. You may well be familiar with it, but if not, this is how it goes. On the desk is a bag of sand, a bag of pebbles, some big rocks and a bucket. The lecturer asks for a volunteer to put all three grades of stone into the bucket. A keen student—there's always one—duly steps up to carry out the task, starting with the sand and then the pebbles. By the time he gets to the rocks there's no room left in the bucket.

'This is an analogy of poor time management,' says the lecturer. 'If you'd have put the rocks in first, then the pebbles, then the sand, all three would have fitted. This is much like time management, in so far as by completing your biggest tasks first, you leave room to complete your medium tasks, then your smaller ones. However, by completing your smallest tasks first you spend so much time on them you leave yourself unable to complete either medium or large tasks satisfactorily.'

That's how learning works. You need to ask questions, accept the answers and reply in a way that is understood. Connect unknown information with known information and things become much clearer to comprehend. It's why I use so many analogies and stories in this book, so you can relate the situations in menswear shops, car showrooms, stationers and so on to your own life experiences.

POWERPOINT

On a business trip to Singapore, my wife and I visited the very impressive National Museum. It detailed the country's occupation by the Nazis in 1941 and featured lots of archive news articles. However, being a modern museum, I also had an audio headset with a verbal commentary. So I decided to conduct an experiment. Having failed miserably to tune in to Five Live for the cricket scores, I moved on to stage two: namely, reading all the articles while listening to the commentary to see just how much I could recall while performing both tasks. Not surprisingly, I learned a lot less than I would have done had I simply chosen to do one or the other.

Australian Professor John Sweller has conducted similar experiments with PowerPoint® presentations. His were a lot more scientific than mine, but I think I beat him hands down in terms of spectacular explosions and human suffering. PowerPoint has become so ubiquitous in the boardroom that it has lost much of its initial sex appeal. Sure, PowerPoint slides are easy to create, cost-effective to produce and look professional, but they're a bit predictable. And, perhaps more importantly, using PowerPoint can actually reduce the effectiveness of a presentation rather than enhance it.

Sweller's research into how we recall things from presentations suggests that it is far more difficult to process information when it's coming at you from all sides at the same time. Choose either the written or spoken word and the human brain can process, digest and retain far more information than if it's bombarded with both.

The fact is that there are limits to the brain's capacity to process and retain information in short-term memory. This is why whenever my wife tells me to decorate the back bedroom it goes straight out of my mind before I've even reached the sports pages.

The problem is information overload. According to Professor Sweller's cognitive load theory, it is simply not effective to speak even the same words that are written. It is far better to show a picture or chart that illustrates the point. The other problem is that most of the time most of the audience are not listening to you. They're thinking about themselves, their problems and their pleasures.

Confucius said, 'I hear and I forget. I see and I remember. I do and I understand'. And he managed to communicate that without a visual aid. So to avoid inflicting death by PowerPoint the next time you do a presentation, use words sparingly. And remember that pictures are literally worth more than a thousand of them. Alternatively, just put the slides on auto and shut up.

29

HOW TO BE A MORE EFFECTIVE COMMUNICATOR

I was once hired to speak at a conference with the specific brief of 'motivating the troops'. Nothing unusual there. I'm a professional speaker. I can be thought provoking, erudite, amusing and uplifting, tell a few well-chosen and relevant anecdotes and hopefully leave everyone with some simple techniques and beliefs to do more and be better.

However, this gig was a bit different. True, I had been warned that the audience of 100 or so senior managers would possibly be in the initial stages of being comatose following a 90-minute Death-by-PowerPoint session from their Big Chief. But what they failed to tell me was the exact content of his presentation and the size of the task ahead. Here, in précis form, is his summary:

'So, ladies and gentlemen, if you are going to remain with the company and be part of the buy-out it'll cost you £10,000. There'll be no more swanning around in business-class lounges and you can forget first-class travel. And remember, we may need to upscale our outplacement programme, so stay on your toes. Now please welcome our motivational speaker, Mr Philip Hesketh.'

I am not making this up.

You can imagine the sight that greeted me. A hundred grown men and women with eyes wide open, jaws to the floor and ears firmly closed. I didn't know whether to try to cheer them up or just go round with some Kleenex. Normally it takes me 15 minutes to get tears running down an audience's cheeks, but the CEO had managed it in one devastating summary. And for the wrong reasons.

One guy on the front row tried to throw himself under a passing tea trolley. He wasn't killed but his suit was ruined. I can't remember what I spoke about. And the point is, neither would they.

It reminded me of the time I watched a marketing director of a leading UK retailer include in her upbeat 30-minute presentation a two-minute summary on the impact of a suicide in the store. And no, it wasn't Top Yourself Shop. No prizes for guessing which bit of her talk the audience remembered. Like me, their minds were probably racing with all manner of possible suicide techniques in a retail environment. Lie across the entry doors on Blue Cross Sale Day, perhaps? Put your head in the till just as the assistant closes it? Or maybe try on six outfits at once and asphyxiate yourself?

BEING MEMORABLE FOR THE RIGHT REASONS

Being memorable as a speaker for the right reasons rather than the wrong ones is actually very easy.

First of all you need to know what the *purpose* of your talk is. When I work with people on presentation skills I ask them to make a 90-second presentation. I then video it and, along with the other delegates, do a critique. I don't worry too much about whether they have their hands in their pockets or whether they are word perfect. What I am most interested in is whether the audience understands what the purpose of the talk was and whether it matches the presenter's purpose.

While running a two-day public course I was asked by one young man if he could do his best man speech, as the wedding was the following Saturday. He delivered the talk and it had all us rolling about laughing. It involved the groom-to-be, clingfilm, lamp posts, alcohol, the booking of a stripper dressed as a policewoman but with a real policewoman turning up and all the resultant misunderstanding and—well, you get the idea.

After I'd dried my eyes I asked him what the purpose of his talk was and he told me it was to make the guests laugh. I asked him how many guests there would be and how many of them would think it was funny. And it was that that caused him to pause and think.

The following day he arrived early and told me he'd been thinking about the purpose of his talk. He'd realized that there were perhaps many relatives, friends of the bride's and groom's parents and so on who would possibly think it inappropriate. He told me he'd decided that the purpose of his talk should be to make the bride's parents feel good about the groom. And could he do it again to the group and to the camera?

And he did. Not as funny, I'll grant you. But he had a great purpose.

He called me the following week. He told me that a number of guests had made the effort to come up to him and say it was the best best man's speech they'd ever heard. He filled up as he spoke to me and thanked me for my advice. And I told him I hadn't given him advice. I'd just asked him questions.

All good presentations come from knowing what your purpose is.

Secondly, you need to know your ABC: A stands for Action, B stands for Benefit and C stands for Consequences. If every speaker at an event structured their presentation with this in mind, more people would go away with the right messages.

So if you have to speak at an event, make sure your presentation makes clear what Action you want the audience to take; what Benefit there is in them taking it; and finally what the positive Consequences will be if they do. By all means have drama in your presentation, but try to avoid any event where someone has lost their life in tragic circumstances.

Conferences are too expensive both in terms of man-hours and the organizing costs to waste time with speakers who don't know their ABC. And if you are going to 'upscale your outplacement programme' among the people who are in the audience, don't have a speaker after that session because the audience will be in shock. Give them a cup of tea and a custard cream.

And leave the clingfilm stories for the pub.

30

THE SEVEN THINGS THAT REALLY MATTER IN RELATIONSHIPS

OR, THE SEVEN SECRETS TO EXCELLENT CUSTOMER SERVICE

A very nice woman called me one morning to say that her boss wanted to book me to speak at their forthcoming conference. He had been very impressed when he had seen me speak at a conference he had attended the previous year. I felt a sort of warm glow deep inside that couldn't be attributed to Ready Brek. She gave me the date of their conference and asked if I was free. I told her that I'm never free but always very reasonable. She chuckled a little and then asked if I could talk about improving customer service.

'Naturally,' I replied, since I have several angles already prepared on the subject, each with their own hilarious anecdotes and witty asides that appear entirely unscripted.

There was a bit of a silence. 'Actually, we've already chosen the title of the talk and gone to print with it. Is that a problem?'

'Only if it's "Great customer service in the Danish fishing industry of the 1970s",' I replied. 'That might stump me.'

Fortunately, it wasn't. The title they had chosen was 'The Secrets of Excellent Customer Service'. I agreed to do the talk on the clear understanding that there aren't actually any secrets. This confused her a little, but she batted on.

'How long will that take then?' she enquired.

'About 18 seconds,' I replied.

She was clearly taken aback by the brevity of what I had planned, but, credit where credit's due, she asked me the cost. When I told her my fee she suggested that it seemed like a lot of money for just 18 seconds' work.

I always find that reassuring. If people never think you are expensive you are probably not charging enough money.

I explained that she wasn't paying for the 18 seconds but rather the 30-odd years of study it's taken to distil it down to less than half a minute. I then added, helpfully, 'But I can also do it in an hour.'

She liked this idea better and enquired as to the price. I told her I only had one fee: the same for 18 seconds, one hour or, indeed, a whole day. If you want me to sing and play guitar, that's a bit extra. She plumped for the non-musical hour, but, curiosity having got the better of her; she asked what the 18-second version consisted of.

'Could you give me your 18-second talk now?' she asked. 'Over the phone?'

Feeling somewhat benevolent, I agreed to do it there and then. But before I did, I explained to her that the seven 'secrets' to excellent customer service were also the 'secrets' to having an excellent relationship where you are trusted and the relationship continues to improve. And here they are for you: the 'secrets to excellent customer service'. Indeed, they are the 'secrets' of running a good business in 43 words and 18 seconds. If you're in business and abide by these words, the improvement in your service will be palpable. Guaranteed. Simply replace the word 'customer' with 'client' or 'friend' or 'colleague'.

Ready?

+ Be nice.
+ Be honest.
+ Ask your customers more questions.
+ Truly care about your customers' needs.
+ Do what you say you're going to do.
+ Exceed your customer's expectations.
+ Do all this every day. Day in, day out.

As I say, for the word 'customer' substitute the word 'life partner', or 'colleague'.

The fact is, there are no secrets.

Case study

I am sitting in Heathrow Airport at 8.30 p.m. My flight to Leeds/ Bradford is scheduled to leave at 9 p.m. but there is bad weather. The authorities know where the plane is, so why don't they tell us? If the voice on the tannoy tells me that the plane is on the ground and that the wait is just for one hour, I can quickly come to terms with it, buy a drink and a magazine and plan what I will do with the hour.

Frustration and anxiety are creeping in as I'm being told either nothing at all or simply that there's a delay. People around me are shifting uneasily in their seats. Will they get home tonight? How long is the delay? Do they need a hotel room? What are the ramifications for tomorrow's board meeting, a son's sports day or a wedding anniversary?

We all have lives to live.

The less you know, the more anxious you become, and it's a constant frustration for me and many other air travellers that airlines and airports don't truly care about their customers. If they did, they would tell us what was happening all the time. Give us the truth; tell us exactly where we stand and tell us right away.

The plane has been on the ground all the time. The plane is to be just 40 minutes delayed. Why not tell us?

Because they don't care.

They think they care. But they don't truly care about their customers' needs. They are not even meeting their customers' expectations, never mind exceeding them.

It could be argued that there are only three things that matter in business: finding customers, keeping customers happy so they stay with you and, of course, making money. But do the fundamentals of business boil down to those three things? For sure you have to get customers or clients in the first place, you have to deliver and do what you say you're going to do and offer a good service (or your clients and customers don't come back), and you need to make sure all the systems and the margins are in place to make money.

But there's more to it than that. And that's why the seven things that really matter include asking your customers more questions and exceeding their expectations. You have to continually be aware of change and motivating your *own* people and colleagues.

THE INEVITABILITY OF CHANGE

You may have heard the 'Serenity Prayer'. The original version was written on a piece of paper by Reinhold Niebuhr as his closing prayer in a church service. Afterwards, on request, he gave it to a friend and it became famous when it was used for his obituary in the local newspaper. Among others, AA (think alcohol breakdown, not roadside assistance) uses the 'Serenity Prayer' and it has brought help to many recovering people as they attempt to accept a disease, take stock of their situation and move forward and make amends. This is how it goes:

> Give me the serenity to accept the things I cannot change, the strength to change the things I can and the wisdom to know the difference.

We live in a world of constant change. Indeed, it's the only thing that's constant. And persuasion techniques change, too.

So if you really want to be more influential and persuasive you need to change. And you need to *want* to change; everything starts with desire. It's a fact of life that both good and bad things will happen to you along the way. Many of the bad things will be beyond your control, so why worry about them? And when the good things happen, don't forget to enjoy them and celebrate every precious moment. But in addition to this, there's also 'inevitable' change.

Some years ago, I read *The Decline and Fall of the Roman Empire* by Edward Gibbon. It's almost as tough as Stephen Hawking's *A Brief History of Time*, but appreciably longer. To save you reading it, let me tell you what happens.

The Romans were ambitious. They grew and grew their empire and, as my mother would say, 'went conquering'. Over the years the upper classes became incredibly idle. They had spread well away from their roots in Italy and there were no mobile phones, laptops and BlackBerries back then to help them stay in touch. So people stopped communicating, particularly at the edges of the empire. Hubris and disunity settled in. They became complacent and arrogant, and at the very heart of the empire in Rome, children didn't want to be anything else but soldiers. The poor had enough bread, cheap meat and wine to eat and drink, as well as chariot races to watch. However, eventually there was no fresh supply of slaves from subject races. Its far-flung borders had become hard to control and the Emperor Constantine in AD 330 established a fine new capital in Byzantium. He even had the arrogance to rename it Constantinople.

Honoruis became leader in AD383 and within his life time the Roman Empire had collapsed. Unlike his macho predecessors, he wasn't at all keen on the military and much preferred poultry farming instead. So when the Visigoth troops came knocking on his door, it was pretty much game over. Or poultry over, if you prefer. After all, there's not much you can do against a savage army when your defence is made up largely of battery hens. Feed them and hope they go away, perhaps.

Recently I read *The Rise and Fall of Marks & Spencer* by Judi Bevan. It's the same story. For Honorius in 410 read Rick Greenbury in 1998. They stopped listening to their customers, they became arrogant and complacent and didn't respond to inevitable change. Like Honorius, M&S had become introspective and obsessed with their own product and had not looked at the change around them. The only difference between the two was their standard of under-wear.

Arguably, Margaret Thatcher was in the same mould: a leader who didn't recognize the time to go. History is full of stories of people who just didn't see it coming. Caesar didn't know Brutus was not on his side until the last minute. And what was the man who chopped down the last tree on Easter Island thinking about?

I've read the biographies of both John Lennon and Paul McCartney about the rise and fall of The Beatles. It took appreciably less time than the Roman Empire and Marks & Spencer, but the story is largely the same. It's one of ambition, growth, desire and teamwork. Then as success takes hold of people's senses, this changes to arrogance and complacency and the setting in of hubris. Poor old George couldn't get his work onto the albums because Lennon and McCartney were hogging the limelight, and they had in-fighting just like the Romans before them and the M&S after them.

Gerald Ratner's story of his rise and fall, which we've touched on before, is the same. He became complacent and insulted his own customers, telling them they were buying crap. If you compare these stories with the collapses of the Mayan civilization at the end of the ninth century, the Anasazi Indians in the late 1200s, Easter Island in the seventeenth century and much more recently the Soviet Union, the common thread is that the steep decline tends to follow very swiftly after the peaks. And that's why there is more to business than just getting customers, keeping customers happy and making money.

That's why there is more to relationships than just getting to know someone and then taking them for granted.

You have to be constantly aware of change and making the people around you feel good about what they are doing. You need to be working at the relationship continually.

For a fine example of change and its inevitability, it's useful to look at the holiday market. In the early 1970s, holidaying abroad was for a very small percentage of people. Indeed, only a handful of Britons held passports. Then, as package tours arrived in the mid- to late 1970s, we all clamoured for package tour holidays to Spain. Benidorm and Torremolinos replaced Blackpool and Torquay and plates of paella were substituted for good old fish and chips. Paella and chips, if you really must.

But then sales of holidays to Spain hit an all-time low in the early part of the twenty-first century, with mass-market operators left with huge numbers of unsold holidays in the peak period of July and August.

Of course, it would be easy to blame the situation in Iraq or Afghanistan, the weather, the interest rates or the football, but that would be dodging the real issue of inevitable change. Two major things have happened to create that change. First, our skill level—or in this case, our desire for adventure—has expanded to such an extent that for many of us, simply going to Spain is no longer exciting.

And the internet changed everything. You don't need to go to a travel agent to book a holiday; you can book online, you can fix up car hire and insurance, and you can pick and choose how long you go for and in what hotels. Add to that the huge growth in low-cost flights available on the web and the acceleration of change is there to see. New Zealand, Australia and Taiwan are no longer regarded as long-haul holidays for the discerning and mature traveller.

We live on planet holiday.

Will the package holiday return? In its current format? Will we go back to Torremolinos and Benidorm in the numbers we used to? Will the Italians run Europe again? Would The Beatles have ever reformed, even when it was possible? Will Marks & Spencer become great again? Well, arguably it has. And it did so by rediscovering what the market wanted and changing itself. The company asked questions of its customers and set about exceeding those customers' expectations.

And that's the real challenge facing all businesses and all relationships: *the desire to seek new ways of doing things.* Persuasive techniques have changed and the classic 'hard sell' that I was introduced to in the 1970s—and, indeed, was a reasonable exponent of—is laughed at by people who have wised up on selling techniques. We need to be persuasive in a very different kind of way. We need to be persuasive by finding out what it is that the other person needs. And that's not only about their logical, stated needs; it's about their psychological needs. It's about understanding what the other person really wants.

It's about not looking and sounding like a vulture that has spotted its breakfast. It's not about persuasion. It's about influence.

Accept that change is inevitable and anticipate it. People who make money out of stocks and shares tell me that the secret is to sell before the market gets to the top. What goes up must come down. The tide goes in, the tide goes out. Yin and yang, Zig and Zag. If you are not part of the steamroller, you're part of the road.

CAN YOU TREAT PEOPLE BADLY WITHOUT CONSEQUENCES?

I have preached honesty as the single most important factor for persuading and I repeat that plea now.

In Ecclesiastes 11:1 it says, 'Cast thy bread upon the waters; for thou shalt find it after many days.'

In today's relationships you can't run the risk of cheating and ripping people off for very long. Not only will you get found out and the law of causality will kick in, but you have to live with yourself too. The law of causality states that for every action there is an equal and opposite reaction, and I believe that to be the case. Deal with everyone honestly and tell the truth, and you'll find in the long term, you'll be well respected and therefore more persuasive.

Remember that if you never tell a lie you don't have to remember anything.

TWO MYTHS

The expression 'If you always do what you've always done, you'll always get what you've always got' is a myth. Its origin is lost in the mists of time and it is often used to make the point that you need to create change. But I think it's horrocks. Everything is either growing or in decline. If you keep doing what you've always done you won't get the same result, you will actually get less. Because the world is changing all around us and you need to keep up with change simply to stand still.

I'm sure you have also heard 'If it ain't broke, don't fix it'. Another myth.

So what about your car, your house, indeed your body? They may not be broken, but they decay and problems occur unless you carry out proper maintenance. So this is horrocks too. You need to nurture all your relationships and ensure that you are continually looking to improve. You need to hone your persuasive skills and expressions all the time.

A friend of mine came to me in tears one day. 'My wife's left me,' he said. 'I haven't done anything.' Nothing more needs to be said.

Myths abound. It's time to talk about trust. Intellectual trust. Let's see how we build trust that lasts a lifetime.

31

HOW TO BUILD TRUST THAT LASTS A LIFETIME

B uilding a long-term relationship is always about trust. And 'intellectual trust' can be measured—by you. It begins with honesty.

Case study

Let me take you to New Zealand and the story of Brent Marris. Marris started Wither Hills in 1994 as a small boutique winery and began blending Sauvignon Blanc, Chardonnay and Pinot grapes from his father John's Marlborough vineyard and his own land, jointly owned with another winemaker in Auckland. Marlborough is an area in the northeast corner of the south island of New Zealand and Marris was good at his job. Awards and recognition followed.

Marris went into partnership with his father, combining their land, and by 2001 they were producing about 10,000 cases a year. That escalated to 200,000 cases—or nearly one million litres of wine. Wither Hills became the most popular Sauvignon Blanc in New Zealand and Marris one of its most decorated winemakers. In 2002 the Marrises sold to Lion Nathan for over NZ$50 million. The then 40-year-old Brent Marris stayed on to keep running Wither Hills as he always had and he kept winning awards.

But by the end of 2006 he had been forced to resign. Despite his wealth he had stress, 16-hour days and a giant question mark hovering over his integrity. He famously uttered these words; 'I wouldn't wish this on my worst enemy.' He was no longer trusted.

His crime? Entering into the New Zealand magazine *Cuisine* wine awards a slightly different wine than the one available on most shop shelves. He called it a technical mistake. Others called it fraud. Personally I'm a fan of Wither Hills. I would recommend its Sauvignon Blanc to you. But in 2007 Marris sacrificed all the medals his prized 2006 Sauvignon Blanc had collected that year, lost his job as chief judge of the country's most prestigious wine awards and placed his reputation at the mercy of the increasingly sceptical wine-drinking public.

In 2003 a group of anonymous Marlborough wine growers had accused Wither Hills of making special small batches of wine, entering them into competitions, and then passing off big-volume runs as the medal-winning wines.

These were rumours, but the rumours reached *Cuisine's* chief judge Michael Cooper. So when Wither Hill's Sauvignon again won gold in the magazine's awards, Cooper decided to test its veracity. He blind-tasted the wine he'd judged against the same wine from his local supermarket and thought they were different. The wines were sent to New Zealand government scientists to test and they found they were chemically different. Cooper called that fraud. Marris said the wines were close enough to be the same. For sure the hoi polloi who actually drink the stuff, and indeed other judges, couldn't tell the difference.

Wine Growers New Zealand subsequently ruled that Marris had not systematically made batches to impress at awards. There was no pattern of sending particular bottling runs to awards and the media. There was no evidence that a special wine batch had been created for awards. Wine Growers accepted that the *Cuisine* incident was a one-off accident. Marris may have been forgiven, but he lost the Air New Zealand wine-judging job and the trust of a nation.

So the first 'ingredient' in developing trust is to be honest. And that is not enough. You need to have verisimilitude, meaning the appearance of truth. If you want to be trusted you must not only be honest but have the appearance of honesty. People must believe that you are being honest.

The second 'ingredient' of intellectual trust is that you must be good at whatever it is you are being asked to do and the third that you must do what you say you are going to do.

My optician, Martin Hoyle, is a first-class example of that. I truly believe that he advises me totally regardless of the commercial consequences to himself. He is very good at his job and 100% reliable. Indeed, if I were scoring him out of 10 on each of the three criteria and multiplying the figures he would score 1000.

And there is a final part to measuring intellectual trust. Once you have multiplied the scores out of a possible ten, you divide them by the level of self-interest you *think* the other person has. And that is often where trust falls down. Do you truly care about my needs and want to exceed my expectations for your own sake or because you are only interested in what you can get from the relationship? Most people who are nice to you do so because they want something. If you behave your way into a problem you have to behave your way out of it.

In the earlier, non-transparent world a company and a person could pretty much determine through advertising and marketing what people thought of their product. But with the internet, out-performing competitors is no longer enough—you have to out-behave them. We can easily find out what companies actually do by reading people's blogs. So to be trusted and develop excellent long-term relationships, you need to have low self-interest. Figure 31.1 shows how it works:

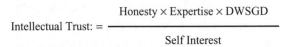

$$\text{Intellectual Trust:} = \frac{\text{Honesty} \times \text{Expertise} \times \text{DWSGD}}{\text{Self Interest}}$$

Figure 31.1 Measuring Intellectual Trust

To use this formula, sit down with someone who is important to you, someone you need to trust you. Then ask them to 'score' you out of ten for each of the four criteria. Do not question their responses. Simply write down whether they *think* you are honest (let's say you score a 9; in other words they think that 9 times out of 10 you are honest), ask them how good they think you are at whatever it is you are doing together (let's say that for expertise you score 8) and then ask them whether they see you as being reliable. Do you do what you say you are going to (DWSGD)? Let's say they score you 7 out of 10.

Multiply those three figures together (in this case $9 \times 8 \times 7 = 504$ out of 1000). Then ask them whether they think you are more interested in you (in which case they score you near 10) or whether they think your motivations are selfish and that you are only really interested in yourself (in which case their score will be nearer 1 out of 10).

Then divide 504 by that number. Let's say they think you see you as fairly high on self-interest and give you 7 out of 10. So 504 divided by 7 is 72, out of a possible 1000.

To be fair, even Martin Hoyle my optician doesn't score 1000. I'd give him a 4: he is genuinely interested in me and my eyesight, but he still is commercial and wants to sell me spectacles. That makes my assessment of him work out at a very, very respectable 250.

But in many respects it doesn't matter what the score is. What matters is to establish *why* you have any low figures on the top line (or a high one on the bottom) and ask why that has come about and what you can do about it. I know a number of clients who have gone on to use my formula with clients and been able to develop the trust in their relationships because they had a mechanism to discuss what trust is, how it's broken down and how to build it back up again.

FEEDBACK: THE KEY TO DEVELOPING INTELLECTUAL TRUST

The key to developing trust is therefore to ask for feedback and take action as a result of it.

I recently had a fridge-freezer delivered by Comet. That's the electrical store, not the celestial body that travels around the sun in a highly elliptical orbit. That would have been too expensive. This was just two guys who were friendly, punctual and performed the task only one step up from perfunctorily. Not a solid frozen mass or gaseous luminous tail in sight.

Then one of them asked me if I'd been 'fully satisfied with the service I'd received from Comet today'. Like most Brits, I quickly answered 'yes', eager not to get involved in an ugly confrontation that might somehow escalate to an all-out fist fight in front of the neighbours. Encouraged by this, he asked me more questions before handing me the delivery note. Finally, he shuffled uneasily from side to side and without making eye contact offered this parting shot: 'I'm not being funny or anything but... thank you for shopping at Comet.'

He couldn't have looked more embarrassed had he bent forward and kissed me on the cheek. Naturally, I would have been forced to revise my opinion of the service had he done so. I'm not saying which way. Obviously he'd been trained in leaving the customer with this final thought, though not in the art of actually delivering it. Later, on the Comet website, I discovered a form I could fill in to comment on the delivery service. The final question—to which the answer was a simple Yes or No—was 'Did the driver say "Thank you for shopping at Comet"?' Well, yes he did. But without an ounce of sincerity. No hint of verisimilitude. Comet now thinks that I'm happy and that its service was in some way superior. There's not even a facility to record my imaginary kissing incident.

A research survey by Bain & Co. revealed that 80% of nearly 400 company executives believed that they deliver a 'superior experience' to customers. The problem is that only 8% of customers agreed. Quite a gap. To close it, companies need to focus on the entire customer experience. They need to recognize that customers perceive interactions differently. Customers don't care about how your departments function or how staff are incentivized. And the ultimate test of any company's delivery lies in what customers tell others about it.

In Chapter 5 I talked about the phone call with Sue Taylor after our sofas had been delivered and she told me I was the first person to call and say thank you. The first! I asked Sue if she ever called customers to check that everything was delivered as planned. And she told me she didn't do that because people might be unhappy and complain to her.

So how do you find out what customers really think? How do you know what people think of you? How do you know if people trust you? How do you know if you have developed intellectual trust? Ask them. And don't ask questions that require only 'yes' or 'no'. Ask to be graded from 1 to 10 on the four key aspects of the service or relationship. And then ask the really brave question: 'What do we have to do to get to 10?' Because the most successful companies don't simply talk good service, they listen to the real voices of customers. In great relationships people truly listen to the other person.

Case study

I am sitting in Pennyhill Park Hotel, which I've made reference to before. As I am preparing myself to deliver a three-hour session, the hotel's managing director, Danny Pecorelli, approaches me. He introduces himself and we chat amiably. He asks if my stay is 'all right'. I say, 'No, Danny. It's not been all right.' I pause for just a second to create a 'special deal'—a hot and cold contrast—and say to him, 'It's way better than all right. It's probably the best hotel I've been in all year and the service is second to none.'

Danny thanked me for that and then he said a very interesting thing. 'Could you do me a really big favour, Phil? Could you give me one area that we could improve on? Any aspect of the hotel or service where we could do better?

I thought long and hard and, quite frankly, couldn't come up with anything at all.

Probably because he has been constantly asking that question of his guests.

My previous two nights had also been spent in hotels. They'll remain nameless to protect the innocent. But their service was nameless and, indeed, even aimless. Interestingly, no one asked me about the quality of the stay. Sometimes a hotel will send me a questionnaire asking for comments and I duly give them but I never, ever, get a response. They never tell me that it's been worthwhile and they never thank me for my time.

Interesting coincidence, don't you think?

The very best service from the best hotels also goes hand in hand with a desire to improve, a desire for feedback. People who don't offer a good service don't want to know about the feedback. Is it that they don't want to know how bad it is? Because for sure, if you ask a question that you don't want the answer to you'd better expect an answer you don't like. But does it all come down to care? As we discussed in the last chapter, things are on the rise or on the wane. Nothing stays still for ever—or as the French put it, *plus les choses changent, plus elles restent les mêmes.*

When you have made a presentation, how often do you ask for feedback whether or not you have won or lost the pitch you were making? How often do you ask your best friend to tell you the most irritating thing about you? If you truly want to be more persuasive and influential, you've got to get feedback on how you are. The Japanese call it *kaizen*.

However, in my experience of asking for feedback, people are often reluctant to give you their real feelings, particularly if you haven't been successful. If you're looking for a tip, ask them for three specific areas that you can 'work on'. For example, three things that if you were given the chance, you would have done differently.

Case study

When we pitched for the Dollond & Aitchison advertising account in the early 1990s, it was at a time when opticians had just been given licence to advertise by the government. Clive Stone, the chairman, Stephan Zagata and their team handled the whole thing very professionally and drew up a shortlist of four advertising agencies to pitch for the account. All the agencies were to present on one day in a hotel in Solihull near Birmingham. We were given the second slot and a maximum of one and a half hours to present.

Dollond & Aitchison's logo was an owl and we had decided to make use of it. We made references to Lloyds Bank's black horse, Andrex's Labrador puppy, the Dulux Old English Sheepdog and so on. Yours truly thought it would be a good idea to have a real, live owl in the presentation and, although it didn't meet with widespread approval among my colleagues, we decided that, on balance, it could be a great idea.

Picture the scene. There are four of us suited and booted, making our presentation to the five good people of Dollond & Aitchison. We have done one hour and 20 minutes of PowerPoint; we have run them through our research, explained our strategy and taken them through the creative work and media plans. And now the *pièce de résistance*.

I had found a guy based in the West Midlands who had an owl. He seemed quite calm at 11 o'clock when we left him outside the room preening his charge and went to make our presentation. But by 12.20, he was getting more and more nervous. At the risk of stating the obvious, this was the first time he'd been involved in an advertising agency presentation for a multimillion-pound account. So when I said with dramatic words 'and now the owl...' and my colleague Bernie May opened the door, the man walked in with the owl. Not only was he petrified, worried and frightened, but he had transmitted his fear to the owl, who promptly wanted to leave the room.

I hadn't been in such close proximity to an owl before and I'm not in a hurry to do so again. It had a wingspan of about ten feet. And although it was tied to its keeper's gloved hand, it made a squawking noise that could be heard in nearby Solihull. Plus it flapped its wings with such drama and purpose that we all scattered to the corners of the room!

'Get it out, get it out!' cried Clive Stone, and, understandably, we ushered the man and his blessed owl away.

The five of us were silent on the drive home. We'd spent the thick end of three months preparing for this account and we were keen to win it. This idea appeared to have blown the account and I was genuinely remorseful as I steered the car back up the M1. I was just glad we hadn't been pitching for the Lion Bar account, because things could have turned out much worse.

When we got back to the office the event had still not become funny. Do you find it interesting that something awful happens but it becomes really funny a month or two afterwards? Holidays that go wrong become funny stories later on. Well, this wasn't funny yet.

By chance it was our board meeting that night and we started at 5.30 p.m. At 7.30 p.m. the phone rang; an odd event in itself. It was Stephan Zagata, wanting to speak to me. My colleagues looked at me and I looked at them as I strode reluctantly to the telephone and picked it up. I felt certain he wanted to know how to get owl faeces off the upholstery and where to send the bill.

'You've won the account, Phil.'

Get in!

I made no reference whatsoever to the owl, but by midnight in the bar had convinced myself (and maybe even my colleagues) that it had been the inspiration that had clinched the account. It was the drama and purpose, it was the bit that made the difference. It was the feather-ruffling finale. I waxed lyrical and went to bed relieved and delighted.

The feedback?

As always, win or lose I asked the client what we had done right and what we had done wrong. I also made a point of asking what other agencies had done to see if there was something we could learn.

It was ten days later that we dined in what was then La Locanda restaurant in Wetherby. Stephan and his team had come for the day and we'd all gone out for dinner: a joyous affair and an opportunity for the two teams to get to know each other. I sat next to Stephan over dinner and as we approached the brandies and coffees I asked him what the other presentations had been like and if there was anything that we could learn.

'Well,' he began, 'you'd never believe it, Phil. One agency brought a bloody owl into the hotel room! We all had to scatter to the far corners. It was a ridiculous idea!' We laughed together and to this day Stephan doesn't know that he confused us with another agency. We'd got away with it. And how many times do you do that?

If you want to be truly persuasive and influential and you want to get better, you have to ask the questions to which you don't necessarily want the answers. If you really want to develop trust between you and someone else, you have to get feedback and take it on the chin.

These opportunities are all around us, but we're not making the best use of them. We're not taking the time to learn, to develop and to get better. We're not taking time to do the right things.

YOU REAP WHAT YOU SOW

I once ran a competition for potential clients where the reward for responding was to be entered into a free prize draw to see the diminutive Irishman Chris de Burgh in concert in Birmingham. There were nine pairs of tickets to be won and the winners, together with my wife and me, would have a special hospitality area at the NEC, watch the concert and then come back to have dinner. It was a worthwhile prize and I notified all the winners by telephone at around 10 o'clock one morning.

Needless to say, they were all delighted. I was leaving the agency that lunchtime when the receptionist said there was a call for me. It was from one of the winners of the prize. 'I don't know how to tell you this, Phil, but since you called me I've been hauled into the managing director's office and I've been made redundant. I am devastated. I should let you know this because obviously I don't really qualify for the two tickets any more.'

I didn't even need to think about it. He'd won the prize and the last thing I was going to do to a man who'd had such bad news was exacerbate the problem by telling him he wasn't welcome at a Chris de Burgh concert.

I reassured him that not only would he and his wife still be very welcome, if there was anything I could do to help him in his career I would be delighted to do so. However, since he was no longer strictly speaking a potential client, I would have to charge him £75 plus postage for the tickets. Only kidding.

He and his wife came along to the concert and we chatted. By this stage he'd got a new job and things were looking good and I was delighted for him.

Now fast-forward six months. I received a phone call out of the blue. Would I like to meet the marketing director of what was then Halifax Insurance, Neil Utley? It wasn't a potential client I was particularly targeting but I was more than happy to meet Mr Utley. The conversation was with his secretary, we fixed an appointment and I turned up at his offices in Halifax. His secretary came to meet me and ushered me up the stairs. She said, 'You don't remember me, do you?' And I apologized and said that I didn't.

'You were very good to my husband some months ago. He'd been made redundant and it made a big difference to him that you still wanted us to go to the Chris de Burgh concert.'

By then, of course, I'd remembered her and that we had had an enjoyable conversation. She then said to me, 'I said to him at the time if ever I can do something for that guy Phil Hesketh, I'll do it. And when my boss Neil Utley said he wanted to speak to some advertising agencies about direct mail, you were my first thought.'

Neil and I have gone on to become good friends and he became a client of the agency and, indeed, has become a client of mine as chief executive of Cox Insurance. It all came down to one opportunity to be honest and sincere and genuine, having a very low self-interest and making a straightforward decision.

You reap what you sow.

HOW LEADERS EMERGE

Whenever people are formed into a group, before long a natural leader emerges. You only have to watch an episode of *Big Brother* or *The Apprentice* to witness this happening. There'll be one person who either takes the initiative in a task and organizes the troops, or, in the case of *Big Brother*, steals a house mate's underwear and runs around the room wearing them on his head. And it's the same with teams. Minus the exhibitionism, obviously. Even if members of a team are all at the same level, without a recognized 'boss' a leader emerges. Why is this?

Research suggests that leaders emerge through a combination of their own outspoken behaviour and how this is perceived by others. In two studies at the University of California by Cameron Anderson and Gavin Kilduff, the behaviour of dominant individuals and how they were perceived by others was closely observed. Naturally there was no shortage of candidates in Tinseltown. Also not unnaturally, their research showed a big gap between the actual competence of leaders and the way in which they are perceived by others.

In one of the studies participants attempted to solve a series of maths problems in competition with another group. The groups were videotaped and the behaviour of their members carefully examined. They found that dominant participants tended to offer more suggestions to the group and were thus perceived as the most competent. Crucially, though, the study revealed that their dominant behaviour encouraged others to see them as competent even when their suggestions were no better. Their voice was simply heard longest and loudest—and was usually believed. A bit like insisting that a country has weapons of mass destruction then discovering that it doesn't.

Of course, outside the laboratory, money and power have more to do with who leads organizations like corporations or nations. In reality, groups of people don't start on egalitarian terms and people don't always 'emerge' from groups of their peers on the basis of who shouts loudest and longest. Again, witness reality television shows to see this in action. The long-time favourite often gets booted out before the end when viewers tire of their dominant behaviour and see little return from it.

Personally I don't think it's about the quality of comments that people make, but rather the quality of their questions that demonstrates to others the validity of their contribution.

So if you are in a group and want to lead, ask good questions.

BUILDING A LIFETIME OF TRUST

This chapter has been about building trust that will last a lifetime. And if there is one thing that a good leader must have, it is the trust of the people around them. If you want to build trust with friends and colleagues that will last a lifetime you have to be honest; you have to be good at what you are expected to do; you must be reliable; and you must be genuinely interested in the other person.

I mentioned Socrates in Chapter 5 and how his questions such as 'What is the most important thing to you about...?' have stood the test of time. His way of questioning is still as relevant today as it's ever been. Not only does asking questions allow you to find the other person's real interests and motivations, it also helps you build trust if you listen carefully to the answers and act on what is said to you.

His 'why?' type of questioning allows you to think more about what the other person is thinking about. Questions such as:

'Why are you saying that?'

How did you make that assumption?

What are the consequences of that assumption?

Why is that happening?

What would happen if...?

Who benefits from this?

How could you look at this another way?

What are the implications of...?

How do you know this?

Is this true?

I am continually surprised at the frequency with which people believe what they are told, read in the newspapers, hear on the radio and see on television. When people give me a view on something and I disagree, I ask them if what they have said is an opinion or a fact. They usually see for themselves that what they have is an opinion, but if they think it is a fact I ask them Socratic questions: How do they know this? How do they know it is true? It is difficult to influence people if they think that what they believe is undoubtedly true.

What good leaders need today is for people to have faith in them. To trust them. If you want to be a leader, build trust and ask more questions. That's essentially what this book is about.

32

MOTIVATION

In business we're always chasing the big prize. It might be winning a new contract, improving sales performance or reducing our carbon footprint. To achieve these goals rarely takes one big effort but rather lots of concentrated bursts. So, for instance, when you're tidying up the office, don't be too discouraged when you've filled up an entire skip but still can't see your desk. Every little helps, as they say at Tesco.

But how do you stay motivated? And more importantly, how can you avoid being demotivated when things don't go to plan? Psychological research by Houser-Marko and Sheldon suggests that the key is to balance up individual tasks against the grand vision. They compared people's reaction to failure depending on whether they were thinking about the individual task or their main overall goal. Participants played a word game that assessed their verbal ability and were awarded points for each individual task. Along the way they were given feedback about how they were doing. However, this was completely made up rather than based on actual performance. Not surprisingly, motivation fell among those who were told they were doing badly. But what the researchers were really interested in was whether their level of focus—either on the individual task or the overall goal—affected motivation.

They found that it did: those who were told they were doing badly, but only on the specific task, didn't expect to do so badly in the future compared to those who were focusing on their primary goal. So it seems that even when things aren't going to plan, it's better to stay focused on the individual task rather than to contemplate the ultimate goal.

Now translate that to your personal target. Whether it's in business or in your personal life, it pretty much always comes down to numbers. Weight, money, sales, miles, that kind of thing. Despite the seasonal peaks and troughs that affect everyone's life, it's human nature to divide the ultimate target by 12 and arrive at a monthly figure. Some months you'll be down, some you'll be up. And when you're neither up nor down you're in some kind of surreal nursery rhyme with king's horses and men everywhere. But try to forget that. The point is that you're more likely to achieve the ultimate goal if each member of the sales team stays focused on the task in hand. Sure, one eye has to remain on the big prize, but when you're actually engaged in the task itself, making a presentation, telephoning an important client, or evaluating progress, it's important to stay task focused.

So if you have a team of people you want to motivate, get them to adopt the approach of a sprint racer. Moments before the race they look off into the distance and focus on the finish line. But as soon as the starting gun fires they stare down at their feet. Now the focus is step by step. Then, towards the end of the race, they have just one focus: the finish line. Okay, someone still always comes last, but you get the idea.

REWARDS

But what *does* motivate people? We are usually either driven or drawn. We are driven away from what we don't want or drawn to what we do want. And often we don't know why we are doing it. Remember those people who buy things they don't need with money they haven't got to impress people they don't like?

We don't always need reasons to be persuaded. We just need emotional satisfaction. Some people buy because they think they are going to save time. To paraphrase The Eagles: 'You spend all your time making money and you spend all your money making time.' Sometimes people buy because they want to be recognized. Why else would the market for personalized number plates be so lucrative? Sometimes there is a real personal pride of ownership, and other times it's a case of keeping up with the Joneses.

Sometimes we do things just for the hell of it. Often we buy something on impulse because we like it and it feels good. But how do you get people to do what you want them to do and enjoy it? That is to say, without payment?

Psychologists have known for a long time that rewards are overrated. Having run a business, I found that whatever reward system was put in place had to be updated and replaced within two years because it became simply part of the salary package. The 'carrot' can be effective under some circumstances, but research with pre-school children teaches us a great deal about the strange effects that rewards have on our motivation.

Psychologists Mark Lepper from Stanford University and David Greene from the University of Michigan were interested in testing what is known as the 'over-justification' hypothesis. They recruited more than 50 children aged between three and four who were interested in drawing. The children were then randomly assigned to one of the following conditions:

1 'Expected reward'
   In this condition children were told they would get a
   certificate with a gold seal and a ribbon if they took
   part.

2 'Surprise reward'
   In this condition children would receive the same
   reward as above but, crucially, weren't told about it
   until after the drawing activity was finished.

3 'No reward'
   Children in this condition expected no reward, and
   didn't receive one.

Now say 'aaaah'.

Each child was invited into a separate room and asked to
draw for six minutes before leaving either with their reward
or empty handed, depending on which group they were in.
Over the next few days, they were watched through one-
way mirrors to see how much they would continue drawing
of their own accord.

The results are in line with plenty of other research on the
effects of rewards. The children in the 'expected reward' group
actually decreased the amount of spontaneous interest they
took in drawing. As for the other two groups, there was no
statistically significant difference between the no reward and
surprise reward groups. So, those children who had previously
liked drawing were less motivated once they expected to be
rewarded for the activity. In fact, the expected reward reduced
by half the amount of spontaneous drawing the children did.
Not only this, but judges rated the pictures drawn by the
children expecting a reward as less aesthetically pleasing.

It's not only children who display this kind of reaction to
rewards. In another study by Curry and colleagues in 1990,
smokers who were rewarded for their efforts to quit did

better at first, but after three months fared worse than those who were given no rewards and no feedback. Indeed, those given rewards even lied more about the amount they were smoking. With the notable exception of very public, hard-to-achieve rewards such as Olympic medals, tangible rewards tend to have a substantially negative effect on intrinsic motivation. The key to understanding these behaviours lies in the difference between 'intrinsic' and 'extrinsic' motivation.

When we do something for its own sake, because we enjoy it or because it fills some deep-seated desire, we are intrinsically motivated. It's *fun*. On the other hand, when we do something because we receive some reward, like a certificate or money, this is extrinsic motivation.

The children were chosen in the first instance because they already liked drawing and they were intrinsically motivated to draw. It was pleasurable, they were good at it and they got something out of it that fed their three- and four-year-old souls. Then some of them got a reward for drawing and their motivation changed. Before the involvement of those bad guys Lepper and Greene, they had been drawing because they enjoyed it, but now it seemed as though they were drawing for the reward. They had become professional drawers. What they had been motivated to do intrinsically, they were now being given an external, extrinsic motivation for. This provided *too much* justification for what they were doing and so afterwards, paradoxically, they drew less.

To be fair to the researchers, this was the over-justification hypothesis they were searching for. People are both motivated and encouraged by sincere and honest praise. We have a deep need to be loved and appreciated.

Rewards are also dangerous because they remind us of obligations, of being made to do things we don't want to do. Children are given rewards for eating all their food, doing their homework or tidying their bedroom. So rewards become associated with painful activities that we don't want to do. The same goes for adults: money becomes associated with work and work can be dull, tedious and painful. So when we get paid for something we automatically assume that the task is dull, tedious and painful—even when it isn't.

This is why play can easily become work when we get paid. Someone who enjoyed weaving baskets, playing the violin, collecting opera programmes or playing Premier League Football suddenly finds the task more tedious once money is involved. Well, perhaps the £100,000 a week footballer's wage cushions the blow somewhat, but you know what I mean.

Yet sometimes rewards do work, especially if people really don't want to do something. Then the reward becomes an incentive. But when a task is inherently interesting to us in the first place, rewards can damage our motivation by undermining our natural talent for self-regulation.

OTHER MOTIVATORS

Often we do things because we feel obliged, as I said when discussing psychological reasons. Sometimes we buy or are motivated to do something because we fear what will happen if we don't. For example, security products make us feel safe from burglars; without them we may feel vulnerable. And sometimes we simply want to avoid the pain of criticism.

I was canoeing in the Canadian Rockies with my eldest son, and the leader in the six-man Canadian canoe was chatting to me about motivation. Unbeknown to me, he was waiting his moment and then at the crucial moment said, 'See that sign over there?' Sure enough, there was a huge sign saying 'Waterfall 1 kilometre. Please leave the river at the next bank.' He asked me if we had seen the waterfall. And we had—huge it was—and certain death awaited anyone who attempted to go over it in a canoe. 'Okay,' he said. 'The current's strong and we've all got to paddle like crazy to ensure we make the bank on the right.' We looked round and all paddled like never before. He tapped me on the shoulder and shouted above the din of the fast running water, 'That's motivation!'

At least it's one form of motivation. It's not a healthy one to rely on in a successful, growing company or a good relationship.

And, of course, there is the small matter of money as a motivator, making it or saving it. It's a big motivator for sure, but often not as important as we think it is.

When we handled the Brentfords retail account, I suggested that we test the effectiveness of advertising by using it for certain stores, but not for others. Given that the size of stores, average weekly sales and type of area were graded anyway, we would match stores against others and we would be able to see how useful the advertising was. The weather would be roughly the same, as would general economic conditions, so we anticipated that stores with advertising would outperform those without.

However, a handful of stores always bucked the trend. Why? Because there was a financial incentive for the managers to beat targets? Not really. What we discovered was that the managers of stores with no advertising wanted to outperform those that had some to show they were better managers; that good management was more important than a good ad. It made them feel important.

In Chapter 1, I explained that I began to write this book on a February morning sitting in Russell, New Zealand. My motivation came from wanting to be the best speaker on the planet and to aid and abet that desire I needed to write a bestselling book. To motivate myself to finish the book, I needed to know where it would be launched and, indeed, needed to picture the book in a bookstore.

So just two days before I started to write this book, I went to a bookstore at the top of Queen Street in Auckland. I'd been told that it was the biggest bookstore in the city, so I went to see where my book would sit. I found the business section and, as the books were laid out in alphabetical order, I found the spot where Hesketh would be. I moved three of the books to one side to make a space for my book, then stood back and pictured it.

I can see it now.

And as I stood six feet back from the fixture staring at this space in the bookstore, picturing my goal, I spotted another book I hadn't seen for some years. Norman Vincent Peale's *The Power of Positive Thinking* has sold over 15 million copies. I picked it up and although I had read it many years before, I thought it was time to buy a copy and re-read it. I looked at the price and it was NZ$31.95. I was in a relaxed frame of mind and scanned the opening pages. The book was originally written in 1953 and has been reprinted many times. I decided to read the preface, the very first words written in any book. This is what the opening paragraph in the book *The Power of Positive Thinking* says:

> At the time I wrote this book it never occurred to me that a two millionth copy anniversary would ever be observed.

I looked at the page and pictured Norman sitting at his old typewriter in 1953 working on the book. I could imagine his buddy calling to see him and asking what he was doing. I imagined Norman saying, 'I'm writing a book.' His friend would naturally ask him what it was about and Norman would say, 'It's about the power of positive thinking. It's about beliefs. It's about how you can achieve more if you really and truly believe that you can do something.'

And I imagine his buddy saying that it was a fine thing to do. 'What are you going to call it, Norman?'

'The Power of Positive Thinking.'

'Excellent,' says his buddy. 'Do you think it will sell many copies?'

And Norman would reply, 'No, not really.'

He wrote a book on positive thinking and didn't think it would sell. I don't make this stuff up.

I also mentioned in Chapter 1 that my own journey really began on the flight back from Harvard Business School with my colleague Bernie May and the then HR director of Arla Foods, Paul Simpson. Paul asked me what it was I really wanted to do. I told him that I wanted to be a lecturer at Harvard. I told him that I wanted to speak at the likes of Cambridge and Oxford universities. I told him that I would leave the agency on my 50th birthday to fulfil that dream. Bernie tapped me on the shoulder and pointed out of the window. 'Did you see those pigs just then?'

In reality, my colleagues were really helpful and 17 months later I went public on my goals. I spent two whole days telephoning clients, potential clients and key suppliers so that they would hear of my impending departure from the horse's mouth rather than a third party.

One of my earliest telephone calls was to Stephen Oliver, managing director of the Union Pub Company, part of Wolverhampton and Dudley Breweries. For the record, he was a client, not a supplier. I'd always got on really well with

Stephen and we'd shared some good times. I explained what I was doing and he said, 'Are you available for bookings?'

On the outside I remained calm and collected, while inside I was thumping the air and turning cartwheels. 'I can probably squeeze you in,' I replied.

He said he was having a management conference in 2003 and that he had faith in me to hold the attention of an audience for 45 minutes or so—would I be interested in speaking? I was speechless. Only kidding. Of course I was delighted and flattered to be asked. He explained the nature of the event and its objectives; he told me that I had a fairly free hand on the content; and then he gave me the date of the event. 'It's on 10 April 2003.'

'Where is it?'

'It's at Oriel College, Oxford University. I'm an old boy of the college and have hired the college for our conference.'

I was born at 7.30 a.m. on April 10, 1953. My very first speaking engagement was to be on my 50th birthday at Oxford University.

The power of positive thinking.

It's amazing how if you have a clear goal, events conspire to help you towards it. Serendipity is a wonderful thing and I regarded that booking not only as the start of a new career but also as a sign and confirmation that it was meant to be.

PEOPLE ARE MOTIVATED TO DO WHAT THEY WANT TO DO

I was speaking at a conference at the International Convention Centre in Birmingham. I was to speak to over 300 delegates at 2 p.m. for 35 minutes. I had my guitar on stage, the audience were beginning to come back in from lunch and I was getting ready for show time. The only thing that remained to do was get my clip-on microphone from a young man called John behind the screen.

As I approached him, it was exactly six minutes to two and I asked if I could be miked up.

'Are you the motivational speaker then?'

'Motivational speaker' is not an expression I use loosely. You'll find it on my website and it's one of my keywords for search engine optimization. But only because that's the most popular expression typed into Google by people look-ing for a speaker. Fish where the fishes are.

I don't believe that motivation is something you can *do* to someone. I'm also concerned that if I'm on holiday and I'm asked what I do for a living and I say I'm a motivational speaker, the other person will say, 'Well, go on then...'

But with the audience filing in and me getting ready to speak and in the right mental state, I took the easy option and said, 'Yes, I am.'

He said, in an insouciant drawl, 'Can you motivate me?' (And he did this in a Birmingham accent...)

Glancing at my watch, I said, 'What is it you want to do?'

And he replied, 'I don't know; I just need motivating.'

Not a word of a lie.

But in many respects he summed it all up. Motivation is about having a goal. Motivation is about knowing what it is that you want to do, but not necessarily why you want to do it.

People are motivated to do what they want to do. So you have to find out what motivates the person in need of motivation. And then work out how to fit that with what you want them to do. When they exhibit behaviour you want to encourage, you tell them how good they are at that. You let them know you think very highly of them. You tell them what they are good at and what you like about them.

And for your own motivation? Well, I believe that if you have the goal, and the emotional desire to achieve the goal, then you have the motivation too. And you can often get the ability later on.

Karl Power had a goal or two. Karl is an ordinary lad from Droylsden near Ashton-under-Lyne. In April 2001 he and his mate Tommy went to Germany to watch Manchester United play Bayern Munich. At their hotel, Karl dressed up in full Manchester United kit before sneaking into the Olympic Stadium. As the two teams took to the field, he removed his tracksuit, ran on to the pitch behind his Manchester United heroes and lined up alongside them to have his photograph taken before kick-off. The next day he was in just about every UK newspaper.

In July 2001 he walked out in full England cricketer's kit to bat in the Ashes series. It was only when he hit four successive boundaries off the first four balls that people began to doubt he was a genuine England batsman. Actually, I made that bit up. The plan actually went awry before he could make it to the crease. Hiding in the wings, his cue to enter the arena was to be three rings on his mobile phone from his mate Tommy. However, unfortunately Karl's young niece called to see how the plan was going and he mistook it as the signal to walk on to the hallowed turf, much to the confusion of the England batsmen who by some miracle hadn't yet got out. He made the news again, though.

In April 2002 he ran out with the England rugby team in Rome and in June 2002 he played tennis on the Centre

Court at Wimbledon just before a Tim Henman mismatch. Rather than being praised for his derring-do, he was rather unfairly vilified by the British press for wearing black socks! Finally, later that month, Karl, his mate Tommy and Tommy's son were photographed on the winners' podium at Silverstone in full Formula 1 driver's kit. Again, they were only rumbled when they tried to cash the cheque. That and quaffing the champagne rather than spraying everyone in sight.

Why did he do it? Even Karl doesn't know. The thing is, he had a picture. He had a goal. He had the emotional desire to achieve the goal and therefore he had the motivation. After that he found a way of achieving it.

Karl was told it was an impossibly stupid thing to do. Stupid maybe, but impossible, no. Because where there's a will, there's always a way.

When I set myself the goal of going to Harvard Business School, part of my motivation was to picture myself in the library at Harvard. On my first free Wednesday afternoon, I went to the library just to sit there and read awhile to capture that magic moment. I went into the Widener library and I'd like to tell you the story of that too.

Harry Elkins Widener came to England from the USA in 1912. He was something of a bibliographer and had come for a holiday with his father. While he was here he bought several important books. Unfortunately, his mode of transport back to the States was the doomed *Titanic*. When the ship went down on 15th April, he and his father, along with many of his books, were lost. The story goes that he was about to step into a lifeboat that would have saved his life when he remembered a newly acquired book (apparently a copy of the second edition of Bacon's *Essays* from 1598) and ran back to get it. He was never seen again.

As a memorial to her son, the wealthy Mrs Widener placed two stone bookends on his grave instead of a headstone. Actually I made that up, but it would have been a lovely touch, don't you think? In reality, her much grander gesture was to donate $2 million for the construction of a building that would house her son's collection so that he would be remembered for ever. That was a very large amount of money in 1912. If you ever get to Harvard, I urge you to go to the library and visit the small museum dedicated to the memory of Harry Elkins Widener.

Some executives believe that money is the ultimate motivator. Some say it's the *only* motivator. I don't believe that to be true. Money is a hygiene factor. So long as people are paid what they believe they are worth, then it's often the feeling of being valued and recognized for their efforts that is more important. Of course, money will always 'talk' and remain part of the motivational process. And it's certainly handy when you go to the shops. But it's not the be-all and end-all.

33

SAY WHAT YOU ARE GOING TO DO AND DO WHAT YOU SAY

I want you to imagine that you and some friends are learning to play tennis. In the first scenario, I want you to suppose that you display a natural talent for the game. With professional help and regular practice you enjoy getting better by the day. Your friends, however, are less Fred Perry and more Fred Flintstone, and fail to achieve your level of improvement.

Playing against them in the first week or two was enjoyable because you were at the same standard. But now it's quite easy to beat them. However, in this first scenario, I want you to imagine that you continue to play opponents less talented than yourself. Frustrating, isn't it? When your skills improve but the challenge doesn't, you become bored and you question whether it's worthwhile to continue since winning has become too easy.

Now let's suppose that instead of being a natural at the game you struggle to master the basics. Like swinging the racket without letting go of it. Or keeping your eye on the ball—even when you're just throwing it in the air to serve. At the intervals you miss your mouth completely with the barley water. Okay, maybe your hand–eye coordination isn't quite as bad as that. However, despite your worst efforts, your tennis coach insists that you continue

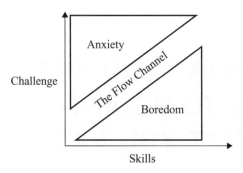

Figure 33.1   Going with The Flow

to play against opponents who are much better. All your friends are improving rapidly, but each time you go on court you know you're going to lose, maybe even be humiliated. How do you suppose that feels? That's right, frustrating too.

You're entering the triangle of anxiety in Figure 33.1 and again, you question whether or not you want to continue to play because there is little or no pleasure.

THE FLOW CHANNEL

The triangles of anxiety and boredom exist in life itself. The secret, of course, is to be in what Professor Mihaly Csikszentmihalyi describes as the 'flow channel'.

This is how films are made. Look at the big blockbuster movies and observe how the producers structure the story so that you become anxious and worried about the hero or heroine. Will Kate Winslet and Leonardo Di Caprio make it off the *Titanic* alive? Will Bruce Willis be able to undo the handcuffs in the burning building? On the Greek island of Kalokairi, will bride-to-be Sophie discover who her real father is before the wedding? And will Pierce Brosnan ever learn to sing?

We don't want to watch a film that takes us into the triangle of boredom. We need a film that grips us, that makes it interesting by taking us into the triangle of anxiety and then back into the flow channel. It's the same principle as the psychological reason 'special deal'. Films that have a 'happy ever after' ending leave us right back there in the flow channel, whereas tragedies such as *Romeo and Juliet* leave us sanguine and reflective as we exit the theatre. *Fahrenheit 9/11* deliberately leaves us in the anxiety triangle. Or at least that's where Michael Moore wanted you to be. *Mamma Mia!* simply leaves you in a good place. It's why it became the highest-grossing movie the UK had seen at the time.

Comedies ensure that our hero keeps making the same mistake. Laurel and Hardy got this off to a fine art. This concept also explains the attraction of watching great sporting events and why football rather than rugby, cricket and golf is our biggest spectator sport. In the FA Premier League, any team can beat another on a given day. We actually enjoy the roller-coaster ride of being taken into the anxiety triangle. Of course, we complain bitterly when our team is losing, but if our team won every single game easily we would simply enter the triangle of boredom.

By far and away my best sporting moment as a spectator was when my eldest son and I went to Barcelona on 24 May 1999 to watch Manchester United play Bayern Munich in the European Champions League Final. My son had his 18th birthday just a few days before and my present to him was a ticket to see the final. (I had been at Wembley in 1968 when United beat Benfica 4–1 and was probably one of only a few thousand in the stadium that night who had been to both finals.) With 90 minutes gone in the game and the fourth official showing just three minutes of injury time left, my subconscious mind was well into the triangle of anxiety and my conscious mind was preparing for the worst—and firmly rooted in the triangle of boredom. When Manchester United scored two goals in the final three minutes to win the trophy—my son and I were behind the goal at El Camp Nou—we shared a very special experience. But if Manchester United had scored two goals early on, the thrill wouldn't have been the same.

So why should you step outside your comfort zone? The answer is that you don't have to. But you run a severe risk of festering in the triangle of boredom for the rest of your life if you don't experience anxiety at some point.

In the same way that all films ever made fall into a handful of categories, there are, in my view, only six types of songs that have ever been written.

1 I love you

Way back in 1976, Paul McCartney wrote, 'You'd think that people would have had enough of silly love songs.' All these years later we still can't get enough of them. In the same song he also wrote, 'Love doesn't come in a minute, sometimes it doesn't come at all.' Today that's still true, but at least you can get treatment. The bottom line is that we'll never tire of telling someone 'you're the first, the last, my everything', though not necessarily in the same rich, deep, husky tones as Barry White. Believe me, don't try it. You just sound like you've got a bad case of laryngitis. By definition, expressing your undying love for someone takes you into the anxiety triangle because you seek reciprocation. If it is reciprocated you enter 'flow'. Unrequited love equals anxiety.

2 I'm leaving you but I'll be back

'Come back; baby come back' sang Eddy Grant and the Equals back in the 1960s. John Denver sang about leaving on a jet plane. Usually this kind of song is about the break-up of a relationship, although in Denver's case it was somewhat more prophetic since he later crashed his plane into the sea and left us all for good. In most instances, however, the anxiety is created by worrying whether or not your loved one will still be there waiting for you when you get back, and not whether your altimeter is going to play up again.

3 I'm leaving you and I'm glad to be gone

Similar to the above but with the cruel twist of a blunt knife. In recent times Green Day said 'Good Riddance', while Stevie Nicks of Fleetwood Mac vowed that she was never going back again. 'I should have listened to my mother' type songs are not that common and rarely make the Christmas charts, but they do have the power to inflict acute anxiety. First because your loved one has left you, and secondly because the manner of their departure and undisguised glee suggest you may be alone for quite a while and end up in the triangle of boredom. And that's not a sexual reference.

4 You're leaving me but I don't want you to

Just like Olivia Newton-John in the film *Grease*, it doesn't matter how hopelessly devoted you are to someone, there's always the chance that they'll push your love aside. And there ain't no sunshine when she's gone; it's not warm when she's away. Just try to make sure that when it happens you're not sitting on the dock of the bay waiting for the tide to roll away or you could get very wet. Ever find yourself wondering if they'll still love you tomorrow or why they don't bring you flowers any more? If he's leaving on that midnight train to Georgia and he's going back to a simpler place and time or if he's bought a one-way ticket, it's called anxiety and tension. A double whammy.

5 You're leaving me and thank God you've gone

Get back to where you once belonged is a famous line from the Fab Four, but it's a sentiment that has been echoed in song lyrics for generations. First she was afraid, then she was petrified, but Gloria Gaynor finally worked out how to survive: 'I should have changed that stupid lock, I should have made you leave your key, if I had known for just one second you'd be back to bother me.' She didn't mince her words, Gloria. 'Go on now go, walk out the door, just turn around now, because you're not welcome any more.' Roughly translated? I've had enough pain and anxiety. Hop it.

6 Protest and novelty songs

The sixth and final category is protest, novelty and miscellaneous. Bob Dylan's anti-war song 'Blowin' in the Wind' was one of the first protest songs, along with his 'The Times They Are a-Changin'', which was all about civil rights issues. Since then, John Lennon implored politicians to give peace a chance and Band Aid asked if we knew it was Christmas to highlight the plight of the starving millions in Africa. The truth is, nobody ever wrote a protest song without in some way feeling angry, anxious and tense.

As far as novelty songs go, I'm at a loss to understand fully what some of them were really all about. So what if Ernie did have the fastest milk cart in the west? And who is really bothered if Puff the Magic Dragon lives by the sea? Unless, of course, you have a beachfront property and it's affecting prices.

Back to the purpose of the chapter.

FLOURISHING IN THE FLOW

Without entering the triangle of anxiety or leaving your comfort zone, how do you achieve anything? How will you ever be more persuasive and influential if you don't start using the techniques we have discussed in this book, today?

All frustration is due to unfulfilled desires, and I hope that after reading this book you will achieve more of yours thanks to your newfound skills at being more persuasive and influential. In addition to the reasons people buy products, services and excuses, we also have certain needs. Naturally, we have a need for food, shelter, warmth and so on. But one of the ironies of life is that we also have a need for certainty and uncertainty. If everything is certain we enter the triangle of boredom, but if everything is uncertain we spend our whole life being anxious. We want to be 'in the flow'.

In its original etymology, the very meaning of the word 'influence' is 'to flow into'. So think of the influence as a river and the influencer as a stream. And think of how natural things are in nature. Good leaders appear to influence people naturally.

When a stream meets up with a river, it joins the current and flows in the same direction. It rarely begins to influence the course of the river until it has established the current. Of course, if the stream is big and strong and the river is small and weak, it can bulldoze as we've discussed before. But you are reading this book because you need to be a 'burgeoner'. And *that* word means to grow and flourish. Influence is about seeing things from the other person's point of view. It's about joining in and listening carefully to objections. It's about asking questions and accepting the answers before you exert your influence.

Interestingly, if man tries to alter the course of a river he builds a dam across it. And what happens? In pushing it into another path, the river reverts to its original course as soon as it possibly can. And if for some reason it can't do that, untold damage is caused behind the dam as the river builds up. You reap what you sow.

Unless you are 'pushing an open door', influencing doesn't work that way. That's why you need to establish the other person's needs and work from that as the starting point, just as the river joins the stream and slowly but surely has to work out the pace, direction and force of the stream before it can truly begin to influence.

As we continue to look at things that matter to the other person, we need to consider their priorities. What are the things that are important to them? In order to do this we need to step into their shoes. This is a strange expression and yet perhaps one we should take more literally; without actually swapping footwear, of course. What would it *feel* like to be in their position? What are the things that matter to them? Rather than trying to second-guess it, put yourself into their position.

Time passes at the same rate, 60 seconds a minute, wherever you are. But it doesn't always feel like that. The time that has passed never comes back. So respect your time here. After all, you're just passing through. Everything in life passes away eventually. So remember to have a certain respect for other people's time.

In my view, the difference between being a 'boss' and being a 'leader' is a simple one. You work for a boss and you do what you have to do because you have to do it. You do what you do for a leader because you want to do it. And that's why leaders are held in high esteem and bosses often in contempt.

The most basic way of persuading and influencing is to use the stick rather than the carrot. It assumes a level of fear. Better than that is the combination of carrot and stick. Better than that is the carrot alone. I've tried other vegetables and it doesn't work. When you can motivate by using only the carrot, that's when you have developed an open and honest relationship with your colleague or buyer. And when you do that you get a long-term commitment.

ACHIEVING MORE

It's impossible to measure your own effectiveness if you don't know what your objectives are. So be sure to have some and always keep them in mind. They could be material or spiritual, or a mix of both. Personally, I would never work for the money alone. The only person who gets job satisfaction from that is your bank manager.

Imagine you are going to die soon and have been granted one last phone call. Who would you call and what would you say to them? And if it's that important, why are you waiting until you're about to die to say it? Remember that happiness isn't the destination, it's the journey. So be sure to have a valid ticket and don't forget to look out of the window occasionally. Work to live, don't live to work. Or as my wife likes to say, 'Put that away now and come to bed.'

If you haven't yet found love in your life, don't give up. And remember, no matter how hard you try, you can't look for love without getting hurt. It just wouldn't be fair on the rest of us.

Be passionate about what it is that you want to do. Have such an overwhelming, burning passion that you set off smoke alarms as you pass by. Know the outcome and be able to measure it. Picture your goal so that you will know when you have achieved it. And don't be limited by what you know when you set your goals. Set your goals with 'no how' rather than 'know how'. Be positive and talk about it. Or, as Linford Christie used to say, 'Go on the B of the bang'.

Talk to people who have done what you want to do and then do what they do. Establish who can help you, discuss with them what you want to do, and ask for their help. You will then create an emotional 'pull' and, in turn, feel an obligation to carry out what you have said you would do. If you don't want to make it public, you probably don't want it enough.

Take massive action and surprise your horse. I achieved my goal of speaking in New Zealand because I bought a ticket to go there. Importantly, I bought the ticket before I had any engagements or anything remotely approaching a commitment from anybody to find me work. If you want to win the lottery, you have to buy a ticket.

Take massive action that is different to what everyone else is doing. They're all looking to take their lead from someone else anyway. As I said in the chapter on social pressure, when the rest of the world zigs, you may have to zag. Stay focused on your own life and goals, and don't get worked up over small, insignificant things. If it really troubles you, see a doctor. Take massive action that says to your own subconscious, 'I have burnt my bridges. There is no way back.'

When I embarked on my new career as a speaker, I told everyone that I would not work in the advertising field again. I wanted to burn my metaphorical bridges. Doggedness, tenacity and persistence are omnipotent. Or, 'If at first you don't succeed, remember that neither did Kelly Holmes.'

Change your habits, your expressions and your expectations. Remember Professor David McClelland's conclusion that the single most important factor in people not achieving their goals was that they had the wrong friends. Avoid negative people and, if necessary, change the people around you. You become like the people you spend the most time with.

And change your language. Success in persuading and influencing is, itself, influenced by your own expectations. Expectation is also critical in negotiation; if you don't expect a top price and go for it, how can you possibly achieve it? And so it is with training your subconscious. Not only do you need to retrain your horse to have higher expectation, you also need to stop saying certain things so that your horse (and by definition you, the rider) becomes more positive in outlook and expects to achieve more.

Here are the top ten things to stop saying if you really want to be more positive, more motivated and more motivating:

1   **'I wish…'** Whenever you wish for anything, you are saying to your subconscious that you're not in control and that only some higher being or 'Lady Luck' can help. 'I wish I was slimmer' or 'I wish I had more money', for example.

2   **'If only…'** How many times have you heard people say, 'If only the client hadn't done that we could have achieved more' or 'If only I'd done things differently.' You did what you did and it's time to move on. Don't say 'If only…', because you are saying to your subconscious that you either should have done something in the past—which has gone for ever—or that success is in some way conditional on something that's out of your control. And if you think it's out of your control, it is.

3 **'I'll try...'** There is no try. There's do and don't do; there's can and can't; there's will and won't. If you invite me to your party and I say 'I'll try to be there', we both know I'm not coming. Stop using 'try'.

4 **'I don't have time.'** Do you know that the average adult in Britain watches 24 hours of television every week? And most of the time most of those people are not watching something they planned to watch. Television is at the same time a great stimulator, entertainer and provider of information, as well as being the greatest single sapper of our time and energy. If you really want to achieve more, watch less television. Because that, as Joan Baez used to say, is where the time goes.

5 **'I'm not too bad really.'** If people ask how you are, don't say, 'I'm not too bad really', because what you're saying to your horse is that you are bad—you're just not too bad really. So, as a consequence, your horse feels negative. Tell people that you're 'buzzing' or have never felt better or that you 'feel great today'. Not only does it cause a positive reaction in them, all the time you're doing it, you're retraining your horse.

6 **'You're wrong on that one.'** Nobody likes to be told they're wrong, do they? Often people don't even need to be told at all—they know all too well.

7 **'I told you so.'** Again, people often know that you told them so and when the realization has dawned is exactly the right time to start talking in positive rather than negative terms. If you do, they'll like you more and, as a consequence, they'll feel indebted to you.

8 **'That's not my problem.'** The mood and circumstance this can create in the listener are quite dramatic. Don't let your people feel that they are not responsible.

9   **'Failure.'** There is no failure, you just didn't get the result you were looking for this time. But you got a result and you can learn from it.

10   **'But…'** There are, of course, some occasions to use the word but, but (!) reduce its usage by 80% and you will be more positive and persuasive. So often people use expressions such as 'I'm not unsympathetic' or 'I'm not one to gossip', and you know it will be followed by a 'but' which completely negates the first part of the expression. And 'with all due respect…' means no respect at all.

DOING SOMETHING ABOUT IT ALL

I'm not in any way a technophobe. Admittedly, I'm not keen on spiders. And, true enough, I'd think twice about riding the Pepsi Max roller-coaster on a full stomach. Nevertheless, when it comes to technological advances in the communications world, I'm as enthusiastic as the next person. In fact, I positively embrace the stuff. I may even give it a cuddle if no-one's watching.

But there's one big drawback to all this technology that leaves me very frustrated. You see, at the same time as ensuring that none of us need ever again be out of contact with one another, it also does an effective job of distancing us from the rest of the world. Let me give you an example.

I was speaking at a conference where some very important strategies were being discussed. Yet instead of giving the speaker their undivided attention, almost everyone in the room at some time or other couldn't resist the temptation to check their BlackBerry or iPhone. Just to see if they'd got any important messages. The fact that all their bosses and colleagues were right there in the room with them didn't make any difference. They still had to check. Because you never know.

This constant checking of handheld devices results in what Linda Stone dubbed 'continuous partial attention'. It's motivated by a desire never to miss an opportunity. Some call it multitasking. And that's fine when the tasks require little cognitive processing. But if we don't differentiate between those and the issues that require *deep thought*, we may miss the big chance.

Does this obsession with being in constant touch make us *more* or *less* productive? Does it help us to understand and deal with the key issues that affect our work and home life, or is it simply a big distraction? The truth is that we're over-stimulated, over-wound and maybe unfulfilled. In trying to process a never-ending stream of incoming data, we put the bigger decisions off.

Henry Ford once famously said that if he had researched the transport needs of people before he built the first car the conclusion would have been they wanted faster horses. The message is clear: switch off the phone from time to time and switch on your full attention. Because if you miss the real message, all you may end up doing is riding a faster and faster horse. A Luddite's view of hand-held communication devices? On the contrary. It is those who are addicted who run the risk of not being able to see the Model T.

Linda Stone also coined the expression 'email apnea', a temporary absence or suspension of breathing while reading emails. Holding your breath contributes significantly to stress-related illnesses because the body becomes acidic, the kidneys begin to reabsorb sodium, and the oxygen, carbon dioxide and nitric oxide balance is undermined, so our biochemistry blows a fuse. Make sure you breathe while reading your emails.

Create time for the things that are important both in your business and personal life but don't seem urgent right now. If you don't do them—if you don't allow time for planning— they grow and become more important and more urgent, and any attempt at managing your time is lost. Differentiate between the time that makes you money, such as seeing clients, telephoning prospects, agreeing deals and so on, and the time that doesn't, such as internal meetings and admin tasks. See a line between the two with all the admin stuff on the left and the making-money time on the right. Always know what side of the line you are on and keep on the right side as much as you can. Know when your prime time is and do your prime jobs then. We all have different circadian rhythms. Do your most important jobs when you are at your best. And don't just choose to do the easy, 'nice' jobs first.

Don't gossip. Don't blurt things out and don't talk about people when they are not there unless you're giving glowing praise.

Last but not least, know what is the most important thing in your life. It's almost certainly your family. So make sure you spend enough time with them. And write your own 'desiderata', not only for yourself but also for your children's children and their children. Mine is set out as the appendix to this book. In Latin desiderata means 'that which is lacking or wanted'. In English, we call it a wish list. It doesn't guarantee happiness or success, but it will help you to define it for yourself. That's the first step to making something happen.

Finally, do what you say you are going to do.

Always.

And do what you say you are going to do when you said you were going to do it and in the way that you said you

were going to do it. In Chapter 13 we talked about expectations and how to manage them. In Chapter 21 we looked
at how we all want a 'special deal', and how 'reason' was at
the centre buying psychology and the fulcrum of how it all
works. If you don't do what you say you are going to do, you
are generating the very opposite of 'special deal'. You are
losing credibility and eroding whatever trust people have in
you. Conversely, if you over-deliver on a promise and go
the extra mile, you are building trust and credibility. Unless
you're a taxi driver, when going the extra mile isn't a great
idea.

Living your life always doing what you say you are going
to do has two enormous benefits. First, your reputation is
built on solid foundations and people will believe in you,
trust you and like you. Secondly, it makes you think more
about the promises you make. And that, in turn, makes for
a happier life, because you're not putting yourself under
unnecessary pressure.

34

INFLUENCE, PERSUASION AND THE PURPOSE OF LIFE

Congratulations in getting this far. You started out on a journey 33 chapters ago and now you're entering the home straight. Far from being the end of the book, think of this as the beginning of a new chapter in your life. When you finally cross the finishing line, take a moment to consider what you have learned and why you have learned it.

To be more persuasive and influential in both business and life has probably been your goal. Hopefully you have acquired the skills and knowledge to become just that. If not, it's too late to have your money back.

But why do you want to be more persuasive and more influential? To be successful? Probably. To feel more satisfied? Most likely. To provide greater comfort and security for yourself and your family? Undoubtedly. Roll them all together and you can sum it up in one word. Here's a clue. If you had miraculous powers and could bestow on a loved one just one gift in life, what would it be? That's right: happiness.

Ask most people what would make them happy and they'll tell you something that's unlikely to happen. Like winning the lottery, owning a Ferrari or dating George Clooney. And that was just a straw poll around *my* breakfast table.

The truth is, happiness shouldn't be about ifs, buts and maybes. It ought to be about stuff we can control and influence and not be reliant on the whims of Lady Luck. Who said you can't be happy unless you have loads of material possessions? As a small child I spent many a happy hour perched on a cold front step with an old wooden spinning top and a bit of string, watching the posh kids ride by on their bikes. But was I miserable? Yes, but only for the first 13 years.

People ask if you're happy with your lot, as if having a lot is the way to true happiness. But ask any of the rich and famous to name a time when they were *really* happy and it will almost certainly be when they were on the cusp of being successful. When it was all still a dream rather than a reality.

Remember, true happiness is about the journey and not the destination. Happiness comes when you can not only choose what to do, but also enjoy doing it so much that you become totally absorbed in it. As Lawrence of Arabia once said, 'Happiness is a by-product of absorption.' He then added, rather confusingly 'You really sink in this sand, don't you?' In other words, if you are absorbed enough in some worthwhile or enjoyable activity, happiness is the spin-off.

The fact is that like sunshine and darkness, happiness and unhappiness coexist in our lives. There has to be anxiety and boredom if we are to appreciate flow. If it were never dark, we wouldn't appreciate the sunshine playing on our face. And if it were never light, we wouldn't appreciate the moonlight dancing on the sand. Though, on the upside, we'd have the perfect excuse for keeping a loved one in the dark.

So here's what to do about being happy and unhappy. Enjoy the one and accept the other. That's nature's way of saying that none of us is really in control of things. And remember, to find true happiness, there must be both a purpose and a pleasure in everything you do. It's only when you are working like you don't need the money that you can ever be truly content in the moment.

And if that doesn't work, here's another thought: 'Nil carborundum illegitimi.' That's right; don't let the bastards grind you down.

GO FOR THE EXPERIENCE

Let's suppose you've got a spare £100 to treat yourself and your other half. What would you spend it on to gain the most satisfaction and happiness? Something experiential like a romantic meal for two at a favourite restaurant, or something material like a set of nesting tables in scrubbed pine? I think you've guessed the answer.

For most people, long-term happiness is more likely to be achieved by spending money on an experience rather than a possession. Having taken my eldest son, David, to the European Champions League Final in 1999, I took my youngest son, Sebastian, to the Final in Rome in 2009. (My middle son missed out on going to the Moscow Final in 2008, which has not escaped his attention.) Anyway, with the possible exception of the 11th and 57th minutes when Barcelona scored, Seb enjoyed every minute of it. You see, even the result didn't spoil the overall experience we shared on our short break to Rome.

Research by Leonardo Nicolao from the University of Texas confirms the theory that for long-term happiness, experiences tend to beat possessions. That's because after a while we only recall the happy memories of the event, like visiting the Coliseum and the Trevi Fountain, and we forget all about the two lucky goals scored against the run of play. Over time, we may even embellish the memory to make an experience seem even better. That's why we remember all those long, hot summers when we were kids, even though there may have only been one or two.

But what if the romantic meal for two turns out to be an absolute nightmare? It doesn't have to involve a crazy, knife-wielding chef spitting a tirade of four letter expletives as he walks round the restaurant, it may be just a disappointing salade niçoise. Researchers who measured people's happiness over a period of time found that those who had made a small but bad material purchase were able to forget about it more quickly than those who made a bad experiential purchase. I'm not sure exactly what this proves, but I think my wife has a wardrobe full of hardly worn clothes that supports it. In fact, the act of shopping for things that you don't really need also proves the theory that it is the *experience* we enjoy, rather than the material gain.

However, there's always an exception to the rule. So if you and your loved one find yourself sharing a bottle of fine wine on a hot summer evening and reminiscing with great fondness about the time you bought that cordless Morphy Richards steam iron, or the years of reliable service you've enjoyed from your Hotpoint twin tub, be sure to get in touch. Just not with me.

My advice is to spend your money on a nice meal or a memorable event. And remember, experiences that are free are likely to bring you even greater long-term happiness.

BALANCING UNCERTAINTY

Uncertainty of outcome is what makes things interesting. But it also makes us unhappy. Anyone who says that 'money doesn't make you happy' has probably never slept rough on the streets or had to survive on the lowest level of subsistence income. The very rich are no happier than those who are rich enough for their needs. However, for the vast majority of us, happiness is enhanced by a few quaint, old-fashioned necessities such as shelter, sustenance and the confidence that we won't be beaten up during the night.

I've met two people who claim to have the best job in the world. One of them is responsible for the Huddersfield Narrow Canal, which runs for 20 miles between West Yorkshire and Greater Manchester, and the other for the highways of a county council. They are both absolutely absorbed by their jobs and they enjoy helping people. Naturally, they have all the regular, day-to-day worries but their life has the right balance of certainty and uncertainty. For them.

When somebody loses their job it creates an uncertain future and leaves them stranded in an unhappy present, with a helpless feeling that they can do nothing but wait for good news from people they want to work for.

It's experiences that matter. Experiences with other people. People you want to be with. And that is why relationships are so important and why your ability to influence people in the right way enhances your happiness. Purpose and pleasure in what you are doing in the moment constitute happiness.

CHANGING THE WEATHER IN FEBRUARY

Right now I'm writing this sitting on Collaroy Beach in New South Wales, Australia. It is early on a Wednesday morning in February. Russell, in the Bay of Islands in New Zealand, where this book began, is some 1300 miles to the south east and it is six years since I wrote the very first words of the first edition of this book. The sun is coming up and an early morning walker ambles by with her dog; the world is at one. It looks like it will be a lovely summer's day with just a little cloud.

I am absolutely not making this up.

So far this month I have spoken in Perth, Adelaide and Sydney.

I'm booked to speak in Melbourne and again in Perth before my wife and I head home via a speaking engagement in Dubai at the end of March. We have decided not just to change the weather in February but in March too. And I am not working in New Zealand this year. Because everything moves on. I have spoken at conferences and seminars there every year for five consecutive years. But then, like everyone else, I needed a new challenge. I set myself the goal of speaking in Australia and, to break the journey, in Dubai.

Everything begins with an idea. And the idea comes to be reality when you take action. This coming Saturday I am playing golf with Graeme Fear, a client I met for the first time 12 months ago. It has been an interesting journey and I am on an interesting path.

It is nice to be here but it has, of course, cost money and effort to get to this point where I have changed the weather in February. For me.

MAKING THE EFFORT

So what has this book been about? As I said at the start, in successful relationships people never stand still. They're always moving forward and evolving to make their relationship even more successful. Happy and successful people do that because they live with hope that things will get even better.

Why is it worth making the effort to be more persuasive and influential? Is it worth it to become, as my mum would say, 'nicer'?

I believe so and I hope you do too. Because it will make you happy.

Why do we pay such a premium for the interior lights in our car to dim rather than simply switch off after a few seconds? Why do we pay a premium for cup holders in our cars that have that nice 'swoosh' sound as they open? Why are the women who sell cosmetics so polite and well groomed? Why do people pay such a premium for first-class travel? Why do expensive shops go to such lengths to create a relaxing and delightful environment? Why can certain cafés and bars charge a premium for a drink as simple as a cup of tea or a glass of beer? How are they able to persuade you to pay the price? Or, more pertinently, how do they influence your behaviour to do so?

Because nice is expensive and expensive is nice.

Why are budget airline staff downright rude? Why do people who work in discount stores not care about service? Why do staff in cheap motels not ask whether or how they can improve their offer? Transient employees often move on because they can see something better. Sometimes they leave because they are not treated well. Why do pretty much all service companies in countries with low unemployment struggle to get cheap labour to give good service? Is it simply because 'nice' people are more expensive? I don't think it's as simple as that.

I live in a small town in the north of England called Harrogate. We have more restaurants and eating places per head of population than any other place but one in the whole of Britain. We are a conference town. We are awash with restaurants, tea shops, cafés, B&Bs, hotels and so on. And yet we are famous because we have a tea shop. I travel all over the world and when I tell people I live in Harrogate they say, 'Ah, Bettys!'

Bettys is the most expensive place in town to buy a tea or a coffee, but people queue up outside it every day. This is the perfect business.

People queue up, even though they know it's the most expensive place in town and that there are plenty of other places to go. And it gets better. When the bill arrives people pay more. It's called a tip. And they go and tell their friends it was wonderful and come back and queue again. The perfect business.

So why do people queue up outside Bettys? Because it's nice. They care.

There are no chipped cups in Bettys. The staff aspire to excellence every day. I know. I go there several times a year. And all that comes from the people who own and run Bettys: a husband and wife team who don't want to be mentioned by name in this book because they prefer the members of the Bettys' team to have the credit. Which is nice.

And that's why it pays to be nice. Because people are willing to pay for 'nice'. People are willing to pay a premium for design, for a belief in a brand, for 'service'. And for 'service' read 'nice'.

We buy emotionally and justify logically.

THE END OF THE BEGINNING

To paraphrase Winston Churchill, is this the beginning or the end for you? Or is it the end of the beginning? Will you live your life in a more persuasive and nicer way from now on? For me, it is simply the end of the beginning.

I have made some progress on playing live with Ralph McTell: I have talked about him at every seminar and conference I have spoken at. I will meet him one day and perhaps achieve my goal. But what then? What do I do from that point on? Plan to play with Sting? Or Eric Clapton?

Happiness is the journey, not the destination.

I have made some progress on becoming the best and most sought-after speaker on the planet bar none. I look forward to speaking at Harvard, Oxford (again), Cambridge and Yale universities. I have written a bestselling book and, of course, I have changed the weather in February. And March.

And it is with hope that I finish this book. The sun is up now. The Aussies are beginning their day. It's time to begin mine.

I have endeavoured to develop loving relationships and make a meaningful, positive contribution. And that is the purpose of life.

The purpose of life is to develop loving relationships and make a meaningful, positive contribution. If in time it turns out to be something else, then send up a flare and let me know.

Life's a game and this book helps you fix the odds. Provided that you do the stuff. It's time to spin the wheel and place your bets.

Good luck.

APPENDIX: PHILIP'S PURPOSE

No book is complete without a 'thank you' to the people who matter most to the author. This book, as with everything I do, every breath I take and, of course, every pound I make, is dedicated to my darling wife, my three wonderful sons and their families. Or, as Sister Sledge once said, we are family, get up everybody and sing. Living life is fun and we've just begun to get our share of the world's delights. High hopes we have for the future and our goals in sight. No, we don't get depressed, here's what we call our golden rule.

Have faith in you and the things you do and you won't go wrong. This is our family jewel.

They are my purpose.

PHILIP'S DESIDERATA

Don't buy cheap bin liners.

Go placidly among the noise and haste and all that.

Be happy that there are some things you cannot change.

Happiness only comes when you accept the things you cannot influence.

Separate opinion from fact but don't let facts get in the way of a good story.

Also separate whites from colours unless you live alone.

Today is the first day of the rest of your life. Do something as though it were the last day of your life.

Pick it up even if you didn't drop it.

'Hang around' sometimes—learn to watch ants and think about why they do all that running around.

Make friends with freedom and uncertainty.

Cry during movies. But only during the soppy bits. And do it quietly.

Assume that anyone driving faster than you and agitating you is suffering some sort of disaster and needs to go that fast.

Stuff happens—true contentment comes from reacting positively to it.

Never stop hugging your kids. That way they still hug you when they're bigger than you. Which is nice.

Never outstay your welcome. Like the Spanish say, guests and fish both begin to smell after three days.

Never book a short break to Spain of more than three days.

Discourage small children from walking around with sharp objects.

Do the same with big children.

Swing as high as you can on a swing by moonlight.

Walk into the sea with your clothes on at midnight. Only do it once and somewhere warm.

Do it for love.

Do it now. The money will follow.

Make people laugh. Wear a paisley shirt with a striped tie.

Do something crazy with custard once in a while.

Read every day. But not out loud.

Learn new words—you can chew them.

Giggle with children.

Say 'Bula' when you arrive home. Every day. Refuse all requests for an explanation.

Don't eat sprouts unless there's someone standing over you.

Don't buy things you don't need with money you haven't got to impress people you don't like.

Always have clean shoes—it says a lot about you.

Write your own desiderata for your children's grandchildren.

Listen to those older than you are. They're getting fewer in number every day.

Write little notes saying nice things to good friends expecting nothing in return.

Say hello to people in lifts.

If you can't be with the one you love, honey, love the one you're with.

Love the one you're with.

Remember, if you're not the lead husky you only ever get one view.

Don't take your shirt off on stage. It's not big and it's not funny.

Remember, the total result of all of your ambitions is to be happy in your own head.

With all its sham, drudgery and broken dreams, it is still a beautiful world. Be cheerful. Strive to be happy.

Remember, the purpose of life is to develop loving relationships and make a meaningful, positive contribution.

So spot when you're doing those two things and celebrate every gorgeous moment.

And trust me on the bin liners.

ABOUT PHILIP HESKETH

P hilip Hesketh is a psychology graduate from Newcastle University and a sales graduate from Procter & Gamble. In 1986 he was the creator, New Business Director and Managing Partner of an advertising agency, Advertising Principles. He sold his interest in the business after 16 consecutive years of growth with the agency billing £48 million and employing 150 people.

Having spent his entire working life studying and practising influence and persuasion, he now speaks on 'The Psychology of Persuasion'. Now firmly established as one of the UK's top professional speakers, Philip Hesketh both commands the attention of an audience and captures its imagination.

It might be an inspiring 60-minute talk or a highly bespoke and interactive two-day seminar. Both are delivered with the same ruthless aplomb that combine a potent mix of thought-provoking, well-researched, persuasive techniques with his own highly entertaining and unique brand of humour.

Having spent his entire working life studying and practising influence and persuasion, he now speaks and runs courses, seminars and workshops all over the world on 'The Psychology of Persuasion and Influence'.

For more details on Philip's current courses and events, go to heskethtalking.com.